Jackie

The best thing for girls – next to boys

Foreword by **JACQUELINE WILSON**

PRION

CONTENTS

Articles

Stories

Patchwork

Quizzes

Craftwork

Reader's True Experiences

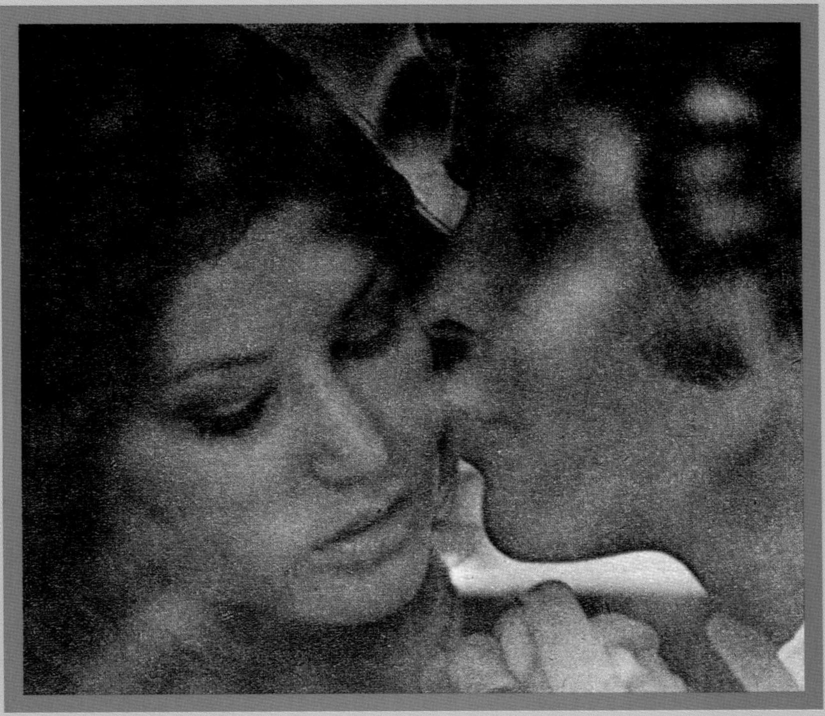

ACKNOWLEDGEMENTS
The publishers would like to thank the team at DC Thomson for all their help in compiling this book, particularly Martin Lindsay, Rory Duncan and Sabrina Segalov. They would also like to thank Irene K. Duncan, Anne Rendall and Hilary Bowman for their editorial contributions.

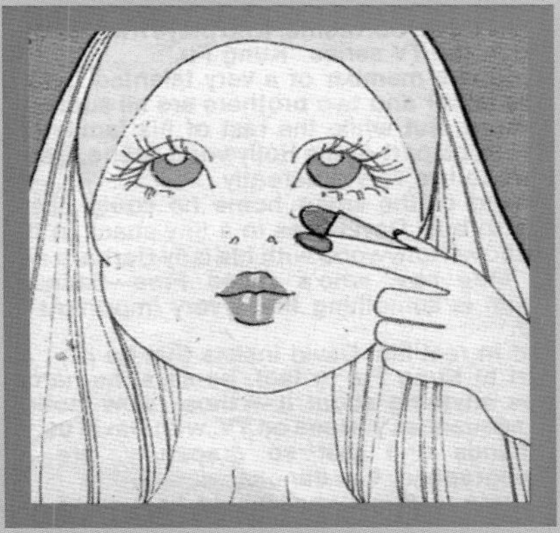

THIS IS A PRION BOOK
First published in 2013 by Prion
An imprint of the Carlton Publishing Group
20 Mortimer Street
London W1T 3JW

A catalogue record for this book is available from the British Library.

ISBN: 978 1 85375 901 7

Printed and bound in China

SO FAR, SEW GOOD
CHEAP AND CHEERFUL FASHION IDEAS.

WELL I NEVER!

Pretty up your wellies! Using copydex or some other strong adhesive, stick on stars or spots, or rows of coloured ribbon, or a lightning flash, or plain bands of colour can be painted on, or paint a splodge of colour round the top (use cryla-colour and roughen the surface of the wellies slightly with sand paper) or trail on some glue and sprinkle on silver glitter. Don't get them too wet !!

QUICK AND EASY RECIPES

GOOD EGG

To make an 'Egg in a frame', you need one large, thick slice of white or brown bread and one egg per person. Cut a hole out of the bread with a pastry cutter and fry the bread on one side 'till golden brown. Turn over the bread, break the egg into the hole and fry 'till the egg sets.

Foreword by Jacqueline Wilson

When I give talks about my children's books to big family audiences I nearly always tell the story of how I started my writing career – and as soon as I say the words "*Jackie* magazine", all the mums in the audience gasp and laugh and nudge each other. Some come and talk to me afterwards, telling me just how much *Jackie* meant to them when they were teenagers.

It meant a great deal to me, too, because it helped me become a professional writer when I was only seventeen. I'd wanted to write ever since I was very little, but my family and schoolteachers all thought this was a silly pipedream. I was made to do a secretarial course and thought I was going to be stuck earning my living as a shorthand typist for the rest of my life. But when I was looking at the secretarial job advertisements in the back pages of the *Evening Standard*, I came across an advert asking for teenage writers. I was a teenager and I very much wanted to be a writer, so I sent off for more information. I was told that the Scottish publishing firm DC Thomson were planning to launch a new teenage magazine the next year, and wanted to compile suitable stories and articles.

I decided to have a go. I didn't write a conventional romantic story about a girl meeting a boy. I wrote a funny article about a girl *not* meeting a boy, outlining the horrors of going to a dance where your friends get off with boys and you're the poor soul left all on her own. I was astonished to receive a chatty letter from the editor Gordon Small, saying that my article had made him laugh and he'd love to publish it. He offered to pay me three guineas – three pounds, three shillings. It wasn't a huge sum even back in the 1960s, but it meant the world to me. Someone was actually taking me seriously as a real writer!

I bombarded Gordon with stories and articles after that. He didn't accept them all, but he always explained why. I was inclined to take an early feminist stance and Gordon sensibly spelled out to me that most of the readers wanted to daydream about boyfriends and liked hero-worshipping pop stars.

However, he offered me a full-time job as a trainee journalist up in the Dundee offices. This was my big chance! My mum was very wary about my leaving home so young. When Gordon and George Martin came down to London and suggested meeting me at the Waldorf Hotel, she was alarmed and insisted on coming with me! I just about died of embarrassment, but they were very sweet and understanding.

So, in October 1963, I got the sleeper train up to Dundee and went to live at the Church of Scotland Girls' Hostel (my mum was very relieved to think I'd have a matron keeping an eye on me). I had to spend my first three months there squeezed into a linen cupboard every night as the dormitories were all full up, but at least it was cosy. I don't think I ever adjusted to the freezing cold wind blowing across the river Tay. I shivered even when I wore my new sheepskin jacket, considered the height of fashion then. I wore Dollyrocker dresses and point boots and perhaps people thought I was a Swinging Sixties chick, knowing about all the latest London trends.

When they realised I was just a shy little mouse from the suburbs, they weren't quite so keen! I was told I needed to train on another magazine first before I could start on the new teenage magazine. I became the junior girl on *Red Letter*, a weekly story magazine nowhere near as glamorous. But it was wonderful training all the same, and I wrote endless stories for them – and even the horoscope column! I hope I predicted that the new magazine would be an enormous success.

I was thrilled when Mr Cuthbert and Mr Tate (in charge of all women's magazines) told me that they'd decided to name their teenage magazine *Jackie*. "It's after you, young Jackie," they said. I'm very much old Jackie now – but I'm still thrilled to be associated with such an iconic publication.

Jacqueline

INTRODUCTION

IF YOU DIDN'T KNOW THE ACTUAL FACTS, you would be forgiven for thinking that *Jackie* was created by a pop music guru or a super-trendy fashionista, but nothing could be further from the truth. The magazine was the brainchild of Gordon Small, a former ex-RAF aero engine fitter who was far from being an aficionado of the music industry or an expert in style.

Gordon was the magazine's founder and became its first editor. Together with a creative team, he produced *Jackie*, an exciting new magazine "for go-ahead teens" which went on to be the best-selling teenage title for ten years.

In the early Sixties the competition included *Valentine*, *Boyfriend* and *Mirabelle*. The sales of these magazines were in decline and the feeling was there was a definite opportunity to grab a share of the teen market. Back then girls didn't have iPads, laptops or mobiles. There was no television in their bedroom. In fact, the family television was more than likely rented and

there was a choice of just three channels – a far cry from today's world of multi-channel television that is accessible 24/7.

As for keeping up with pop music and the charts, teenagers listened to the hits on Radio Luxembourg under the bed blankets! (Duvets hadn't hit homes in the UK.) So it's not surprising that their magazine played a major role in the lives of teenage girls – it was the highlight of their week.

Girls who had read *Bunty* and *Judy* were looking to move on to something far more grown-up and exciting. Little did they know it was just about to hit the shelves!

Jackie launched on Thursday, 11 January 1964. The very first cover featured a youthful Cliff Richard and the magazine came with a free twin heart ring. If that wasn't enough to excite a typical Sixties teenage girl, add the promise of full-colour pin-ups of their favourite pop stars, tips on how to be more kissable, dreamy love stories and way-out exclusives on their idols, and girls across the UK were speedily reaching for their purses, happy to ▶

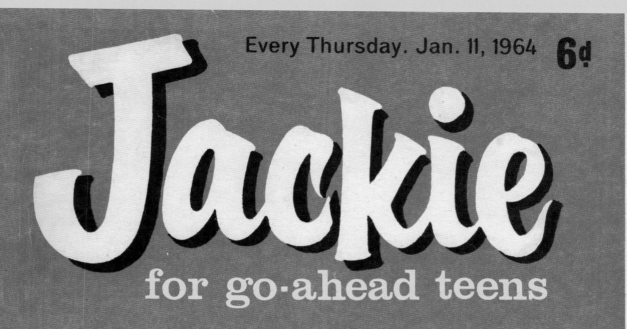

Every Thursday. Jan. 11, 1964　6d

Jackie

for go-ahead teens

N°1

FREE
WIN HEART
RING

SUPER FULL COLOUR
PIN-UPS OF CLIFF,
ELVIS, BILLY FURY
and The BEATLES

PERFUME TIPS FOR A
MORE KISSABLE YOU

DREAMY PICTURE
LOVE STORIES

COLOUR PICTURES OF
OUTFITS TO MAKE
YOU PRETTY IN THE
RAIN 'N' SNOW

PHOTO FEATURES AND
WAY-OUT EXCLUSIVES
ON ALL THE POPSTERS

Above: The cover of the very first edition of *Jackie*.

FAKING IT!

part with their pocket money. At just 6d, the equivalent of 2½p today, *Jackie* was the must-have mag if you wanted to be up to date on what was hip and happening. In the same way, *Top of the Pops* was the must-see popular music programme on television. *Top of the Pops* launched just ahead of *Jackie* with the first show airing on 1 January 1964.

The name *Jackie* was chosen from a list of girls' names. There was a slight concern following the assassination of President John F. Kennedy in 1963 that it might be associated with his widow, Jackie. Incredibly, every newsagent was contacted and informed that there was no connection and the original choice remained.

Jackie's address printed in the magazine was 185 Fleet Street, Fetter Lane, London EC4A 2HS, but in reality it was actually produced hundreds of miles away in the north east of Scotland. It was created in Dundee, a city in Tayside famous for its jute, jam and journalism. The thinking behind the London address was to give the title more kudos and to make it appear as though *Jackie* were produced at the centre of the cool capital.

The magazine bridged the gap between being a little girl and a young woman; *Jackie* was like the reader's big sister and knew exactly what she wanted and aspired to be.

The content was a lively mix of fashion and beauty tips, pop gossip, horoscopes, fun quizzes, love stories and life advice, including the all-important tips on how to get a boy – and keep him!

Jackie was a hit right from the start. Every Friday the circulation figures came into the office (for the editor's eyes only) and every week they continued to rise, reaching an all-time high in the early Seventies when sales peaked at over a million. Gordon Small remembered it being, "a wonderful feeling".

Former editor, Emil Pacholek, worked on the magazine from the late Sixties to the early Seventies, as he recalled, "I started off as what was called the production editor which meant I did a bit of everything, but I also learned everything. I wrote picture story scripts and text stories before becoming the editor. Every issue had an Ed's letter and I can remember writing one in particular which was all about hippie dippy sayings!

"I've never surfed in my life, but I feel I know what surfing feels like because the atmosphere in the *Jackie* office was exhilarating. It was hard work, but it was fun. You couldn't wait to get there!

"*Jackie* met its market brilliantly. Gordon Small, who was the magazine's founder and first editor, went on to become Managing Editor of all the DC Thomson teen titles and women's publications. He was a gifted man. I always thought he gave the staff their heads."

Ed Walker was a designer on *Jackie* in the late Sixties. He, too, felt that Gordon Small was fundamental to the success of the magazine:

"Gordon had a different style of working to what was the norm in those days, he was very inclusive. He'd get all the staff round his desk and would ask for their input. He listened to everyone and took on board what people thought, even the youngest members of the team.

"I used to travel to work by train and every Thursday it was full of girls reading their copies of *Jackie*. I think the pin-ups were a key factor in achieving the amazing sales."

Posters of pop idols such as David Cassidy, Donny Osmond and David Essex adorned the bedroom walls of thousands of teenage fans.

Fashion also played a major role in Jackie and throughout its life an amazing array of weird and wonderful gear graced the pages, including jeans with enormous flares, maxi skirts and the proverbial huge platform shoes. Bright purple was all the rage and Biba was big news. In the early years of *Jackie* the fashions were drawn. The artwork was striking and very stylised.

Jean Haxton, who worked on *Jackie* from 1967 to 1974 remembered one particular artist: "Gabrielle Stoddart produced amazing drawings of models who had super-slim legs that went on forever!"

And Gabrielle will never forget working for *Jackie*:

"I very much remember the day Gordon Small walked into the office of Helen Jardine Artists in London's Covent Garden where twelve fashion artists worked for the newpapers, magazines and advertising agents. I shared the weekly commissioned work with a friend.

"We were able to go out to choose the clothes, taking them back to the studio to draw and try on. Gordon allowed us to design and create a theme for the double-page spread. Of course, we had a deadline and I remember

A JACKIE QUIZ
HOW COMPATIBLE ARE YOU?

Either you have or you haven't got it! Compatibility we're talking about—that's the ability to get on well with people!

But it's not so easy to cultivate if it doesn't come naturally.

Tell you what. It'll take hours saying what it is and how to get it, but it'll be much more fun and easier to explain if you just do our quiz! Then you'll know if you've got it or not . . . and if not, why not! What could be easier?

So . . . come on, do the quiz!

1. Your boyfriend's sister is getting married soon, and she's said she'd like you to go to the wedding. You love romantic white weddings, so you'd love to go, but your boyfriend is very unorthodox and he's completely against the idea of making a big, expensive fuss about getting married. He says he won't encourage her by going along and helping celebrate. He thinks she ought to have more sense and put the money by! So when she asks if you'll be coming, do you say . . ?
a) "Uh . . . I don't know if I can make it, yet."
b) "Ask Pete!"
c) "Of course—nothing would keep me away!"
d) "Afraid not—Pete would go mad if I did!"

2. A girl at work is having a trying time at home, and you keep falling over her, crying her eyes out in the loo! You get the feeling that this isn't going to get sorted out until she finally makes the break and leaves home, but you know (because you both get the same wage) that she can't possibly afford to live away from home at the moment. So would you . . .

b) Be very sympathetic and encourage her to tell you about her woes?
c) Act very cheerfully and try to get her mind off her worries by telling jokes and asking her to join some social activity with you?
d) Ask her if she wants to talk about it, and just listen, if she does?
e) Suggest she talks to someone who can help her sort things out, such as the personnel officer at work, or a welfare official?
f) Think there is no easy solution, so tell her she has just got to toughen up and make the best of it, learn to cope, like everyone else has to?

3. How many of the following statements seem to you to be very true:—
a) Older people have more experience, so they must know better.
b) If you want to settle an argument fairly, everybody concerned must be prepared to give in a little bit.
c) Everybody has SOMETHING nice about their nature, and if you look long enough you can find it.
d) People who share the same interests are bound to get along better than people who have nothing in common.

4. There are three boys who are interested in you (bet you like this sort of problem!!) BOB is very much the same sort of person as you are, and he likes the same sort of things. He is not terribly exciting, but nice. If he has a fault, it is that he is a little bit sensitive and would be very hurt if you two-timed him.

LEN is not like anybody you have ever been out with before. You are not sure your parents would like him much, if they met him. You hardly ever agree with the things he says or thinks, but a date with him is very . . .

JEEPERS CREEPERS
— HAVE YOU GOT NICE PEEPERS?

If you have, and you actually like the thought of being judged on looks alone, then the Miss Eye Dew Contest 1980 is for you. Entry leaflets containing full details are now available from Eye Dew stockists throughout the country, and all you have to do to enter is send a photograph of yourself in black and white or colour with one pack top from Eye Dew — the closing date of the competition is September 30. The six finalists will be notified by the end of October, and invited to London for the final judging. During their two-day stay in the capital, they'll be shown the sights, visit a West End show and be photographed by a leading beauty photographer. The winner will be awarded the title "Miss Eye Dew 1980" and will receive the first prize of £2000 worth of diamond jewellery!

Even if you can't find a leaflet near you, just send off an s.a.e. to Miss Eye Dew 1980, 51 Green Street, London W1Y 4BT, and one will be sent to you. Eye Dew Drops give you sparkling clear eyes, and a few drops before making up will get rid of that horribly red bloodshot look. A pack costs around 90p.

WEAR A RAINBOW

MAKE-UP 1

Pinky colours are back with a bang, especially for lips and nails! Blues and greys look best on eyes, though, pink shadow looks rather strange except as a highlighter on brows.

For lips try Pink Tinge or Hideaway Pink from Yardley's Magic Moisture lipstick range, 48p each; Soft Centre Pink and Soft Centre Rose, 55p each from Gala's Soft Centre range; Pink Sorbet by Rimmel at 31p. Match up your nails with colours like Cornelian by Cutex, 29½p, Pink Tinge and Hideaway Pink by Yardley, 43p each and Cheeky Rose by Rimmel.

Grey looks super with pink, so try grey shadow on your eyes. Look for Yardley's Smooth-On Grey, 39p, Helena Rubinstein's Winkie Smoke, 59p, Boots No. 7 Gunmetal Eye Slicker, Rimmel's Grey and Silver Pressed Shadows, 16p. Add a hint of pink to your cheeks with Boots 17 Blush Powder in Tawny Pearl, 14p, Yardley's Blooming Cheek Blusher in Toasted Almond, 51p or Rimmel's Pearly Blush Stick in Pearly Pink, 31p.

MAKE-UP 2

Blue suits most people and blue eye colours are really flattering. Go for deeper pinks for lips and nails and make sure cheeks are glowing with deep pinky blusher.

Look for Yardley's Romantic Rose lipstick, 48p, Gala's Soft Centre Rose and Soft Centre Poppy, Rimmel's Rosy Shimmer, 36p. Paint your nails with Romantic Rose polish by Yardley 43p, Boots 17 Heliotrope polish, 24p, Boots 17 Midnight Hour, 20p or Rimmel's Rose Shimmer polish.

Choose super blues for eyes, like Helena Rubinstein's Oh So Blue, Dizzy Blue Dazzle and Derby Blue Dazzle, 59p, Smooth-On Blue Shadow from Yardley, 39p, Boots 17 Pearly Azure or the Blue Blue Eyes Eye Tones kit, 29p, Rimmel's Navy Pressed Shadow 15p. Cheer up cheeks with Yardley's Burgundy Oyster Blooming Cheek Blusher, 51p or Rimmel's Translucent Blush in Russet, 53p.

Super blue and natural twinset with v-neck slipover and edge-to-edge card, from the Focus Range by Balmswear. Cardi Style No: 2860. Price: £4.75. Fabric: Courtelle cotton slub/rayon. Colours: Harebells/ecru, pale green/ecru, face powder/ecru. Sizes: 34 to 38. Slipover Style No.: 2849. Price: £4.00. Other details as above. From Henry Wigfall, Brandon Street, Sheffield; Phillips & Hope, Hove; Thos. Ellis, Aberystwyth; Inverness Stores, Inverness; Lindy's, 80 Cornwall Street, Plymouth; Retail Ltd, Halifax; L. W. Baumer, 86a Westbourne Grove, London W.2.

Calf-length navy cord skirt with pleats from the waist, from Laura Ashley. Style No.: MSK 87. Price: £8.00. Fabric: Corduroy. Colours: Assorted, prints and plain. Sizes: 10 to 14. From all Laura Ashley shops.

Pretty pink and blue hat from Bermona. Style No.: GS229. Price: £3.50. Fabric: Cotton. Colours: Blue, pink, cream and green. From Sydney Smith, Kings Road, London S.W.3. Enquiries to Tony Porter, Bermona Hats, 37 Maddox Street, London W.1.

Bronze T-bar with slim platform and heel, from Dolcis. Style No.: A11/10051 Elfa. Price: £7.99. Fabric: Leather. Colours: Bronze, black. Sizes: 3 to 8. From all main branches of Dolcis.

---

working into the evening to get it all done to be ready to send up to Dundee for print.

"It was an exciting time to be in London working in the mid-Sixties as there were so many opportunities for young people. Everything was new. We were quite influenced by the artwork coming over from America and I believe the *Jackie* drawings must have got me some freelance work with the influential American fashion paper *Women's Wear Daily* where the drawings were very inspiring with very long legs!

"I also did a regular beauty strip for *Jackie*. I'd go around the shops to find new make-up and then write tips and provide illustrations on how to apply the products.

"I have to thank Gordon for his trust in me."

As time went on, the magazine also moved on and *Jackie* changed from using drawn artwork to photographing "real" models on location.

Jean recalled, "We were always on the lookout for new and different places to shoot the fashion and I can vividly remember sessions taking place at Leuchars Railway Station (near St Andrews) and Errol Railway Station (between Dundee and Perth). Even now, all these years later, when I'm out in the car I can't help myself thinking about possible locations that would have worked well!

"I think the secret of *Jackie*'s success was it had the right mix of material. You could go from working on a feature about David Bowie to writing about David Cassidy. There were so many different types of music covered in the pages. ▶

9

Adam Ant

"At one point I did the doctor's column. I worked closely with the doctor who happened to live in Dundee. She was a regular visitor to the *Jackie* office.

"I can remember meeting famous bands. Steve Winwood and Spencer Davis came to the office and chatted away. Another time I met the Walker Brothers at the Taypark, a local hotel in Dundee. They were all wearing eye make-up including eye-liner.

"Working on *Jackie* was just fantastic. We had great laughs and would discuss television programmes we'd watched the night before, such as the comedy *Monty Python* which was one of a kind."

Judith McLaren was a graphic designer on *Jackie* in the late 1980s. She remembered high jinks in the *Jackie* office, particularly on one occasion which involved the designers going "on strike"!

"We were working on the issue that was going on sale at the beginning of April and decided to have a laugh. All the designers downed tools and the journalists had to lay out the pages of the magazine. Not surprisingly, when the magazine went to press it looked absolutely ridiculous! There were pieces of sticky tape keeping pictures in place and images of scalpels and brushes scattered all over the pages!

"The 'strike' was even highlighted on page three where the readers were told about the designers' action. The truth was eventually revealed in the final pages that it was all an April Fool's joke and everything would be back to normal the following week. It was great coming to the office! The work was divided equally between the layout team, including designing the all-important front cover, so you got a taste of everything. They were very happy times."

Mandy Hendry, who was the editorial typist from 1988 to 1991 completely agreed that the *Jackie* office was a fun place to be:

"The laughs and the humour were fantastic!

"I started at DC Thomson in the mail room, where the letters were sorted out and then delivered to the individual offices. From there, I moved to the typing pool where twenty-two women tapped away at huge cumbersome typewriters. I couldn't believe it when I was picked to be the '*Jackie* typist'. I felt really apprehensive as the office was so trendy, but I needn't have worried. Nobody was ever moody. There was no stomping around.

PATCHWORK

SO FAR SEW GOOD
Cheap and Cheerful Fashion Ideas

bombers away!

Cut the old cuffs and waist band off your bomber jacket and put on new ones of stripy hessian braid. Cut a piece of braid for each cuff 23cm. long and join each one to make a cuff just big enough to slip your hand through. Cut the waist band the same size as the one you've taken off and sew it on the same way.

STOWAWAYS
Stowaway sounds so romantic . . . sigh! They're three fantastic perfumes with faraway names to excite even the most unimaginative among us!

There's Dawn Flight (our favourite) which is crisp but subtle at the same time with extracts of Jasmin, Hyacinth, Cedarwood and Lily of the Valley. Sleepy Lagoon is a sophisticated and sensual combination of lemons from California, African Neroli, Bergamot of Calabria and a hint of Parma Violet and Oakmoss Musk Orient Express, on the other hand, is exotic and spicy with Sandalwood, Hyacinth and Muguet for a touch of mystery!

Stowaways are on sale in most chemists and department stores packed in aluminium sprays, price £1.05 each.

STOWAWAY

SLEEPY LAGOON

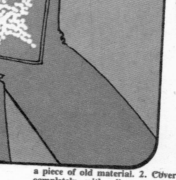

STARSTRUCK!
Now you too can be a star — thanks to "Jackie" reader Johanna Warren of Derby who sent in this great idea to "Your Patch," and won £1 for it. We think her star patch looks much nicer than an ordinary one, and it's easy to make, too!

Just: 1. Cut out a star shape from a piece of old material. 2. Cover completely with silver sequins. 3. Sew on to your jeans.

We guarantee you won't be lost in a crowd wearing this!

Have you any ideas for "Your Patch?" If so, we'd like to hear from you! Write to: Your Patch, Patchwork, Jackie, 185 Fleet Street, London EC4A 1HS. Your idea could win you £1.

"Looking back it was like Ab Fab! The dress code was 'come as you are'. Everyone had their own style. The editor at that time was always dressed in ethnic gear. Nobody wore smart suits, or shirts and ties. Hair was big and the bigger the better – perms were 'in'.

"The television soap *Neighbours* was at its peak when I was on Jackie and there were loads of features about Kylie Minogue and Jason Donavon. I can still picture Kylie Minogue singing 'Tears on my Pillow'!

"The working practices back then were so totally different compared to today. The editorial team didn't do any typing. Their copy was all hand written and given to me to type. Even making a phone call had its own ritual as no one had an individual handset. Any external calls were made, or taken, in a strange little booth that was in the office and every call had to go through the main switchboard.

"When I worked on *Jackie*, my face was used on the 'Ask Amanda' page which was named after me! The photographer took loads of pictures of me wearing lots of different outfits and in a variety of poses – glasses on, glasses off, pencil up at my mouth looking thoughtful and so on!

"But 'Ask Amanda' wasn't my only claim to fame. I also starred in some of the photo stories, which was great fun. I had a brilliant time on *Jackie*."

Photographer Gordon Reid worked for the magazine from its early days and experienced first hand how the top-selling teen title evolved to stay in tune with its readers, ensuring it was always bang on trend.

Of course, photographic equipment also changed over the years becoming far more high-tech, compact and transportable. Digital was a distant dream in the *Jackie* era. Gordon lived locally and, just like the doctor who answered the medical problems, was also a regular visitor to the *Jackie* office.

"The magazine enjoyed a close relationship with its readers, it was very interactive. I did a wide variety of work for *Jackie*. I photographed pop bands, including the Undertones, Thin Lizzy, UB40 and Duran Duran. I did fashion and cover shoots. I also worked with the editorial team on the photo stories and provided pictures for the problem pages and emotional features.

"I often found myself in challenging situations, but thankfully I always got through them. I like people, I've infinite patience and I'm an expert at blagging, which always helps! As a photographer, it's essential you can communicate well and think on your feet.

"Taking cover shots was far more complicated than you would imagine. I didn't just need to think about the model and make sure she was smiling, as happy faces were essential. If there was a free gift being given away with the issue, I had to consider the size of the item and where it would be positioned. I found it was always best to talk to the layout team before a shoot to avoid any disasters and do the best job.

"The British weather could cause real problems as it's so unpredictable and changeable. There were days we spent hours hanging around praying for the rain to go off and often by the time it cleared the light could be fading fast so I had to be super quick."

But it wasn't just the weather that could cause trouble. Working with animals could be very testing, even if you had the patience of a saint. Gordon recalled one particular fashion shoot in a local park that involved a dog.

"The theme was black and white polka dots and some bright spark thought it would be a great idea to use a Dalmation. I was busy organising the model, getting her in the right pose, and I turned round to find the dog lifting his leg on my camera box!"

Jackie was a fabulous magazine that was loved by everyone who read it and everybody who worked on it, so in the words of David Cassidy, could it be forever?

Sadly no. With sales declining to 50,000, the decision was made to shut the title and the presses rolled for the last time on the issue dated 3 July 1993.

It was maybe "Bye bye baby" but there's no doubt that the magazine still holds special memories for millions of women who will never forget the huge part that *Jackie* played in their teenage years.

Irene K. Duncan

V-NECK TOP
ONE SHOULDER TOP

SIMPLY SOCKING

Whatever the weather, socks are great. Wear plain ones under trousers or long skirts, or fantastic stripy ones with your tartan trousers if you're a Bay City Rollers fan.

We've found three different kinds to buy and even a way of making your own plain socks stripy! Read on and find out how!

Super stripy socks with you-know-who up the side, from British Home Stores, No Style Number, Price: 45p for shoe sizes 9 to 12; 12½ to 3½ and 4 to 7 are 49p. Fabric: Nylon. Colours: Pale blue/red/yellow stripes. From most branches of British Home Stores.

Long woolly socks to cover your knees and wear under skirts, from Sunarama. No Style Number Price: Over-knee 95p, below-knee 75p. Fabric: Acrylic. Colours: Black, yellow, navy. Size: One size only. Write to Janet Girsman Promotions Ltd., 34 St. George Street, Hanover Square, London W.1. for a list of stockists, or send for them direct to the same address (mail order 15p. extra).

Tie-dye white or pale wool or nylon socks using Dylon Multi-Purpose Dye. To make them stripy, bind the socks tightly with string at intervals and remember that the broader the binding, the wider the stripe you'll get.

You'll have to begin with the lightest colour you want, so bind the areas you don't want to be dyed with string, then dissolve the dye according to the manufacturer's instructions and simmer the socks for 15 minutes. Then rinse thoroughly. Bind over the dyed area and remove original bindings. Using the next colour you want repeat the process, then remove string and rinse until the water runs clear.

Bright stripy socks by Sunarama. Fabric: Nylon. Price: Over-knee 65p, below-knee 50p. Colours: Assorted stripes. Sizes: One size only. Stockists as for fig. 2.

THE BEATLE BEAT WAKENS ME EVERY MORNING

I have a cute little flat. Everything's fab, except I can't get up in the morning. I just sleep on and on.

So I dreamed up a crafty plan. First, I connect my record player to the light socket, then I tie a piece of string from the bell key on the alarm to the light switch.

Before I go to bed I put on my Beatle's LP and the alarm clock on the very edge of the table.

At seven the alarm goes off, winding in the string. This pulls the clock from the table, and the weight puts on the light switch.

The string stops the clock from falling to the floor, and as the record player warms up, the Beatles serenade me from sleep! It's the greatest idea since sliced bread. No more tellings-off from the boss!

Marjorie Thomson,
Norwich.

(Samantha says—A copy of the disc " Hootin' Blues " is on its way to you, Marjorie. It's the nearest thing to a freight train. Guaranteed to waken the dead!)

I have a week's holiday coming up and would like to go ski-ing. But the money won't run to the Continent. Any ideas?
Diane Stewart,
Leeds.

The Scottish Council of Physical Recreation, 4 Queensferry Street, Edinburgh, 2, should be able to fix you up. There are lots of super ski-ing places north of the Border—with an opportunity for "he-ing" in the evenings.

The Scottish Youth Hostels Association run weekly courses costing 10 guineas, inclusive of ski hire and accommodation. Their address is 7 Bruntsfield Crescent, Edinburgh, 10.

ATTENTION ALL GIRLS!

Why, why, why must all girls think it's essential to look exactly alike?

Whether they are blondes, brunettes or redheads, once they've had their hair styled the same way and put on that mask they call make-up, they're not individuals any more.

Give me a girl who's not ashamed of her natural looks, and leaves her hair soft, not pulled and pushed with the aid of grips and lacquer into the latest fashion fad. You usually find she is also intelligent and has a mind of her own.

Brian Wilson,
Sheffield.

I'm open for replies.—S.

SCALPED

When I had my beehive hairdo, I'd one very embarrassing moment. I'd got my false bun not so tightly tied-up under the built-up hair and was sitting in the bus on the way to the office. A man with an umbrella was just getting off and, as he passed me, he picked up my bun on the point of his brolly.

But a real Cockney bus conductor saved my blushes when he yelled, " 'Ere, Sittin' Bull, no flippin' scalpin' on my bus!"

Angela Aitken,
Stepney.

Bet you went red to the roots of your hair.—S.

PLATTER BETWEEN PLATES

If you find that one of your records has become warped, a simple way to flatten it out is to place it between two sheets of glass with a heavy book on top. It should be quite flat again in a couple of days.

Janice Black,
West Hartlepool.

(Ingenious. Even our pop gossip man, Pete Lennon, can see through it!—S.)

SHAKE RATTLE

The boy next door has an ancient sports car which bears the proud name, Lucunder. I'd never heard of this name before and asked if it shouldn't be Lucinda?

" Oh, no," he said, " that's it's name all right. You see, there's something loose under the bonnet."

Virginia Maxwell,
Kent.

(We can't know EVERYTHING, can we?—S.)

LONGING

My boyfriend is in the Merchant Navy, and when he's away he writes a long letter to me every day and puts each of them in a separate envelope. When he reaches his destination, he sends them off and I get an enormous pile on one day.

Last week it took me two-and-a-half hours to read them all!

Ann Currie,
Birmingham.

(Send me his address, please, Ann. He deserves a dozen ball-point pens free.—S.)

PLUMP, PLEASE

Why is it that all the girls who get the handsome hunks in the love stories are as slim as can be?

My boyfriend, and lots of other boys I know, prefer a girl to be on the plump side. They say they're jollier and more fun to be with.

So how about a heroine who's frankly fat once in a while, just to keep everyone happy?

Valerie Brooks,
Southampton.

(Art Editor, please note.—S.)

LIGHTER SIDE

My boyfriend was engrossed in watching a football match on TV. He took out his cigarettes and matches, and, without taking his eyes from the screen, put a match in his mouth and tried to light it by scraping a cigarette along the match box!

Melinda Yeaman,
Dundee

(It's amazing what a boy'll do just for kicks.—S.)

There y' have it! Your first letters page.

Write to me about anything under the sun. A quid for every letter I print—and two for the pick of the bunch.

The address? Samantha's Page, " Jackie," 12 Fetter Lane, Fleet Street, London E.C.4.

THE EDITOR SAYS . . .
Like your St Christopher luck charm? Here's wishing you many happy journeys with it. But once you get to your destination, don't be like one pop star, who, on a visit to New York, put his in a coffee machine in mistake for a 25-cent piece. He didn't get any coffee—but a cascade of small change clattered on to the pavement.
See you,
The Editor.

✦ A LITTLE BIT OF ROMANCE ✦

ONE OF THE HIGHLIGHTS OF *JACKIE* WAS THE LOVE STORIES told in pictures. During the first few years of Jackie – from 1964 to circa 1966–67 – the stories, which were drawn by various artists, seemed to be aimed at an older readership. The drawings showed people who seemed to be in their twenties rather than their teens – but since you always aspired to be older than you were, that was fine. The girls were all very sophisticated, and the men were suave and mainly wore sharp suits and ties and drove flash sportscars. The girls had impossibly long and big hair – very like a Barbie doll really, with very long eyelashes and big lips – when you look at some of the "celebrities" of today, not much appears to have changed!

The scripts were written by freelance writers and were pretty formulaic – boy meets girl, girl falls in love, boy behaves badly, girl goes off in a rage, boy woos girl with sweet words and wins her back and they live happily ever after.

A perk of the job was a trip to London to meet the writers and discuss scripts with them. The staff came up with ideas for scripts, often based on a current song. There was a record player on all the time in the office and the titles of the songs sparked off loads of great ideas. So, we would be listening to say, Adam and the Ants' "Prince Charming" and think, great name for a story, let's go with that!

The scripts were then sent off to artists to be drawn. In the early days, they were drawn in Spain by a group of artists – cleverly called the Spanish

artists! They were sent the script and the drawn artwork would be back several weeks later. Everything had to be planned well in advance, because all of it had to be done by snail mail – i.e. the Post Office, in those days. They were all in black and white and very detailed. Sometimes, things were lost in translation – one script called for a one-armed bandit, i.e. gaming machine, to be drawn and when the storyboard came back, we had a gangster minus a limb …

As soon as the artwork arrived, it was whisked off to the balloonists in the art department to have the script inserted in speech balloons. In those days, that was every bit as skilled as working with software such as Photoshop is now.

In the late Sixties, the magazine started to use photos – for example, there was a picture story based on Sean Connery in a scene from one of the famous Bond movies, *Thunderball*, featuring a black-and-white still from the movie and then drawn artwork about him.

This occasional use of black-and-white photography to start the stories continued throughout the Seventies, but the rest of the stories were still illustrated by artwork. Then in the early Eighties, one of the problems sent in to Cathy and Claire was used to make a picture story. It was called "What's your problem" and it became a regular feature, firstly using a photograph to start it off, then illustrated artwork, but in 1981 the first fully photographed problem was used. Within a couple of issues, there was no turning back and it was entirely done using photography and real people. Most of the time, these were staff – but the magazine did use ordinary people, whom staff found by going out to the busy High Street just yards from the office, and asking people if they would like to be in Jackie. From memory, they were paid the princely sum of about £3. Surprisingly, most people agreed. Occasionally, one page of the photostory would be in colour – but film was expensive and also only certain pages could be in colour. Being in charge

Should I Lie To You?

ALL 4 LOVE

of a photoshoot was a bit like being a director on a movie, you had to remember who was wearing what in which scene.

In the latter half of the Eighties, the format of the magazine changed – it was smaller, but with more pages and there were much more pop and gossip pages – including television stars from soaps of the day such as Brookside. The quality of both the printing and the photography itself improved hugely, so that resulted in a much better looking magazine. The readership also got younger by the decade so that by the late Eighties the average reader's age was probably around thirteen.

In 1989, the magazine went to full colour and with almost double number of pages of the first issue. The photo stories were also produced in full colour, but there was a greater emphasis on celebrity culture and the influences from cinema, television and the music industry. It became more about aspiring to be famous than being content with your own life.

Anne Rendall

The 5TH. proposal

FOUR PROPOSALS IN A WEEK ISN'T BAD GOING, HUH?

ONE IN SAN FRANCISCO, ONE IN NEW YORK, ONE IN BERMUDA, ONE IN MONTE CARLO. AND WHO KNOWS WHAT'S IN STORE FOR ME IN LONDON?

ALL RIGHT—SO I'M CHEATING A LITTLE. THE FIRST THREE WERE FROM THE SAME BOY. THAT JUST SHOWS HOW PERSISTENT HE IS.

Persistent — that's Greg all right. And his first proposal, in San Francisco, came right out of the blue.

I KNOW IT'S SUDDEN, JULIE—BUT I'M CRAZY ABOUT YOU.

I THOUGHT YOU WERE STRICTLY A BACHELOR CAREER PILOT.

I WAS—TILL YOU CAME ALONG. THE PLANE HASN'T BEEN BUILT THAT HAS YOUR SWEET LINES. AND IN THIS STATE, YOU DON'T NEED TO WAIT. PICK UP TWO WITNESSES AND WE COULD BE MAN AND WIFE IN FIFTEEN MINUTES.

YOU'RE VERY PERSUASIVE, GREG, AND I'M A LITTLE IN LOVE WITH YOU. BUT GETTING MARRIED ...WELL, IT'S NOT A THING I PLANNED TO RUSH.

ALL RIGHT. I WON'T CROWD YOU, HONEY. BUT THE MINUTE YOU DECIDE, LET ME KNOW.

Next night, in New York, the scene was different, but the theme very much on the same lines.

I HAVEN'T MENTIONED THIS TO ANYONE, BUT I PLAN TO HAND IN MY NOTICE IN A COUPLE OF WEEKS.

YOU'RE LEAVING THE AIRLINE? WHY, GREG?

I THINK I CAN GET FINANCIAL BACKING TO TAKE OVER A SMALL, THREE-PLANE OUTFIT ON THE WEST COAST THAT'S GOING FOR A SONG.

PROPERLY RUN, IT WOULD BE A GOLDMINE. YOU'VE GOT EXPERIENCE, PERSONALITY, LOOKS. WORKING TOGETHER, WE'D HAVE IT MADE IN A COUPLE OF YEARS!

By the time we got to Bermuda, it was all I could do not to surrender to the atmosphere of romance in the warm air.

IF I KEEP ASKING, I RECKON YOU MIGHT SAY "YES" IN A WEAK MOMENT. LOOK—EVEN THE MOON'S ON MY SIDE.

I WON'T KEEP YOU WAITING MUCH LONGER, GREG, DARLING. I PROMISE.

Two more nights under that Caribbean sky, and who knows what might have happened? But then Fate took a hand. Another stewardess took ill and I was rushed out as a replacement. Next day I was in Monaco.

I'LL MISS GREG. BUT I NEED A FEW DAYS AWAY FROM HIM TO GET THINGS STRAIGHT IN MY OWN MIND. DO I REALLY LOVE HIM?

Curiosity brought me to the Monte Carlo casino.

IT DOESN'T LOOK AS EXCITING AS I'D IMAGINED.

Still, nothing ventured . . . I changed ten francs for a blue chip and slipped into the first vacant seat.

PLACE YOUR BETS, MESSIEURS, MESDAMES.

MY BIRTHDAY'S ON THE TWENTY-SIXTH. . . . I'LL TRY RED 26.

BLACK NO. 5. I COULDN'T HAVE BEEN FURTHER AWAY. OH, WELL, SHORT AND SWEET.

But as I turned to go—

PLEASE STAY, MÂM'SELLE. YOU HAVE BROUGHT ME MY FIRST LUCK OF THE EVENING.

The accent was clipped, the voice commanding.

AT LEAST—STAY UNTIL THE NEXT SPIN?

I watched, fascinated, as his pile of chips grew. Blue ones, green ones—and the coveted thousand-franc whites. Then he gave a signal to the man behind the table. nonchalantly tipped him—and took my arm.

EXTRAORDINARY. FROM THE MOMENT YOU SAT DOWN BESIDE ME, I FELT A SPECIAL AFFINITY, AN ATTRACTION. AND NOT ONLY BECAUSE OF YOUR BEAUTY.

YOU MUST DO ME THE HONOUR OF HAVING SUPPER WITH ME, MÂM'SELLE—?

THANK YOU. SOME OTHER TIME, PERHAPS. I PROMISED TO MEET SOME FRIENDS BACK AT THE HOTEL.

And that was that, I thought. Until next morning, when my room-mate Sharon woke me . . .

WHAT PRINCE CHARMING WERE YOU WITH LAST NIGHT? THESE CAME FOR YOU.

The note read—"Some meagre recompense for the luck—and pleasure—of your company last night. — Paul Rojet."

I DIDN'T TELL HIM MY NAME—OR WHERE I WAS STAYING.

MONEY BUYS INFORMATION LIKE THAT—IF YOU'VE ENOUGH MONEY.

AND PAUL ROJET IS LOADED RIGHT UP TO THE GILLS. SORRY, HONEY—I COULDN'T RESIST PEEKING AT THE CARD.

PRETTY RICH, IS HE?

LET'S JUST SAY HIS WIFE ISN'T GOING TO HAVE TO TAKE IN ANY WASHING. THAT'S HIS YACHT OUT IN THE BAY. THE BIG ONE.

MMM. PITY, IN A WAY. I'M DUE OUT OF HERE ON THE NOON FLIGHT TO LONDON.

But as I checked the passengers aboard—

GOOD MORNING!

BUT...YOUR NAME'S NOT ON MY LIST.

A Cathy & Claire Special on going out with a boy for the first time

WHAT ARE YOU DOING TONIGHT?

)O you sometimes think some girls, and not even always the pretty es, seem to attract boys like magnets, while ners wait miserably day in day out for a boy ask them out?

At times like that, you think it's really ten when everyone else seems to have tes, and you don't. You begin to wonder ether there's something wrong with you, d your self-esteem goes down to nil.

Sue, for instance, is a pretty girl of 14, who nfesses that she feels on the shelf because hasn't yet been out with a boy.

'I want a boy to ask me out, but if one ever I just wouldn't know what to do," she d us. "It's funny, but I just can't imagine yone wanting to go out with me.

'I hear other girls talking about their boys d I think, wouldn't it be lovely to be like em! But I never talk to boys, I haven't got y brothers and I go to a girls' school, so ere's not much chance of meeting yone!"

Well, Sue is obviously keen to start going t with boys, but is too unsure of herself to anything about it. So firstly she should aw comfort from the fact that there's no ed age when a girl should start going out th boys. Sue's biggest stumbling block is at she has built it up so much in her mind at the idea of going out with a boy ems like some incredibly romantic and possible dream.

In short, she takes the whole thing too iously and dramatically. Going out with a y is in fact one of the most natural things in world, as she'll discover when she's erested and mature enough.

Boys are only human and friendships tween human beings are only normal! The ore natural and down-to-earth your itude towards boys, the easier it will be for u to cope with and enjoy going out with em.

So, if you haven't yet started going out th boys, how do you begin?

As Sue pointed out, if you never talk to ys and if you never go to places where ys are likely to be, it's obviously a no-no. s surprising how many girls complain they n't meet boys when all they're doing is ing at home moping and moaning about at a dull social life they lead!

For a full social life, the first essential is to out and mix with people, or to join a club ere there's a ready-made group (including s of dishy boys!) to welcome you.

There are youth clubs, dances, discos, imming pools, skating rinks and other ces of entertainment where boys abound. Really you'll find boys everywhere — re's no need to join a class on car intenance or heavy engineering. Whater interests you develop, you'll find boys re developing them as well!

A girl we know had a smashing time at an hery club, and another girl, who's a good ger, joined a local choir full of lovely ors and baritones! There's bound to be ne club or organised activity to cater for ur interests in your area. The church, too, good meeting place, and most churches e young people's groups where it's easy make friends.

VE know it takes courage to join a club all on your own. But, if can't find a friend to tag along with you, ve it alone, and remember that people are ically kind and friendly.

Everyone has experienced that awful ling of being an outsider, so if you're in situation, you'll find that most people want to make you feel at home.

f you don't believe us, listen to Jeannie, d 15, who plucked up the courage to join a th club.

When we moved to Bradford last year I n't know a soul," she said. "My mum kept nagging at me to join a youth club and make friends, instead of mooning round the house, but I dreaded the thought of it and kept putting it off.

"But then one evening I was so fed up, I just walked into the club. I felt really self-conscious and shy, but the organisers were very kind, and after the first few times, I began to enjoy it. I think it's great now, and can't wait for the evenings when I go there to come around!"

Thanks to the club, Jeannie has a fabulous crowd of friends, and a boyfriend, Rick, who she's been seeing for the last few weeks.

Of course, joining a club or going to a disco doesn't guarantee instant success in getting a boyfriend, or even a casual date, but you can do a lot to help yourself.

One thing it will definitely pay you to remember is that boys are often too shy to approach a girl, especially if they fear they may be snubbed or made to look foolish. If you appear to be friendly and approachable, boys will more easily pluck up the courage to make the opening move.

It's logical that the girls who are least shy and most extrovert have a better chance of being approached than the shy girls, who tend to give the mistaken impression that they're difficult, moody or aloof.

So try to relax, talk to other girls, look lively and interested in what's going on around you. If you find that a particular boy keeps looking at you, smile at him and, if he still doesn't take the hint, you can always try casually wandering up in his direction.

In Victorian times a girl used to drop a white hankie at the boy's feet to indicate that she liked him, but that's a bit dated these days and might not have the desired result!

Still, it may be up to you, sometimes, to make the first move if you feel a boy is obviously interested but too timid to make friends. In a club or a social occasion, it's quite acceptable for a girl to start chatting to a boy.

This is easier said than done, we know, and the trouble is that opening gambits are always corny and make people feel a bit silly — Hello, what's your name? Excuse me, could you tell me the time? Do you come here often? Haven't I seen you somewhere before? Horrible weather we're having! Isn't this a lovely record? Phew, it's crowded in here!

None of these are great conversation pieces, but the point is that an opening line isn't supposed to be a great, profound or witty statement. It's simply a way to get into conversation and get to know someone better.

Remember, nothing ventured, nothing gained! If the boy doesn't want to know, he'll respond, answer your comment or question and turn away, but if he's interested, the conversation can then branch off from the corny starter.

IF you're too scared to approach a boy on your own, you could enlist the help of a friend, or ask to be introduced to the boy who takes your fancy, or even get your friend to tell him you quite like him.

If a boy approaches you with a weak and corny intro like: "Do you come here often?" don't laugh at him. Make it easy for him by being as friendly and easy-going as you can. Don't leave him to wrack his brain for the next thing to say. He'll find it too much hard work and go in search of a nice chatty girl to pass the time with.

Another point is that the more you practise talking to people (especially to boys) the easier it becomes. So even if the boy chatting you up doesn't seem the answer to every girl's prayer, at least give him the benefit of the doubt and contribute to the conversation.

This will have two good effects — it'll make him feel ten feet tall, and it'll also give you practice in being able to get on well with boys. Never burn your boats, 'cause you might find he's got a really nice guy as a friend and then you'll be eating your heart out.

It's always best, especially if you're not too sure of yourself, to avoid being clever. Some girls have the ability to flirt, to put on an act, and even tell whopping lies to make themselves appear fascinating, worthy people. It's fun to be a flirt, but the best way of getting boys to fall for you is simply by being your natural self.

If you're natural and friendly, the boy will feel encouraged to try to get to know you better. If you go silent and look at him with great moony eyes, he'll probably get scared off.

Eventually, a boy *will* ask you out, and if it's your first time, you're bound to be a bit nervous and unsure of yourself.

The first thing to remember is that the boy is probably just as nervous as you are, and just as anxious to make the date a success, so it's up to you to help things run smoothly.

The second thing to remember is that the boy asked *you* out. He had to pluck up courage and take the initiative. That means he chose you because he liked you more than the others and wanted to know you better. Again, it's up to you, if you like the boy, to show him that you're complimented and happy about the arrangement.

THE object of going out with someone, apart from getting to know them better, is to enjoy each other's company and have a good time.

You can't enjoy yourselves if you're too tense and worried, so try to relax. Also try not to take it all too seriously.

Very often, when the girl expects a very serious romance, the boy gets frightened that he can't live up to her expectations, and it's a tense, fraught outing. Other times, when the girl is too shy to respond, the poor boy spends an uncomfortable evening trying to make conversation, and probably loses confidence in the mistaken belief that the girl is bored, or doesn't like him.

There are lots of things you can do to help. You might feel shy, but you must try to overcome it for your own sake. You can probably natter non-stop to your best friend for hours, so there's no reason why you can't joke and laugh and chat with a boy in the same way.

You can also help by being appreciative, telling him how much you enjoyed the film, and that the beefburger and coffee were quite the nicest you've ever tasted!

If you like him, you'll find it natural enough to be warm and affectionate to him. And he'll respond happily. After all, there's nothing people like better than feeling needed. So remember, it's up to you, as well, to show that you care.

For instance, it's off-putting for a boy when he asks you where you want to go or what you want to do, if you say, "I don't mind" or, "It's up to you." He asks you because he wants to know the sort of entertainment you enjoy. In other words, he wants you to help him make the decisions.

The most important thing, however, is not to worry. You don't have to make incredible, witty conversation all the time. If you really can't think of anything to say, don't try to force things — look happy and put the boy at ease. Each subsequent date will be easier and the more you're able to relax the more you will enjoy yourself.

However, if, after all that, your first boy doesn't phone you and disappears into the blue, try not to see it as a reflection on you as a person. It's just that this time, things didn't work out. But that's no reason to suppose they won't in the future.

Remember that not everyone's well suited, so it's a good idea to go out with lots of people, have different dates, and always keep in mind that there are other fish in the sea!

Go out in a crowd sometimes, and enjoy the company of both boys and girls. The friendlier you are, and the more people you mix with, the easier it'll be when it comes to enjoying yourself with boys, and, afterwards, choosing that very special steady boyfriend.

All this may be easier said than done, but believe us, it's worth doing. So what are you waiting for?

REMEMBER UNCLE ANGUS?
YOUR SCOTTISH UNCLE WHO WENT TO A PARTY ON NEW YEAR'S EVE 1973 AND HASN'T BEEN SEEN SINCE?
THE VERY ONE, WELL, HERE'S A CARD FROM HIM
SO HE MADE IT HOME AT LAST!
NOT QUITE, IT SAYS...
"HAPPY NEW YEAR MIKE, HAWAII IS TERRIFIC, CHEERS, UNCLE ANGUS"

FRILLED TO

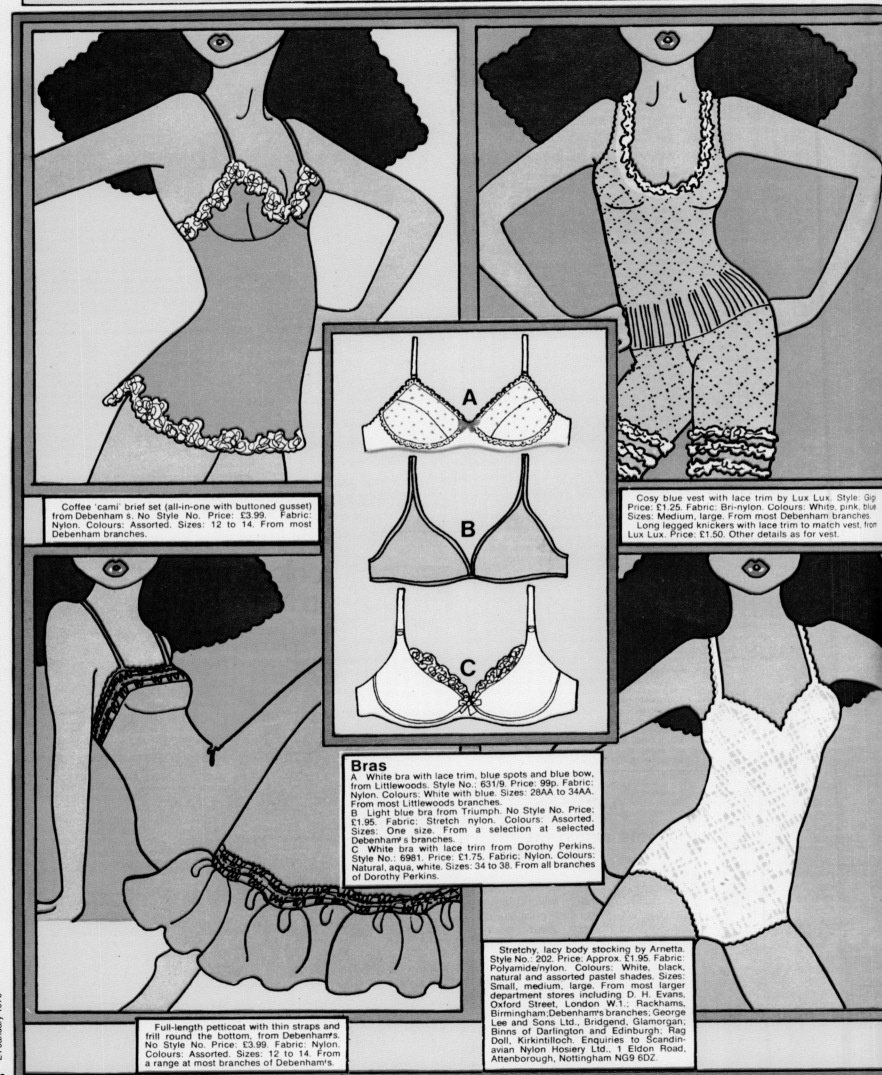

Coffee 'cami' brief set (all-in-one with buttoned gusset) from Debenham s. No Style No. Price: £3.99. Fabric: Nylon. Colours: Assorted. Sizes: 12 to 14. From most Debenham branches.

Cosy blue vest with lace trim by Lux Lux. Style: Gigi Price: £1.25. Fabric: Bri-nylon. Colours: White, pink, blue Sizes: Medium, large. From most Debenham branches. Long legged knickers with lace trim to match vest, from Lux Lux. Price: £1.50. Other details as for vest.

Bras
A White bra with lace trim, blue spots and blue bow, from Littlewoods. Style No.: 631/9. Price: 99p. Fabric: Nylon. Colours: White with blue. Sizes: 28AA to 34AA. From most Littlewoods branches.
B Light blue bra from Triumph. No Style No. Price: £1.95. Fabric: Stretch nylon. Colours: Assorted. Sizes: One size. From a selection at selected Debenham's branches.
C White bra with lace trim from Dorothy Perkins. Style No.: 6981. Price: £1.75. Fabric: Nylon. Colours: Natural, aqua, white. Sizes: 34 to 38. From all branches of Dorothy Perkins.

Full-length petticoat with thin straps and frill round the bottom, from Debenham's. No Style No. Price: £3.99. Fabric: Nylon. Colours: Assorted. Sizes: 12 to 14. From a range at most branches of Debenham's.

Stretchy, lacy body stocking by Arnetta. Style No.: 202. Price: Approx. £1.95. Fabric: Polyamide/nylon. Colours: White, black, natural and assorted pastel shades. Sizes: Small, medium, large. From most larger department stores including D. H. Evans, Oxford Street, London W.1.; Rackhams, Birmingham; Debenham's branches; George Lee and Sons Ltd., Bridgend, Glamorgan; Binns of Darlington and Edinburgh; Rag Doll, Kirkintilloch. Enquiries to Scandinavian Nylon Hosiery Ltd., 1 Eldon Road, Attenborough, Nottingham NG9 6DZ.

BITS!

Green v-neck vest with white lace trim, from Marks & Spencer. No Style No. Price 99p. Fabric: Cotton. Colours: White, green, beige. Sizes: 32 to 36. From major branches of Marks & Spencer.
Green knickers to match vest, also from Marks & Spencer. No Style No. Price: 49p. Sizes: 34 to 38 hip. Other details as for vest. From major branches of Marks & Spencer.

White lacy vest with 1 inch wide straps, from Woolworth. Style No.: 1964. Price: 69p. Fabric: Cotton. Colours: White. Sizes: 10 to 14. From larger Woolworth branches.
White frilled calf length petticoat with drawstring waist, from Laura Ashley. No Style No. Price: £6.00. Fabric: Cotton. Colours: White. From all Laura Ashley branches.

Bras

D Coffee-coloured bra from Warners. Style No.: 1846. Price: £2.75. Fabric: Nylon/Elastane. Colours: White, coffee. Sizes: 34 to 36 A, B and C cup. From selected Debenham branches.
E Black bra with adjustable straps comes from Dorothy Perkins. Style No.: 6972. Price: £1.25. Fabric: Lycra and net lace. Sizes: 34 to 36 A and B cup. Colours: Black, aqua, white. From all branches of Dorothy Perkins.
F Pretty white bra with adjustable cups, from Dorothy Perkins. Style No.: 6955. Price: £1.15. Fabric: Nylon. Colours: Natural, white. Sizes: 34 to 36 A and B cup. From all branches of Dorothy Perkins.

Square-necked cream vest with ribbon trim from Marks & Spencer. No Style No. Price: 99p. Fabric: Cotton. Colours: White, green, beige. Sizes: 32 to 36 bust. From major branches of Marks & Spencer.
Cream knickers to match vest also from Marks & Spencer. No Style No. Price: 49p. Sizes: 34 to 38 hip. Other details as for vest. From major branches of Marks & Spencers.

All-in-one 'cami' brief set, from Wolsey. Style No.: M67. Price: £2.50. Fabric: Celon. Colours: White, black. Sizes: 10 to 14. From D. H. Evans, Oxford Street, London, W.1.

RISE AND SHINE

FIND it difficult to get up in the mornings? We all do it . . . stay in bed far too long and then panic round trying to remember all the things we're supposed to do and finally go without breakfast!

The answer is a good routine, of course. A master plan to help you get up and out of the house without too many problems, looking and feeling ready for the day ahead!

So, here goes. We're bringing you a complete guide to getting up from the awful moment your alarm goes, to the minute you rush out of the house.

7.45—You'll need about an hour for our system, so set the clock accordingly the night before. If you have to leave the house at 8.45, for example, you must set the alarm for 7.45.

The great thing is to get out of bed a few minutes after you've woken up. The longer you lie there, the harder it is to drag yourself away from the cosy blankets. Sit up in bed and do a few deep breathing exercises until you are fully conscious and realise that it is in fact morning!

7.50—Get out of bed (leap out if you're feeling energetic) and touch your toes a few times or whirl your arms like a windmill

several times. This is to let your body know that it should be awake, and to get the blood pounding through your veins in fine style.

Running on the spot is a good idea, or, if you're running a bit late (ugh!) with your schedule, you'll have to make up for it by running downstairs later!

7.55—Now to the bathroom. Morning baths or showers are super, and if you're a quick

dresser you'll probably have time for one. Other people may object to you hogging the bathroom, however, so you'll have to hurry.

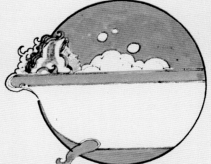

Washes are quicker, though, so have a good one and brush your teeth. (You'll have to brush them again after breakfast, remember!)

Apply your deodorant and give it plenty

of time to dry. Sprinkle yourself with talc so that you're smelling really sweet. If you wear cologne or perfume during the day, now's a good time to apply it. That way you won't spill it all over your clothes.

8.00—Make-up next. Apply lots of moisturiser first and let it sink in. This will protect your skin from the horrors of the day, and also from all that make-up you're about to put on. If you're still at school and are not allowed to wear make-up, it's still a good idea to put a layer of moisturiser on first.

Foundation comes next if you are wearing make-up. Make sure it's even and you haven't got any tide-marks round your chin and neck. Then for your eye make-up. Take

your time over this, making sure you get it right. If it goes wrong, be patient, remove it and start all over again.

Morning's a bad time for applying mascara. Eyes are still sleepy and you're more likely to blink and spoil it all. If you can't trust yourself not to blink, try putting a folded tissue under your lower lashes to protect your cheeks until it's all over and your mascara is dry.

Blusher is the next step, so here goes. Never put blusher too close to your nose, as this has an ageing effect. Keep colour to your cheek-bones, depending on the shape of your face, and put a hint of colour right between your eyebrows above your nose for subtle highlights.

Set the whole lot with translucent powder, making sure you don't leave any blobs behind, and then you're ready for your lipstick.

If you're a messy eater or tend to leave lipstick behind on your toothbrush, you may prefer to leave lipstick until you're just about ready to go out.

Now for your hair. Brush it well and make sure it looks really nice and tidy. If it looks very greasy and you can't bear to leave it that way, why not try using a dry shampoo to give it a boost.

8.15—After all that, you should be ready to get dressed: Take your time over this, making sure that tights are the right way round, and bra is properly adjusted and fastened, otherwise you'll be uncomfortable all day. Plan what you're going to wear, either the night before or while you are washing, etc. If you don't do that, you'll be tempted to throw on the first things that come to hand and spend the rest of the day worrying about how you look.

If buttons are missing or hems are down, don't wear the clothes. Think of something else if you can, because there's nothing more likely to spoil your day than worrying about loose threads and saggy hems. If you've spilled something on your skirt or trousers the day before, either wash them or take them to the cleaners immediately. If marks are left, the material will eventually rot and disintegrate, so beware!!

8.30—If you're one of those people who likes to have breakfast but ends up gulping half a cup of cold coffee and eating one bite of toast, then you'll be relieved to find that you've got at least ten minutes left to have a really good breakfast.

Even if you don't really like the thought of anything too substantial so early in the day, you can at least enjoy a nice cup of tea or coffee, or a glass of milk before you go out.

If Mum's been slaving away over a hot stove to make you a cooked breakfast, you'll have time to do it justice, and maybe even time to wash up your own dishes afterwards . . . you never know!

While you're eating, think of all the things you'll need for the day, and try to remember where they are. Have a look outside to see if it's raining and decide whether you'll need hat and brolly, or not.

If it IS raining, you may have to decide on something else for your feet, boots instead of shoes to keep your legs warm and dry and you'll need a coat instead of a jacket to keep the rest of you dry especially if you've got some walking to do. It's really depressing to have to sit around in wet clothes and even worse to end up with a cold or chill.

8.40—Now to put all that into practice. First, clean your teeth, then collect your handbag, making sure you've got tissues or a hankie, brush or comb and absolutely everything you're going to need during the day. Collect books, pens, pencils and things . . . notebooks, address book, things you can't do without at work or at school.

Put them all together in the bag you're going to take with you, then put on your hat and coat, say goodbye to Mum (and anyone else who happens to be around) and off you go.

It all sounds quite easy written down on paper, but there are lots of things that can interrupt and hinder your schedule. Don't be too put out, you'll just have to hurry along and make up the time somewhere else.

You really will feel so much better if you don't have to hurry and rush in the mornings, and the chances are that you'll have a much better, happier day for it. If you've always got up at 8.55 to be out of the house at 9.00, here's your chance to reform and be early to work for a change . . . it certainly won't do you any harm to try it!

NEW YEAR NEW YOU

THIS is the time of year when everyone makes wonderful resolutions they hardly ever keep! But this year's going to be different — isn't it?

Of course it is! Because with our help and a lot of will-power, you should be able to glide into 1975 looking immaculate in every way — that's if you follow our beauty resolutions — and promise to keep them!

1 I MUST take off my make-up every night no matter how tired I am.

Make this a rule, like always cleaning your teeth at night, and you'll find you can't bring yourself to break it.

If you break it, woe betide your skin! Pores will soon become clogged, and once the walls of the pores have been stretched, it's almost impossible for them to regain their original tightness. So you end up with open pores and all sorts of nasty things.

If you have a normal or dry skin, try Anne French Cleansing Milk (23½p) or Love's Creamy Face Wash, (55p) to remove make-up. For oily skins, try Love's Fresh Lemon Face Wash (55p) or Pond's Lemon Cream (25p).

2 I MUST not wear holey tights.

It's amazing how much those tiny holes you thought you could get away with seem to grow and grow until your legs look like a sieve! If you want to avoid this (and who doesn't), try each night to look out the next day's tights — clean and perfect. Of course, there's an easy solution if you just can't keep tights whole — wear trousers all the time and you can wear socks underneath!

3 I MUST try to be tidier.

This can result in some lovely, unexpected beauty bonuses. No frantic last-minute, unsuccessful searches for, say, that new, rust eye shadow you bought to wear with today's jumper.

Three times a year, thoroughly tidy and clean wardrobe, drawers, handbags and their contents. Place certain things in certain places so that you don't need to strain your memory and search. You'll be able to place your hand speedily on what you want if you hang things in your wardrobe according to their colour. All browns, greens, blues etc. together.

4 I MUST not snip bits off my hair!

Unless you're a trained hair-dresser, resist snipping off those long ends in the fond belief you'll achieve a professional fringe or razzle-dazzle curls. The result could be chaos! So why not invest in a small supply of coloured hair ribbon, plain hair grips and fancy slides, which will keep over-long hair prettily under control till you can make that much-needed appointment with a hair-dresser.

5 I MUST dispose tidily of my nail clippings.

Reminds us of the (joke?) "Do you file your nails?" "No, I throw mine away." (Groan!)

The best time to cut toe nails is after your bath, because then they are soft and pliable. Nail cuttings should be wrapped in a piece of paper and put in the waste paper basket, not left scattered here and there on the bathroom floor. Ugh! And double Ugh!

Once your toe nails are tidily cut, you can make them look even nicer with the stunning nail colours which are around just now. Choose from the Max Factor Whipped Cream range (49p) in Dewy Rose or Enamel Red. Or Woltz Italiana's "Uffizi," a succulent orange colour at 30p for the mini size.

6 I MUST learn to walk elegantly.

There's a very simple but effective exercise designed to improve your walk and your posture in a moment. And it's simply this: when you're walking along, pretend someone (or something!) is pulling you up by the ears. Sounds silly, I know, but try it and you'll be amazed at the results!

You'll find that your shoulders straighten, your tummy flattens and your bottom tucks in nicely. All the ingredients for an elegant model walk!

7 I MUST learn to speak clearly.

First rule, especially if on the phone, is to sound cheerful. This isn't easy if you're feeling down-in-the-dumps, are worried about something, or because he hasn't rung. But a cheerful welcoming note when you speak can earn you the reputation of having a lovely voice on the phone. Don't go mad, though, and laugh uproariously when you answer the phone. That could be disastrous!

The second rule is to listen to what you're saying and relax. An instructor at a drama school says the voice will be at its clearest if you stand or sit with your spine straight, your shoulders loose, not stiff, your shoulders loose, not pushed back, and your chin parallel to the ground, not up or down. Try it and see if she's not right!

And remember — tension is fatal to clear speech. The keyword is relax, relax, relax.

8 I MUST keep warm this winter.

This is important, because it's impossible to look really nice if your nose is blue with cold and your fingers red with chilblains. Hot milky drinks are wonderful for central heating! So never leave the house in the morning without breakfast and a hot drink.

Wear thicker underwear and more clothes. Sounds obvious, but it's surprising how many shivers are caused by ignoring this simple rule. Chunky woollens are the fashion look for this winter, anyway, so you'll be completely in style if you're styled for warmth!

9 I MUST keep my accessories clean.

That means: dirt-free hand-bag or shoulder bag; shoes cleaned every night so that in the morning they're ready to light up the pavement; glasses (if you wear them) shining clean because you've wiped them with a chamois or a soft tissue. And not only the lens, but the sides and bridge as well, because if these are left in a greasy state, they can give you a spotty skin.

Handbag combs should be washed more often than your dressing-table brush and comb. Just leave to soak in warm, soapy water for a few minutes, scrub with a nailbrush to get rid of all the horrid bits, rinse thoroughly and — you've got a sparkling clean comb!

Brushes take a bit more time, because you'll have to pick out the stray hairs, but it's worth it!

10 MUST not top chipped nail varnish with layer after layer of new nail varnish.

Quite right. For a smooth, lovely nail surface, there must be a fresh application of nail polish. Cutex 'Basecoat' used beneath the varnish, ensures a smooth flow of polish. A layer of 'Basecoat' over your varnish gives a stronger resistance to chips.

You should really also leave your nails polish-free at least one week in three, to allow them to "breathe" and recover their strength for the next onslaught of paint or glitter!

11 I MUST not be scared to go to the dentist.

Very important if you want to have a nice smile this year and the next and the next . . . You can help, too, of course, by brushing your teeth regularly every morning and every evening — and after a particularly sweet or spicy meal. If you just can't manage to brush after a meal — eating an apple is the next best thing to keep your teeth sparkling and your breath fresh and sweet. And remember — bad breath won't do anything for your new 1975 image, so make sure your breath is fresh by carrying some Amplex tablets or Gold Spot with you.

12 I MUST keep all my resolutions.

And a tip to help you keep your beauty resolutions: a reward! After a month of continuous good beauty behaviour, reward yourself with a little treat. Eat a cream cake (just one!), buy some new make-up, or invest in a new perfume. That always makes you feel luxurious! Yardley's "Shanida", warm and subtle, is super, and costs 80p for the Mini Spray, or Mary Quant's "Havoc" spray perfume is really luxurious at £1.70.

So there you are — twelve resolutions which (if kept!) will make 1975 your most beautiful year yet!

THE WAY TO HIS HEART!

THEY say the way to a man's heart's through his stomach — and there's certainly nothing more impressive than being able to produce an attractive, tasty and satisfying load of food for a starving guy!

If you haven't got round to finding out what he loves to eat, though, there's a good way of doing it without even asking. All you need to know is his birth-sign, then you can follow our Zodiac guide, which'll tell you whether to make him something light and luscious, sweet and spicy or just fantastically filling!

What's more, you don't have to be a kitchen wizard to produce these. The recipes we're giving you are almost as easy as boiling an egg. So get out the pots and pans, and you'll be on your way to winning his love!

CAPRICORN
(Dec. 21 — Jan. 19)

Capricorn boys can be serious, practical sort of creatures and they usually prefer simple food.

You'll have to break the monotony of their diet! They'll be pleasantly surprised with the zesty flavour of onions, lemon juice and vinegar. The last'll match the sharpness they can show but they have a sweet side, too! This should satisfy both sides very well!

SWEET 'N' SOUR APPLE FRITTERS

INGREDIENTS (for 2)
2 medium cooking or green sour apples
2 level tbsp. butter
1 level tbsp. caster sugar
1 level tsp. cinnamon
1 small can thick cream or evap. milk
UTENSILS
Frying pan
Plate or small bowl
Wash apples and slice into half-inch thick rings. Cut out the pips and centre core of each ring. Mix the caster sugar and cinnamon together on a plate or in a small bowl. Melt the butter in a frying pan over a medium heat. Fry the rings for 2 to 3 minutes on each side until just turning golden. Don't overcook or the rings will become mushy. Dip the rings in the cinnamon and caster sugar and serve with a tbsp. thick cream or evap. milk.

AQUARIUS
(Jan. 20 — Feb. 18)

Aquarius is a real Air sign, and Aquarians will love light dishes with mild, delicate flavourings. Their ruling planet, Uranus, gives them a liking for things new and unusual, and their love of travel makes them interested in foreign food. You'll be right on the mark with this fresh, delicate dessert recipe.

FRUIT IN SNOW

INGREDIENTS (for 4)
One jelly (any flavour)
2 oz. can evaporated milk
1 can of fruit (peaches, apricots etc.) — drained.
UTENSILS
Mixing bowl
Rotary or electric beater
Prepare the jelly according to directions on the packet, only using ¾ pint of water. Allow it to half set, then beat with a hand or electric mixer, adding the evaporated milk a little at a time until the jelly becomes frothy and pale. Fold in the drained fruit and allow to set until firm. Spoon into dessert dishes and serve.

PISCES
(Feb. 19 — March 20)

Pisces is a water sign, so it's not surprising Pisces boys enjoy fish dishes more than any others. Like all the water signs they're big eaters, but they get bored with the same old things and go for imaginative, new, original recipes. Anything rich and highly seasoned appeals to them! You could easily overspend when you're catering for them, but these Fish 'n' Cheese Dreams should satisfy your pocket and his taste!

FISH 'N' CHEESE DREAMS

INGREDIENTS (for 2)
2 slices of bread
1 small can salmon spread
¼ lb. cheese (Cheddar, Gouda, Edam etc.)
Grate the cheese. Spread the salmon on the bread. Sprinkle the cheese over the bread. Grill the bread until the cheese melts and begins to turn golden brown.

ARIES
(March 21 — April 20)

Arians love eating but you won't interest them in anything exotic! Hearty, simple food appeals to them most, but since Aries is a fire sign they need a dash of spice in it. This taste may also come from the red hot rays of Mars, the Arian ruling planet. Arians can be a bit "peppery," so this recipe should suit them fine!

CHILLI-FRIED BEEF

INGREDIENTS (for 4)
1 10 oz. can baked beans
1 10 oz. can tinned tomatoes
½ lb. mince
1 medium onion (diced)
salt, pepper, chilli powder
cooking oil
UTENSILS
Frying pan
Large saucepan
Heat 2 tbsp. cooking oil in frying pan. Add the onion and cook over a medium heat till soft and golden. Add the mince to the frying pan. Mix the onion into the mince and allow the mince to fry well on medium heat. Occasionally spoon off any fat from the mince. When the mince is well cooked (about ½ hr.) drain off any fat and put mince and onion into the large pot. Mix the baked beans, tinned tomatoes, salt, pepper and a dash of chilli powder (it's super-hot so a little goes a long way!) into the mince. Bring the mixture to the boil over a medium heat then allow to simmer for 5-10 minutes over a low heat before serving.

TAURUS
(April 21 — May 20)

Taurus is an Earth sign ruling practical, down-to-earth people, who love rich, hearty, mild-tasting food. In particular, Taureans enjoy dishes garnished with cream, such as creamed mushrooms or chicken in sauce. Keep them happy with this rich, sweet dish!

SPICED BANANAS

INGREDIENTS (for 2)
2 bananas
2 tsp. butter
1 level tsp. cinnamon or mixed spice
2 tsp. sugar
1 small can thick cream or evap. milk
UTENSILS
Frying pan
Place butter in frying pan and melt over a low heat. Add sugar. Peel the bananas, slice lengthwise and fry lightly in the butter and sugar over a medium heat, 4 to 5 minutes on each side. Be careful not to overcook or the bananas will become mushy. To serve sprinkle with cinnamon or mixed spice, and top with a large tablespoon of cream.

GEMINI
(May 21 — June 20)

Gemini is an Air sign, which tells you your Gemini boy's a light eater. He'll love airy, easy-to-prepare dishes like souffles and omelettes. Since theirs is the sign of the twins, Gemini boys enjoy a meal with several elements to it. For example, something sweet and sour, or a casserole with two different kinds of meat. The following's bound to catch his eye and please his palate!

FOUR-LAYERED TRIFLE

INGREDIENTS (for 4)
2 packs of different flavoured jellies
custard powder
milk
sugar : small carton double cream
chocolate vermicelli
UTENSILS
1 mixing bowl and spoon
Large glass bowl
Prepare half a pint of one jelly according to the directions on the package. Pour into the bowl and allow to set firmly — about 3 hours. About 2 hours later prepare half a pint of the second jelly. Allow this to cool for about an hour, till it's half set, before pouring it over the first layer of jelly in the bowl. Make up half a pint of custard and when it's cool, pour it on and sprinkle with chocolate vermicelli. Since it takes at least three hours for each layer to set firmly, you should start making it in the morning if you want to have this for tea.

CANCER
(June 21 — July 21)

Cancer the crab is a water sign, ruled by the Moon. This tells us that Cancerians love eating, so watch you don't encourage them to overdo it! Seafood's their favourite, but unlike the other water signs they don't like spicy foods. Make something bland and filling for them; fish and potatoes will definitely appeal!

FISH AND POTATO CAKES

INGREDIENTS (for 2)
4 medium sized potatoes
1 5-6 oz. can tuna or salmon
cooking oil
salt, pepper
UTENSILS
1 frying pan
1 saucepan
1 mixing bowl
Boil the potatoes. Drain them well. Mash well in the mixing bowl. Crumble the fish into flakes and mix into potatoes. Add salt and pepper to taste. Coat the bottom of the frying pan with oil and heat over medium heat. Form the potato fish mixture into patties half an inch thick and about 2 inches across. Fry until dark golden brown on both sides, adding more oil as it is absorbed. Then eat them with fried eggs!

LEO
(July 22 — Aug. 21)

You'll find your Leo boyfriend takes quite a bit of catering for! Leos go for everything that's extravagant, rich and satisfying!

Don't try anything too exotic or spicy, though. Hearty meat dishes are their favourites, with just enough of a tasty tang to them. This should keep them happy.

TANGY HAMBURGERS

INGREDIENTS (for 4)
1 lb. mince
4 soft rolls
1 onion
cooking oil
salt, pepper
¼ cup tomato ketchup
Optional.
hamburger seasoning, relish, sweet pickles, mustard, garlic salt or diced clove garlic, pinch of mixed herbs (origano, tarragon, parsley, sage, thyme etc.)
UTENSILS
Frying pan
Large mixing bowl
Chop the onion as finely as possible. Place the mince in the mixing bowl. Add the onion, salt, pepper, ketchup and any of the optional seasonings or herbs. Put just enough cooking oil in the frying pan to lightly coat the bottom. Heat the frying pan over a low heat while you start making your patties. Take a lump of mince the size of a medium tomato and press it between your hands into a smooth ball shape. Make sure the ball is well pressed together. This helps to keep the pattie from falling apart while cooking. Begin gently pressing the ball into a flat shape that covers your palm. Try making the pattie thin (¼ inch thick is best) since cooking will make it shrink and thicken. Place the patties in the frying pan and turn the heat to medium. Cook the patties till they are well done, about ¼ hr. on each side. While the patties are frying, split the rolls and toast under the grill. Serve the hamburgers with any of the following: ketchup, mustard, relish, sweet pickles, slices of tomato or onion.

VIRGO

(Aug. 22 — Sept. 21)

Be careful when you cook for a Virgo boy, they're often fussy and finicky eaters!

But you'll be all right if you remember they're an Earth sign, so they enjoy simple dishes, usually with vegetables that grow beneath the ground, such as turnips, potatoes and onions. Our recipe should win the heart of even the fussiest Virgo.

FRENCH ONION SOUP

INGREDIENTS (for 2)
1 can consomme soup
1 onion
¼ to ½ cup grated cheese
2 slices bread
UTENSILS
Saucepan with lid
Slice the onions as thinly as possible. Break the slices into rings. Place the onions in the pot with the consomme. Over a high heat, bring the soup to the boil. Turn the heat to low, allowing the soup to simmer slowly, covered, for about 10 to 15 mins. until the onions are soft. While the soup is simmering cover the bread with grated cheese and grill until cheese has melted and a golden crust begins to form. Cut bread into quarters. Pour the soup into bowls. Float the toast quarters in the soup and serve.

LIBRA

(Sept. 22 — Oct. 22)

Since Libra's an Air sign, Libran boys will prefer light dishes which are mildly savoury. They're impatient, so don't cook elaborate meals that take ages, but make sure you make something elegant and sophisticated! You'll really please him with this light savoury French dish for tea.

GRATIN POTATOES AND SAUSAGES

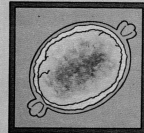

INGREDIENTS (for 4)
4 oz. grated cheese
1 medium onion
1 oz. butter or margarine
4 to 6 medium potatoes
4 sausages
2 eggs
1 cup milk
½ tsp. salt
½ tsp. pepper
UTENSILS
Large ovenproof baking dish
Small frying pan
Small mixing bowl
Preheat oven to 375 deg. F. or Mark 5. Chop the onion and fry slowly in butter for 5 mins. or so until tender. Put aside on a plate. Fry the sausages until well done. Peel the potatoes, slice and boil for ten minutes. Butter the bottom and sides of baking dish. Spread half the sliced potatoes over the bottom of the dish, then half the cooked onions. Cut the sausages lengthwise and lay on top of the potatoes. Sprinkle the rest of the onions over the sausages and then the remaining potato slices. Beat the eggs in the mixing bowl. Add the milk and salt and pepper. Pour the eggs and milk over the potato, onion and sausage mixture. Spread on the grated cheese. Dot the top with butter. Bake for 30 to 40 minutes until top is nicely browned. Serve at once.

SCORPIO

(Oct. 23 — Nov. 21)

Scorpio's a water sign ruled by Mars, which tells us that Scorpio boys are attracted to fish and strongly spiced foods. Their meals must be rich and filling and like Taureans they're very much affected by the colour and smell of a dish! This spaghetti sauce will please his eye and the rich spicy smell will have him hanging round the kitchen! Try it with meat balls or fish.

SPICY SPAGHETTI SAUCE

INGREDIENTS (for 4)
1 lb. spaghetti
cooking oil
1 medium onion
salt, pepper
1 small (5 oz.) can tomatoes
Optional: clove garlic or garlic salt
oregano, tarragon,
grated Parmesan cheese.
UTENSILS
2 large saucepans
Large frying pan
Mixing bowl
Dice the onion and cook slowly in a saucepan for 5 minutes in a tablespoon of cooking oil. Add the tomatoes and the garlic, oregano or tarragon if you have them. Leave this pan on one side for a moment. In a large pot, bring 2 pints of salted water to a boil over a high heat. Add the spaghetti and boil until it's soft and the strands have increased by almost double (about 15 mins. of rapid boiling). While the spaghetti is boiling bring the sauce to a boil over a medium heat then turn heat to low and simmer, covered. When the spaghetti is cooked, drain in a colander (taste a few strands to make sure they are not sticky or starchy). Add to the sauce.

SAGITTARIUS

(Nov. 22 — Dec. 20)

Sagittarians have healthy appetites, are easily bored with the same dishes and enjoy trying new recipes. Being a Fire sign, they enjoy spice in their food, and it's got to be something hearty and filling! They've also got a taste for smoked things — bacon or kippers will be a favourite. The following recipe should leave a Sagittarius boy full and happy!

FRENCH CANADIAN SMOKED BEANS

INGREDIENTS (for 4)
1 large can baked beans
1 smoked rasher per person
1 onion
1 level tsp. American mustard or
¼ tsp. mustard powder mixed with 1 tsp.
vinegar
salt, pepper
cooking oil
UTENSILS
Frying pan
Large pot with lid
Fry the rashers very well till they are crisp and most of the fat has been cooked away. Put aside on a dish. Dice the onion and fry in one tbsp. of the bacon fat until soft but not browned. Cut the rashers into 1 inch pieces and place rashers, onion, beans, mustard, salt, and pepper in pot. Simmer beans over very low heat until they come to the boil. Add a little water if the beans become too thick and begin sticking to bottom of pot. Serve with bread and butter.

THE BEATLES believe in dining in style—their own style! Which means tomato rolls and ice-cream, hamburgers, the lot!

That's what Paul, Ringo and George were scoffing when we dropped in at their flat. But, hey, where's John?

"Oh, he's around," the others told us. "Been in the kitchen for the past 15 hours. Why don't you look in there?"

We did, and discovered John craftily grilling Welsh rarebit. Watch your nose, John!

John's quite liable to burn a kettle of water, so Paul keeps a watching eye on things.

Life must go on. Even Beatles have dirty shirts, and they must be washed. Paul puts in some practice.

Jackie PIN-UP PAUL

SOMEONE LIKE YOU...

The steely arms of the law closed around me...
there was no escape... I'd been arrested!

ALL RIGHT, YOU. JUST COME ALONG QUIETLY.

BUT IT'S ALL A MISTAKE. I'M INNOCENT!

DISGRACEFUL. THE STREETS JUST AREN'T SAFE NOWADAYS WITH ALL THESE CRIMINALS AROUND!

When they got me to the station...

HERE SHE IS, SARGE. SHE SAYS HER NAME'S LUCY SMITH. PROBABLY AN ALIAS.

BETTER KEEP YOUR EYES ON HER, MEN. SHE'S A REAL DESPERATE LOOKING CHARACTER IF EVER I SAW ONE.

WHO, ME?

The sergeant told me I could make one phone call. He advised me to call a lawyer.

BUT I DON'T KNOW ANY LAWYERS!

TSK, TSK. WHAT A PITY. NEVER MIND THOUGH, YOU CAN ALWAYS PLEAD INSANITY.

Then I thought of somebody. Andy Cartwright. He was a law student and he lived in the same block of flats as me.

BUT WE DON'T KNOW EACH OTHER ALL THAT WELL JUST TO PASS ON THE STAIRS. IT'D BE AN AWFUL CHEEK FOR ME TO ASK HIM.

But I didn't have much choice. So...

HELLO... ANDY? EM... THIS IS LUCY, LUCY SMITH. IF YOU'RE NOT DOING ANYTHING DO YOU THINK YOU COULD COME ROUND TO THE POLICE STATION FOR A MINUTE? I'M IN THIS TINY LITTLE BIT OF TROUBLE.

So Andy arrived on the scene.

WHAT'S GOING ON? YOU HAVEN'T REALLY MANAGED TO GET YOURSELF ARRESTED, HAVE YOU?

IT'S ALL A MISUNDERSTANDING, ANDY. HONEST.

WHAT'S THE CHARGE?

AHEM... JUST A MINUTE. I'VE GOT THE LIST OF OFFENCES SOMEWHERE.

LIST? YOU MEAN THERE'S MORE THAN ONE?

HE'S EXAGGERATING. IT'S NOTHING MUCH REALLY.

DISTURBING THE PEACE. COMMITTING GRIEVOUS BODILY HARM. ATTEMPTING A SMASH AND GRAB RAID ON A JEWELLER'S. DAMAGING PRIVATE PROPERTY, ASSAULTING A POLICE OFFICER IN THE EXECUTION OF HIS DUTY...

SEE? I TOLD YOU IT WAS NOTHING MUCH.

NOTHING MUCH! HOW DID YOU MANAGE TO MISS OUT KIDNAPPING AND HIGH TREASON?

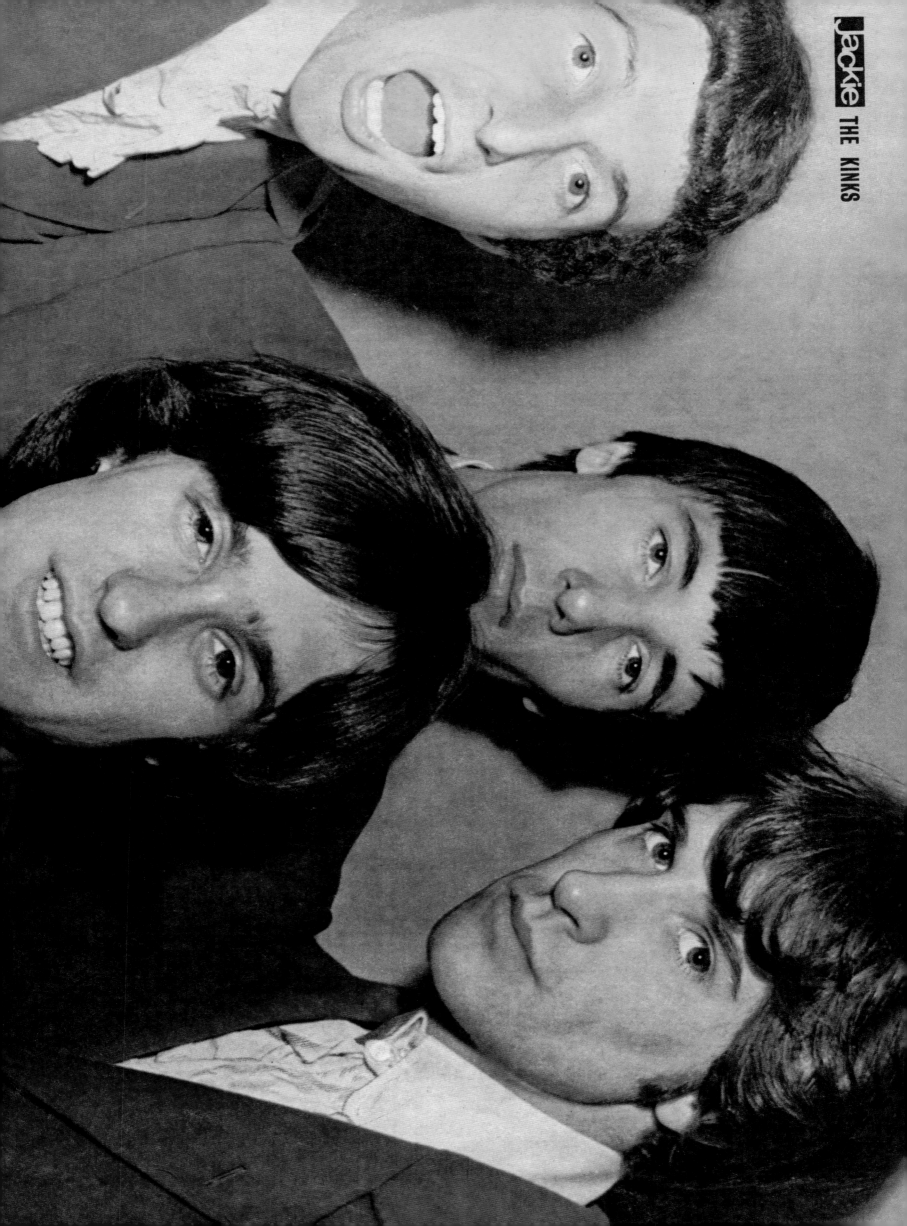

HOT GOSSIP

WHEN *JACKIE* FIRST CAME OFF THE PRESSES IN 1964, there was a relatively small number of really big names – people whom you would call celebrities now. The Beatles of course were a phenomenon unlike anything ever seen, at least in the UK. The nearest thing to that sort of fame would have been Elvis in America. Looking back, there were some unlikely candidates for pin-ups too – John Alderton, who at that time was starring in the television drama, *Upstairs Downstairs*, was one of them. The first few issues also carried pin-ups of film stars such as Steve McQueen and Sean Connery.

There was very little actual gossip about the stars' private lives. A column entitled "Pop Gossip" in the first issue had a snippet of news supplied by Paul McCartney saying that fans had started sending him green toothpaste, having heard he shaved with it … apparently, he did in fact use green shaving foam, but they had got the wrong information – truth is stranger than fiction!

Moving through the Seventies and Eighties, pop became more important and new magazines came on the market, like *Smash Hits* and *Just 17*. They were printed in full colour and were based in London, so *Jackie* had to up its game to succeed. Looking back to those days, you realise how little scope there was for getting information. There were no celebrity style magazines, there was no Twitter, no Facebook, so we had to rely on information from the music industry – the old A and R (Artists and Relations) people. There was the ever-present time lag problem as well: because we were working three months ahead, getting good, timely copy was always a problem. The solution was to have people on the ground in different cities. We commissioned reporters based in London and some of the bigger cities such as Birmingham and Manchester to interview pop stars. We spoke to people in the pop industry about their stars – there were very few stars we were interested in other than music ones.

Information came in mainly via the phone! We sometimes had problems with the telephonists who answered the phone from the central switchboard. Again, it is difficult to believe, but there was only one phone in each office, on the editor's desk, except in the *Jackie* office. By dint of it being the foremost magazine in the teen stable, it had its own phone cubicle as well. Sometimes, stars themselves would phone through to speak to the editor. On one memorable occasion, one of the lovely ladies on the switchboard phoned the editor and said that she had a Mr Elton John on the line – she suspected it was a hoax call and asked if she should just tell him that she could not put him through?

SEARCHIN' for IDIOTS

POP GOSSIP with pete lennon

I caught The Searchers surrounding a litter-bin the other day. Mike was doing the Sherlock bit, complete with deerstalker and telescope.

"What are you doing?" I said.

"Sssh," they replied.

"What are you looking for?" I asked.

"Be quiet!" they said.

"Please," I said. "Tell me what's going on."

Chris looked at me and said, "We are studying this litter-bin, so that people with nothing to do will come and ask us what we are doing. You are the 15th we have caught today."

Toe-ing the line

We know stars like Shirley Bassey and Dusty Springfield prefer to record in their stockinged feet—but I can tell you that Frank Ifield goes even farther out than that. I met him the other day as he was about to go into a recording studio—and he was preparing to take off his shoes and his socks!

Said Frank—"There is a special reason why this makes me feel relaxed. I spent so much time in the Australian bush when I was in my school-days—and in the bush it's the normal thing for kids to run around barefoot. So taking off my shoes 'n' socks somehow takes me back to those days—and real happy days they were. Makes me feel without a care when I sing."

Frank certainly bares his sole when he's putting those numbers on disc!

Railroad Joe

Called to see Joe Brown at the house he has bought in Essex—and we had to talk pretty loud. Reason—the rumble of electric trains at the bottom of Joe's back garden.

"People said I was crazy, living right by the railway," said Joe. "But, dad, I dig it. Sit in my bedroom at night watching the trains flash past. All the lights and the noise are fine by me."

Then Joe laid a finger alongside his nose and let me in on a secret. "Another good thing about living here, mate. I'm thinkin' of tapping the electric rail for free 'juice'!"

Toothy tale

Met those ring-a-ding Dakotas on their way to a disc session the other day. "Like a Coke, Pete?" they said. "I'm always oke for a Coke, fellers," I replied.

As they took their straws in their mouths, I remarked on how razzle-dazzle their teeth were. "That's Billy, man," said Tony Mansfield—meaning Billy J. Kramer, natch. "He says you gotta spread a little happiness—which means a good grin—which means good teeth. Forces us to go to the dentist every three months or else."

"Does anyone make him go?" I asked. "Betcha life," said Mike Maxfield. "We make sure he goes in first. After all, he's the boss. It's up to him to set a good example, by gum!"

Waste of "time"

Bobby Vee recently let me in on one hobby that he's just a wee bit ashamed of—it's breaking alarm clocks!

"I know I shouldn't do it," Bobby told me, "but I sometimes have to work very late AND have to be up very early next morning. It's then that I occasionally blow my top, grab the alarm clock and throw it across the room. Man, I feel real good for a few minutes afterwards. But then if I find the clock is damaged beyond repair, I figure that—even though I'm not worried about the cost of a new one—it is still a waste and is therefore wrong."

Maybe so, Bobby. But I guess most of us know how you feel. Try what I do. Leave the clock on the mantelpiece and throw a slipper at it. At that time of the morning, you'll always miss!

WE took this Beatle-pic after rehearsals one day and boy, do they look whacked, wack? Guess even a Beatle has...

POP GOSSIP

TOPS...

Slade and Elton John both played concerts in Sydney on the same day recently — Slade in the afternoon and Elton and his band in the evening.

As you might expect, the two groups decided to stick together while they were there. Firstly, they turned up at each other's concerts, and then, in the evening, after they'd finished working, they had a big party in Elton's hotel suite.

I was lucky enough to be invited to the party, too, and I spotted Elton and a slightly merry Noddy Holder deep in conversation. Their chat didn't last too long, however, because the next time I looked, Noddy's hat had fallen off and he'd dropped off to sleep! Somehow, I think it was the effect of the infamous beer they have here in Australia that caused Noddy to drop off, not Elton's conversation!

At the same party I got talking to Dave Hill, and I asked him how his new companion, his Great Dane, was getting on. (If you remember, Pete told you about the dog a few weeks ago in Pop Gossip.)

"He's huge!" exclaimed Dave. "When he stands on his hind legs he's nearly a foot taller than I am, and he's not even fully grown yet!

"And the way he eats is incredible. I've never seen anything that could eat as much as he does!"

To make matters a bit more chaotic, Dave has also been having a bit of trouble with his pet's training.

"He doesn't pay any attention to me," he said. "I try to be stern with him, but he just won't listen. In fact, he'll only respond to female voices —my mother's or some of my girlfriends'. I think it's something to do with the shrillness of their voices —he can hear the higher notes more easily. I must admit, though, I'm not convinced. It seems a bit unfair. I mean, I can't rush off trying to find my mum every time I want him to sit!"

DOWN UNDER

Mike

SHE'S B...

Yes, Sandy... We could... clump... Sandy... normal... that!). So... no...

...her triumphant return, complete with plaster. ...long before we saw her — clump.

...couldn't just break her ankle like any other... ...act to have a very unusual break (she's proud of...

...three whole weeks before she'll be back to ...as she ever gets a), ...h, you'll be sad to know that Sandy's injury ...ging. She sounds just as bad as ever! Pete

...nothing ...ter than ...on he was ...m in Los ...ago, he ...ome round ...essing room ...mong them ...o bought 35 ...show!), Steve ...Ross, and ...nis player.

...e from the ...one other ...— Tatum ...probably ...at lovely

Elton and John his manager, with Tatum.

...special ...ct he ...his big for Tatum(!), but it's the ...thought that counts, isn't it?

Unfortunately, it was just a bit too

"I'd been with Gary for eight years," said John, "and in that time I'd had a lot of ideas, but I'd no time to develop them while I was with the group.

"So I felt it was time to move on and create new things. It was a hard decision, but I felt I had to do it.

"You'll be glad to know that, despite the split, John's still great friends with Gary and the rest of the boys.

"I discussed it with Gary and the group before I left," said John, "and they agreed and wished me luck. And, of course, they're really interested in what I'm doing now. And so are we!

ROSS-ALL ALONE

As you know, John Rossall of the Glitter Band recently left the group in order to fulfil a long-standing ambition of his — to become a solo star.

And John is thoroughly enjoying his new career!

HELLO TO SUCCESS!

Speaking of Gary Glitter, another group who're associated with him are Hello, the young group from London who recently had a big hit...

ROLLING HOME

Eric Faulkner of the Bay City Rollers had a lot of trouble finding himself a place to stay last year. In fact, he even resorted to living in a hotel for a few months!

But in December he finally moved into his new home — a cottage just outside Edinburgh.

"It's a lovely place," said Eric, "and I'm really glad I've finally found a place of my own at last.

"The best thing about it is that it's in a very peaceful area, so when I'm there, I can really relax and get away from everything — for a few hours at a time, anyway!"

There were some very talented people working as the magazine's pop editors. They would go down to London regularly and check out new bands. If they thought they were going somewhere, quite often we would ask them to appear in a fashion photoshoot with a model. They were keen to get the exposure and would turn up ready and willing to be dressed in the clothes we had borrowed for them.

One memorable photoshoot featured Bucks Fizz and it was only when the photographs came back to the office that we noticed that there was a bulldog clip visible holding together an outfit which was too large at the shoulder! Sometimes, though, there were some great coincidences, particularly when a band that we spotted with potential reached the top of the pop charts at the same time as we featured them on the cover. That was the flip side of the long lead time – it gave their song time to be a success – and created a win-win situation.

Occasionally, we used particular agencies or photographers who had great access to the stars. One of those was a guy called Harry Goodwin. He was the photographer on *Top of The Pops* so he got some great shots for us and we would make up a story around a particular shot. Or we would save them for pin-ups. A great selling point for us was using a pin-up over three weeks. The first week you would get David Cassidy's legs, then his torso, and finally his head. That meant we were sure the readers would buy it for those three weeks. Some things were worth waiting for!

Anne Rendall

Pop Gossip

I'M DAVE, FLY ME!

Dave Paton, lead vocalist of Pilot, recently told me of the day he managed to live up to the group's name.

"We were flying over to Belgium in a five seater plane, and as there were six of us, I had to sit in the co-pilot's seat. Half way across the plane said he wanted to catch up on his book work and asked me if I'd like to take over the steering.

"It really was a nerve-racking experience, because I had to keep looking at the dials to make sure that I remained at a certain height and that I steered in the right direction. Needless to say, we kept going up and down and backwards and forwards. In fact it was probably the longest flight to Belgium anyone could make!

"But at least I can now boast that I've been a real pilot, though perhaps next time I'll let one of the others take over!"

L to R: Dave Paton, Stuart Tosh, Ian Bairnson, Bill Lyall.

SEEING STARS

This week is the first decanate of Scorpio, which starts on October 23 and ends on November 2. Though people born at this time seem very detached, cool and restrained on the surface, deep down inside they are extremely passionate, fiery and strong-willed. For this reason they should be careful about the jealousy they fall prey to when they're in love.

Pop people born under this decanate include:

Bill Wyman (Rolling Stones) 24th October.

Denny Laine (Wings) 29th October. Trevor White (Sparks) 30th October.
Jimmy Saville 31st October.

POP PUZZLE

First the answer to last week's pop puzzle. Your jigsaw man was that young rebel, Steve Harley (Sparks). And now for something really tricky . . . below are the real names of certain pop stars. Do you know the names they're better known as?

OK. Get working; as usual I'll give the answers next week.

1. David Jones 4. David Cook
2. Barry Green 5. Bernard Jewry
3. Reg Dwight 6. Paul Gadd

STANDING OVATION

The pop world's a tough business and stars frequently have to take quite a few knocks. And that's what literally happened to Wigan's Ovation lead singer Jim McClusky.

"I was walking back to my mum's house after seeing some friends when a crowd of girls asked me for my autograph," he told me. "As I was standing there, happily signing, five guys came up to me, knocked me to the ground and started beating me up."

Another inspiration for Bryan is his record collection. A lot of Bryan's songs come from the 20's and 30's, so when he's not watching the screen, he's usually playing 78's from his record collection. And if you don't know what 78's were — ask your mum!

L to R: Jim McClusky, Alfie Brooks, Phil Preston, Pete Preston.

boys admit to being true country folk at heart. "London is a great place and the people are so nice, but it's miles too fast for me," Jim explained with a smile. "I just want to get back to Wigan and relax, play darts and do a bit of fishing.

Though the other members of the band like to relax as much as Jim, they all have one burning ambition. "We'd like to reach the musical standard of the Stylistics with whom we appeared at Manchester recently, Jim confessed. "It must be wonderful to be so professional that you get a standing ovation every time you play."

Well, if their name's anything to go by, we're sure they'll succeed!

BAKER USES HIS LOAF!

FERRY LONG AGO

When Bryan Ferry isn't performing in his own intimate and romantic style, you can usually find him — watching telly! "I'm an avid TV viewer," he told me recently. "I find myself watching all those films from years ago. I'm particularly fascinated watching the dress and manners of other generations. It gives me ideas for my stage shows."

A FIT STATE!

If you've ever seen Status Quo perform, you'll know how hard they work and the tremendous amount of energy they use up.

"Yes, we do get pretty hot up there," drummer John Coghlan told me with a grin. "But it's a great way

"I can play drums as well (!!!)"
Adrian confessed . . .

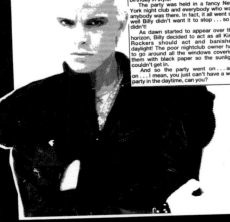

Hot Gossip

IF IT'S HAPPENING IT'S IN HOT GOSSIP! ● IF IT'S HAPPENING IT'S IN HOT GOSSIP! ● IF IT'S HAPPENING IT'S IN HOT GOSSIP! ● IF IT'S HAPPENING IT'S IN HOT GOSSIP! ● IF IT'S HAPP

SNIPPETS

Nick Rhodes says that the large number of Duran Duran books on the shelves are "rip offs" . . . Frankie Goes To Hollywood are split over performing Bruce Springsteen's song, "Born To Run"—two of the band can't stand it . . . Tracey Ullman thought George Michael looked like an orange with a wig on in his "Careless Whisper" video . . . Edwyn Collins reckons he looks like a 50-year-old . . . Brian Hibbard and Red Stripe of The Flying Pickets have entered their dog's name in the phone book! . . . Roger Taylor's got a black Mercedes sports car . . . The Thompson Twins have rented an apartment in Paris just across from the Eiffel Tower.

DREAM COME TRUE!

Watch out for Dream Team, a great new, all girl band who look set to take the charts by storm with their new single, "Boy George."

Tami Hamilton, Caroline Hamill, Ruby-Marie Hutchinson and Salli-Anne Stairs, who make up the group, are all big Boy George fans, so they were delighted when they heard the Boy himself actually liked the record!

If you fancy winning a copy of the single for yourself, just send the answer to the question below, on a postcard to Jackie Dream Team Competition, 185 Fleet Street, London EC4A 2HS. The first twenty-five names picked out on March 7 will each win a copy of the record.

Q. A famous pop star's sister sings with Dream Team. Is it . . .

a. Limahl's?
b. George Michael's?
c. Paul Weller's?

Jackie + Wendy.

Wendy's not speaking to anyone today. She's just discovered that the love of her life—Billy Idol—is 29! I suppose that means we're both back to fighting over Paul Young again!

WHO'S THAT GIRL?

Cyndi Lauper is really fed up at being swamped with fans everytime she steps out of her house in New York—so she's come up with a novel way to avoid them!

"I just put on one of those really silly masks with the glasses, nose and moustache attached, you know the ones with the bushy eyebrows," she laughs. "Nobody ever bothers me when I'm wearing it!"

SOUND OF SILENCE

Ian McCulloch reckons that the greatest problem for the Bunnymen is that he just can't speak to the rest of the band.

"The other members of the band all live in the same house but I live with Lorraine, my wife. I only seem to be able to communicate with the rest of the band when we're playing.

"That's why I did my solo single 'September Song'. I reckon it's just what we needed to get us all talking to each other properly."

Looks like all our fears about Mac's solo careers breaking up the Bunnymen were unfounded. Hope so, anyway.

THE IDOL RICH!

Billy Idol really celebrated his 29th birthday in style.

The party was held in a fancy New York night club and everybody who was anybody was there. In fact, it all went so well Billy didn't want it to stop . . . so it didn't!

As dawn started to appear over the horizon, Billy decided to act as all King Rockers should and banished daylight! The poor nightclub owner had to go around all the windows covering them with black paper so the sunlight couldn't get in.

And so the party went on . . . and on . . . I mean, you just can't have a wild party in the daytime, can you?

WILD BOY?

Believe it or not, this guy could've been the sixth member of Duran Duran! Andy Wickett left Duran before they hit the big time, but he's now claiming that he actually wrote the music and most of the words to "Girls On Film."

A rather upset Andy told us, "They owe their success and fame to me. Even now they still play the song as a finale at their concerts. I helped to make them millionaires!"

Andy also claimed he was offered £600 on the condition he would have no further interest in Duran, but on average, the group would have made £36,000 on royalties from the record!

Never mind, Andy, we're sure you'll make just as much money when your solo career gets off the ground!

HAPPY BIRTHDAY

Many happy returns to "The Most Beautiful Man In The World," David Sylvian, who has a birthday on Feb. 23rd.

COME BACK DAVID

Have you been wondering why we haven't seen much of David Bowie lately? Yes, I know he's been in the news with the release of his new album "Diamond Dogs", but the man himself hasn't been seen in Britain for quite a while now.

The reason is that David is in America at the moment, giving the people living around New York and the East Coast a chance to see his new show.

This week, in case you're interested, he's playing in Pennsylvania, West Virginia, Tennessee, Georgia and Florida. So, as you can see, he's being kept quite busy!

The tour ends next month, and all we can do is hope that, when he's finished, he'll decide to come back and pay us a visit!

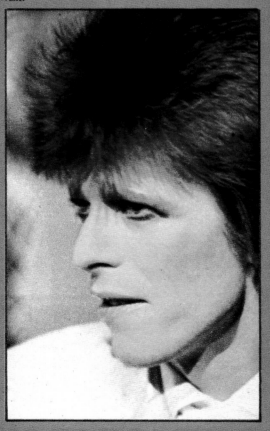

33

pop gossip

Just as spring inspires everyone to clean up their homes, so summer seems to influence us to change them — or that's the way it appears to be in the "Jackie" office. At the moment, practically everyone in here is looking for a new home. The Ed, being born lucky(!) has just discovered the most beautiful flat overlooking the sea and miles of silvery sandy beaches, and is all excited about moving in. It's secretly driving the rest of the girls mad with jealousy!

Alison, Sandy and Cheryl thought they'd struck it lucky too, when their landlord informed them that their flat was to be re-decorated — at his expense. There was only one snag — they're having to move out, because he wants it redecorated for himself!

Jean and Pam, both of whom have recently got engaged, are looking for lovely little cottages in the country, where they can live in domestic bliss for evermore. Everybody say "Aaaah"!

Me, I'm quite content to stay in my luxurious penthouse suite — it suits me so well. Oh well, we can all dream, can't we . . . ? *Pete*

Hairy Story!

You've probably dreamed about meeting your favourite pop star. But if it actually happened, and you found yourself face to face with him, what would you do — and what on earth would you say to him?!

Lots of groups — like Slade, for instance — really enjoy talking to their fans, and they try to meet them whenever possible. And that means there are lots of girls who've been lucky enough to have a chat with Noddy, Dave, Don and Jim.

So what do they talk about?

"Well, believe it or not, a lot of them want to know if my sideboards are real!" said Noddy. "I usually let them give the hair a tug to prove that they are — as long as they promise not to pull too hard!

"I'm very proud of my sideboards. They're coming on very well. It's all because I water them regularly, you know!"

WHAT KATIE DOES

That happy brother and sister duo, Mac and Katie Kissoon, recently made it in Britain with their hits, "Sugar Candy Kisses" and "Don't Do It Baby." But their British success hasn't made that much difference to their lives — because over on the Continent, Mac and Katie have been famous for years!

"Of course, things are more hectic for us now," said Katie, "but we don't mind that. We're just relieved that we've had a hit at last after waiting so long for it!"

The Kissoons' success means that they now have less spare time than before, but when she does get the chance to relax, Katie likes to stay at home and do some dressmaking.

"I make most of my stage clothes myself," she told me. "I usually make them from a basic pattern, and add my own ideas to that.

"Normally I go around in jeans and casual clothes, but onstage I like to wear really feminine clothes, in fabrics like chiffon. I think it's important to look as good as possible when you're onstage."

And Katie certainly succeeds in that!

GETTING THE NEEDLE!

Have you seen that ad on TV recently? You know, the one where Noel Edmonds is persuading us to part with some blood — all for a very good cause — the Blood Transfusion Service! Well, Noel may look completely calm and at ease on the film, but the truth is that, at the time, he was feeling far from brave!

"I've always fancied giving blood, because it's such an essential service," he said. "But at the same time, I've got this absolute horror of hypodermic syringes!

"For the film, we had to do several hours of rehearsal before the cameras did the real 'take,' and all the time I was quaking in my shoes at the thought of this needle going into my arm. I didn't feel in the least bit brave! I was imagining all sorts of ridiculous horrible things — like my dying for an extremely noble cause, and becoming a national hero at last!

"Yet when it came to the actual moment, and they finally did extract a pint of blood from me, I hardly felt a thing. It was all over in no time — and I felt a real fool for having been such a coward beforehand!"

FLAME AND FORTUNE

L. to R: Dale Vernon, Peter Gill, Michael Wilson, David Wilson.

Speaking of Slade, there's a brand new group on the scene who have the same name as Slade's first film, "Flame."

You'll perhaps already know what the group sound like from their first single, "Teenager In Love," which you may remember was the Power Play on Radio Luxembourg a couple of weeks ago.

But as you can see from the photo, the boys don't just make nice music — they look pretty good, too!

They're all very young — Michael Wilson is the youngest at 12, while Dale Vernon, at the grand old age of 17, is the eldest — but despite that, they manage to produce some very tough, rocking music.

"I'd hate people to think of us as some kind of child protegees, just because we're still fairly young," said 15 year old David Wilson. "I formed the group years ago with my little brother Michael, and since then we've played hundreds of live gigs.

"So we've all been working together very closely for a long time now, and I think that's very important. We all understand each other."

ICE-CREME!

L to R. Back, Kevin, Lol. Front, Graham, Eric.

Before he became a professional musician, 10CC's Lol Creme tried his hand at a couple of other jobs — neither of which were very successful!

"Like most other students, I used to take on summer jobs while I was at art college," said Lol. "One summer I went into business selling ice-creams from a cart, but that failed because my partner, who was a girlfriend of mine, had absolutely no head for business!

"The kids would come up and ask for a sixpenny ice-cream, and she'd say, 'Are you sure your mum didn't say a threepenny one?' and she'd end up giving them threepenny ones instead!

"And as well as that, she also loved ice-cream — and she kept treating herself to some. In fact, she literally ate all the profits!"

So next summer, Lol decided to try something completely different!

"I'd heard that a local firm were looking for lorry drivers," he said, "so I decided to go along and try for the job. I'd never driven a lorry before, but I figured it couldn't be too difficult. So when the foreman asked me if I had any experience, I just said, 'Yes of course!'

"But it turned out to be not quite what I'd expected. I'd never imagined lorries were so big inside! When I was sitting in the driver's seat, I couldn't see out of the window — and my feet couldn't reach the pedals!

"That job only lasted a day!"

And maybe that's just as well! I think Lol might be safer sticking to music!

PET HATES

This week — John Richardson of the Rubettes.

"I hate flying! Unfortunately, I have to travel quite a lot by plane because I'm in a group — but I still haven't got used to it!"

WHAT'S A GREEK URN?*

The girls in Pan's People really enjoy their job. Even though they admit it involves a lot of hard work, they wouldn't ever want to do anything else!

So it came as a bit of a shock when we discovered recently that Dee Dee had decided to give up her dancing career. Actually, Dee Dee doesn't intend to forsake dancing altogether. She'll still keep practising in her spare time. But she's exchanging her career for a life of domestic bliss — with a Greek tycoon, no less! (See what kind of people you're likely to meet if you're a Pan's Person?!)

And though everyone's sad at Dee Dee's departure, they're very happy with the new member who follows in her footsteps. The lucky girl is Caroline Argylle. Caroline, who's 18, was picked straight out of stage school to join the group, and is still a bit dazed by it all herself.

It is believed that Caroline was chosen from a short-list of highly talented dancers, which, strangely enough, did not include our own Jenny from Jackie . . . !

● Millions of pounds and a beautiful new wife!

POP GOSSIP
WITH PETE LENNON

So here I was the other day, just sitting here snooz-er—
working hard, when the Ed came over, smiled (yes, he really
did!) and announced that as part of his New Year Resolu-
tion to be nicer to me from now on, he was going to take
the Ed's letter off Pop Gossip and leave the space to me.

Isn't it exciting? I've got a whole column to fill up
any way I like! What's that Alison? Alison, our Beauty
girl, has just asked me to mention her, so here you are
Alison . . . oh, all right, Dorothy, I'll mention you as
well. Aargh! Sandie has just threatened to sing if I don't
mention her! Anything rather than that . . . here you are,
Sandie.

Oh, for Goodness' sake . . . no, Marilyn, Sam, Willie,
Susan, Nina, Cathy, Claire, Sheila, Eileen and Daphne, I
am not going to mention you too!

Now to get on with my letter—oh, that's funny, I seem
to have run out of space! Ah well . . . *Pete*

THAT'LL BE THE DAY . . .

Incidentally, Maurice
Woodruff predicted some time
ago that David would break
into musicals, and now he's
got the leading role in one
. . . so don't scoff too much
next time you read YOUR
horoscope!

Here's a bit of a mystery for you! I was looking through
our old files the other day when I came across this piece of
gossip.

It's about David Essex, who was then appearing in a
show called the Fantasticks. And the amazing thing
about it is that it appeared in Jackie on January 6th,
1968—three years before Godspell started!

Little did we know at that time just how right that
prediction of Maurice Woodruff's would turn out to be!
Don't know about you, but that sends little shivers up
down my spine . . .

HOUSE IT GOING?

As you know, Gilbert O'Sullivan has never gone in
for the grand life—and that turned out to be a great
advantage to him when he moved to his new house last
Autumn. To most people, moving house is a great upheaval,
and requires lots of patience and planning—but Gilbert
has such a small amount of furniture, he just hired a small
van, and threw everything in!

In fact the only piece of furniture that caused him
any trouble was his piano, one of his favourite possessions,
which he was determined to keep.

"I couldn't possibly leave that behind," said Gilbert.
"It's just an old upright piano, but it has sentimental value
for me—I wrote most of my early hits on it."

BLUE WITH COLD

The saga of Blue's Hughie Nicolson's new flat con-
tinues—he says he's just bought a fridge for it!

"It's fantastic," says Hughie. "I've never owned a
fridge before and I'm really thrilled with it.

"I keep opening and shutting the door to watch the
lighting switching itself on and off!"

Well, whatever turns you on . . .!

UN-DAWNTED!

We all know who Dawn are and what they look like,
but a couple of years ago it wasn't quite so easy to
tell. You see, at that time, there were 14 Dawns going
around!

Explained Tony Orlando: "I used to work for a music
publishing firm in America, and one day I was playing
around in the studio when I came up with a song called
"Candida". Everyone who heard the song said it would be
a hit, so we recorded it under the name Dawn and put it
out.

"It did become a hit, but even then I didn't intend taking
a group out on the road. However, in the end I had to.
You see, because no one knew what Dawn looked like,
some people thought they would make money out of it—
and all of a sudden, 14 different groups appeared, all
going under the name Dawn. So then, of course, I had to
do a tour to show people the real, live, authentic Tony
Orlando!"

A LANE ALONE

Ronnie Lane has left the Faces now, but he hasn't lost
any of their style—or their sense of fun! To launch his
solo career, Ronnie hired Chipperfield Circus for the night,
invited lots of friends and had a huge party.

The entertainment included typical circus fare—clowns,
acrobats and trapeze artists—and then they were followed
by Ronnie himself, playing a two-hour set, with some
of his musician friends backing him. By the end of the
night, everyone was in the ring, dancing all over the
sawdust!

Meanwhile, the Faces have been kept busy. After
their recent British tour, and their Christmas party at the
Edmonton Sundown, they have a new album called
"Overture for Beginners" which should be out any day
now. It was recorded live in Philadelphia, New York and
Los Angeles during their last American tour. Promises to
be lots of fun!

THE RIGHT SPIRIT

Have you noticed how many people are taking an
interest in Marilyn Monroe these days? First of all
there was "Candle in the Wind", Elton John's beautiful
tribute to her on his "Goodbye Yellow Brick Road" album.

Then, when I took our tame (well, almost tame) Geordie
Susan along to see Lindisfarne on their recent British
tour, we noticed that the group supporting them, a duo
called Darien Spirit, included a lovely song "Elegy to
Marilyn" in their act.

Since then, the two boys who make up Darien Spirit,
Harry McDonald and Jack McAllister (how did you
guess that they're Scottish?!) have brought out an album
of the same name. They wrote the title track, they say,
because of their interest in Marilyn and the legend
surrounding her.

Harry and Jack with a model of their heroine.

DOUBLING

Beach And Bedroom

No use wasting space by carting along a dressing-gown *and* a beach cover-up on holiday, so buy something that'll be great for both.

We chose this short-sleeved robe from Marks & Spencer, Style No: 167/4011. Price: £5.50. Fabric: Cotton/polyester. Colours: White, gold, brown, green. Sizes: 10 to 16. From selected branches of Marks & Spencer.

Spotted baby-dolls are from Woolworth. Style No.: GS3/5. Price: £1.99. Fabric: Nylon. Colours: Pink, turquoise, brown, navy. Sizes: 12 to 14. From larger Woolworth branches.

Brown bikini with brown, yellow and orange striped top comes from Marks and Spencer. Style No.: 1175/3308. Price: £2.99. Fabric: Nylon/Lycra. Colours: A range of prints and colours. Sizes: 10 to 14. From selected branches of Marks & Spencer.

Beach And

Special dresses for the beach can be expensive, especially if they're so summery you're not likely to wear them when you get home! A wraparound skirt is the answer — wear it on the beach with a bikini top then wear it again in the evening with different tops and T-shirts for the disco.

This wraparound skirt comes from Jean Lee. Style No.: LS/828. Price: £4. Fabric: Vincel/Cott Colours: Royal/white, P White, Brown / Wh Yellow/White, Green/Wh Sizes: W and WX. Fr branches of Debenha Goldbergs branch Shephards of Gatesh and district.

The white bikini has a p white top and a gilt buc trim on the briefs, fr Littlewoods. Style No.:

UP!

THERE'S no point in buying two lots of holiday gear when one will do, so think before you spend and see how you can double up

Disco

Night And Day

Don't clutter up your case with millions of tops and T-shirts, think carefully and don't buy two where one will do.

Our V-necked T-shirt with huge rose motif is from Jump Knitwear. Style No.: 4248. Price: £3.95. Fabric: Cotton. Colours: Light blue, green, fawn, dark pink. Sizes:Small, medium, large. From Dickins & Jones,

Oxford Street, London W.1.; Renee Shaw and branches; Joyce of Bromley; Carleys of Blackpool; Bradmore, Essex Road, London N.1.; Jane and I, Blackheath.

White shorts with elasticated waist from Littlewoods. Style No.: 60/40. Price: £1.99. Fabric: Crimplene. Colours: White, salmon, navy, blue. Sizes: 12 to 16. From most Littlewoods branches.

Long skirt with ties at the back and frill at the bottom, from Dorothy Perkins. No Style No. Price: £5.99. Fabric: Cotton. Colours: Assorted. Sizes: 10 to 14. From main branches of Dorothy Perkins.

SCARVES *are*

GUESS what's hitting mod bods' headlines? Our old standby—the scarf! Suddenly, it's fashion plus! But you just can't wear a scarf looking like a scarf.

Take a square, fold it thisaway or thataway and tie it in whichever style is fave! Try out some of these swish square-ways, or mix 'n' switch around from these ideas to a different, zippy way that is just you. 'Cos it's girls with zing that catch a guy's eye.

where to wear

. . . under soft lights

At dances, parties, twosome-type dinner-dates. The finest, prettiest, tied into a smooth bandeau, often with a tiny jewelled pin clipped to one side.

. . . at get-togethers

Just a twosome or with the gang, teamed with gadabout casuals for anything from Trad-dad stomps, the Shake sessions or on the Beatles Beat!

. . . in bowling alleys

Smitten kittens go for squares. Look great—and no strands of hair flop dizzily in front of your eyes as you're about to bowl!

. . . around town

Worn by town-bods, they add zing to town-type togs! No more arriving at work looking like Dragalong Droopy's sister. Be a doll.

. . . on the beach

Match your scarf colour to your swimsuit—sensational! For that extra something, try wearing that scarf under sunhat 'n' specs! Mystery snares the males!

Plain chiffon squares from Fenwick, Bond St., London, W.1.
Patterned silk squares by Richard Allan of London.

Fave rave.

Scarves rise to dizzy heights when you fold a crisp square into a triangle, then turn back the long edge about an inch to form a cuff. Tie so that the ends are flying at the back.

Double-up Datester

A twosome as the name suggests. Match a pair of scarves in a super colour combo that plays up your eyes, hair—or get-up. Each scarf is folded separately into a narrow strip. Next tie them together to form a wide bandeau.

Zing, zing, zing!

Has real male-appeal when you choose the colour that's YOU! Go for an extra big square. Fold it into a triangle, cross the ends under your chin, then tie the ends OVER the point at the back, ends flyaway.

eye catchin'— and guy catchin'!

Sphinx-minx.

It IS a scarf—designed as a scene stealer for long-haired mods. Make a triangle again and tuck point in to form a wide bandeau with a covered-in top. Ends are tied cheekily at the side in a small butterfly knot.

Snazzy square.

If this one makes you stop, it'll do the same to the boys. Tie a triangle-shaped scarf securely at the nape of your neck, then fluff out the sides a la Cleopatra. You'll look really super if your square is slightly starched.

Slinky?

Pert, pretty—and practical! Make a three-inch-wide bandeau and flip round topknot, leaving ears showing. Ends are tied at the side and brought forward over shoulder. Wear one earring at knotted side of scarf for extra dash!

Twistin'.

This is the one we're really mad about! Long-haired bods simply swirl their hair up into a high ponytail, bind a narrow-folded square round twice and tie the ends into a double bow, plonked on top. Simply sensational.

Beachnick!

Ahoy, there! For beach days and any day, get with the pirate look scarf-wise. Form a triangle again, tie scarf round head and push well back behind ears in folds. Tie in a long knot and pull ends round either side of neck.

Topknot tie-up?

A floppy bow! It's the very thing to give you the little-girl look! Tie a folded square loosely round your topknot, then whip the ends up as in the picture. Looks zany—and really cute.

DON'T watch this space — doodle in it! Don't think too much about it, just casually pick up a pencil and start scribbling.

OK? Well, you didn't realise it, but while you were idly doodling away without a thought, your sub-conscious mind was working ten to the dozen revealing your inner feelings and releasing the dark, hidden side of your nature!

You see doodles can tell you general things about your character and they can also pin-point a certain mood which you happen to be going through. Most people stick to the same type of doodles, with the same basic shapes and patterns, but they vary their doodles according to how they're feeling, by altering the boldness, size and texture.

For instance, a bold, flowing doodle indicates a happy, confident mood, and a light, squirly doodle points to a quietly happy and contented mood. If you feel madly happy or fantastically in love, your doodle might look wild, free and uncontrolled.

If life is difficult, you're likely to draw something heavy and over-complicated. If there are a lot of rather unpleasant things on your mind, your design will be cluttered, knotted up and frankly a bit of a mess; while if you're in a calm, serene frame of mind, your doodle is likely to be gentle and delicate, with plenty of airy, white spaces.

So have a good look at the doodle you've drawn in our blank space, then read on and look at the doodles we've illustrated. Which one most resembles yours? Your doodle is probably a mixture of several we've shown. So find out what the hidden meanings are, then piece the information together, to get a reading of your character and your mood of the moment!

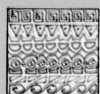

This type of doodle is fairly conventional. The pattern is neat and regular, and the person who draws this is likely to be a practical person who has no pressing problems, and who sails through life quite easily. It shows a friendly, sociable nature and a liking for a fairly well-ordered life. This person knows what she is doing, is very capable and works hard without being too vain or ambitious.

This doodle looks black, depressed and angry, and would go with a very bad mood of black despair and misery. If you're suffering from 'flu, a broken heart or just a fit of the blues, this could be your doodle. You are expressing despair because things look so heavy and black, and you feel that there's no way out, no escape from the turmoils of life.

This doodle tells quite a different story. The face may symbolise you, but you've made a dreadful mess of yourself. You're not pleased with yourself and you're trying to blot out the bad faults in your nature. Alternatively, you are trying to hide and cover up the truth about yourself. Could be, of course, that the face is your worst enemy and you've made a lovely job of getting your own back on her.

You are a romantic if you've done a pretty doodle like this. You're feminine, gentle, dreamy, in love with someone, or just romantically in love with life itself. You tend to be unrealistic about life and to shut yourself away in a dream world. This doodle could also indicate a longing for a beautiful romantic life which you don't have at the moment. Only you know if your doodle symbolises life as it really is for you, or life as you would *like* it to be . . .

A doodle which looks like nothing more than a scribble could show a lazy careless person, but it's more likely to be an indication of someone who doesn't know her own emotions. Perhaps you are scared to unravel yourself for fear of the home truths you will come up against; perhaps you are deliberately running away from yourself. Or it could be you are going through a stage of confusion about yourself; finding it impossible to make an important decision, or perhaps life has thrown you into a situation with which you cannot cope.

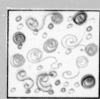

This is several doodles in one, really. Lots of people draw circles. The hollow, bubbly ones show good humour and pleasant feelings; the tightly curled circles point to an introverted nature, the squirly circles and patterns show self-confidence, but also rather vain self-centred qualities.

Strange shapes, often looking rather like pieces of a jig-saw puzzle point to someone who lives a great deal in her mind. If you've done a doodle similar to this, you like working for a purpose, and you enjoy a challenge. You are always searching for answers to life and delving into things. You don't want to be told — you want to experiment and work things out for yourself.

If you've done a very simple doodle like this, perhaps just one bold pencil line, finished off in a flash, it could be that you are a super confident person, who has nothing to fear, no problems or hang-ups. It could also be, though, that you did this doodle because you were absolutely determined not to give anything about yourself away. Come along now, what are you hiding?

This doodle is almost a work of art, and obviously a lot of thought and care has gone into working out a finely-drawn, intricate design like this. You are obviously either a Picasso or a perfectionist, or both. The truth is, though, that you put too much thought into your doodle rather than letting your mind run free. You, too, are covering up rather than revealing yourself!

This doodle indicates a horrible feeling of being hemmed in and confused. It is like a trap from which you can't escape, and even if you could escape you wouldn't know which way to go. This points to a feeling that life is unsatisfactory — you are bored and fed-up, or have a deep unhappiness you find difficult to pin down. Any doodle which goes into the centre, rather than comes out from it indicates this mood, as though life is closing in around you.

If you draw a face, you could be thinking of someone special, or the face could be you. Trees and plants usually represent people; buildings and square shapes represent security, or a longing for security, lots of flowers and pretty objects show a longing for peace and love. In this doodle, the face would represent you, and the sun would represent happiness and pleasure, meaning that you feel good, and that in general you are pleased with yourself as a person.

These round, fluffy cloudy shapes indicate contentment and peace. They show someone who is not ecstatically happy, but at peace with themselves, and getting quiet satisfaction and enjoyment from life.

A small design like this in the centre of the square could indicate a cautious nature. It would most probably be drawn by a rather nervous person, who finds it difficult to express her feelings. It shows the self-contained nature of someone keeping herself on a tight rein and not being able to let herself go much. If you're feeling not very confident and rather shy and withdrawn, your doodle could turn out like this.

This rippling, wavy type of doodle shows generosity, pleasure-seeking, and a rather sensual nature. If you've drawn one like this, you are enjoying life at the moment, or perhaps you are the sort of person who is a pleasure lover at heart — you enjoy comfort, luxury and all the good things life has to offer. You float along from one treat to another. You could be accused of being irresponsible and lazy, but let's just say you're having a great time!

This type of doodle shows a lively mind; it shows self-confidence, enthusiasm for life and a very ambitious nature. If you've drawn something like this, you are excited by life in general. You refuse to be held down or restricted. You want to make the very best of yourself, and the sky's the limit. The swirling lines in this design look as though they want to break out of the square and expand in all directions.

This sort of doodle, which looks a bit like a maze, also shows an unhappy feeling. Perhaps it is a feeling of being weighed down and obsessed with problems and worries, but unlike the previous doodle, there is some hope. It looks as though there is going to be some way out of your problems. The person who draws this doodle faces up to her problems and tries to be constructive about them, looking for logical solutions.

This one is also maze-like and complicated, but it's light and airy as well, and although it is usually drawn by a very complicated and thoughtful person, it isn't an unhappy doodle. It indicates someone who thinks deeply about life, someone who is curious by nature, and always wants to get to the heart of the matter and to understand what is going on around them. It shows a deep fascination with people and life.

DOODLE?

finally...

everyone doodles differently, and doodles are so individual that it would be impossible for us to show all the different varieties. If we haven't covered your doodle, here are a few things to notice if you want to analyse your own (or other people's) doodles. How much white space is there compared to black filling in? The more space there is, the happier the Doodler is.

● Are the lines and shapes straight and forceful, or curving in a more relaxed pose? Are the shapes jagged and fearful looking, or smooth and rounded, or fluffy and gentle?

● Are the pencil lines hard and pressed into the paper (which shows strong feeling or tension), or are they delicate and light (which shows calm and happiness). Are the pencil lines very faint and hesitant-looking? (In which case the person is shy and unsure of themselves.)

● Cluttered designs usually point to conflict and problems, whereas widely spaced designs show open-heartedness and a happier approach to life.

● Heavily shaded drawings point to depression, outlined shapes with a lot of white hollows can indicate either a calm relaxed nature (if the shapes themselves are fairly bold and well-defined) or they can indicate a rather timid, frightened personality (if the shapes look too woolly, sketchy or badly controlled).

Don't worry if your doodle has shown nothing but bad characteristics and black despairs — try another doodle next week when your luck, or your mood, has changed, and see how different it'll be.

It's often best not to concentrate too much on your doodle, so that it isn't forced. Try doodling while watching telly, listening to your favourite group, or talking to your friend on the phone.

happy doodling

EYE EYE!
beauty bazaar

WHAT big eyes you've got— or have you? Since eyes are one of the first things people notice, it's quite a bonus if you've been blessed with a pair of huge, sparkly peepers! But if you haven't—then here's how to pretend you have!

By using eye make-up cleverly you can disguise small eyes and make them look bigger and one of the first rules to learn about making eyes look bigger is — use a light-coloured eye shadow.

Dark shadows tend to emphasise the smallness of the eyes, so it's best to stick to paler shades like blue, green, lilac, white, yellow, etc.

It also helps to pluck your eyebrows, so that no stray hairs obstruct the shadow area.

Now, start applying the shadow to the lid and slightly extend it above the socket, almost to the eyebrow. This immediately gives the eyes a wider look.

If you take the shadow a fraction beyond the outer corner of the eye, and very faintly round underneath the lower lashes you'll notice the difference right away.

Your eyes will appear larger and wider apart. You can also add a touch of white highlighter to the corner. This gives a sort of outer ring to the eye, which appears to increase the size of the natural white and makes the eye itself seem larger.

Now you can apply your mascara. Unless you have very dark hair and quite a dark skin to match, black mascara is rather strong and would probably ruin the whole effect.

It's better to use a brown-black or just plain brown and try not to get your eyelashes clogged together.

Wait till the first coat has dried then apply a second coat. It's a good idea to clean up an old mascara brush and keep it for separating the lashes.

And there you are! If you take time and trouble, you'll find that small eyes needn't be a drawback and can, in fact, be made to look just as nice as naturally big eyes!

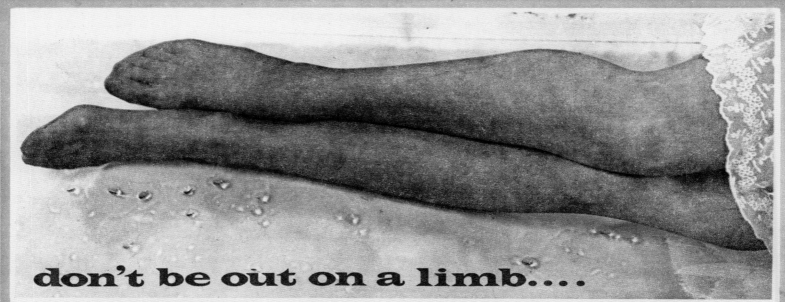

don't be out on a limb....
DO YOUR LEG WORK NOW!

THE season of big dance dates and dashing about to get just the thing for your best girl friend's Christmas will be here before you have time to stand on one leg.

And, talking about legs—how are yours shaping up? Will they be able to stand up to hours of trudging round the shops and not ache for ages afterwards? Can they be seen in sheerer than sheer nylons and pass the test?

Start pampering your pins now and you'll waltz (or should that be shake?) through it all.

Exercise for toning-up muscles, slimming plump legs and adding curves to thin ones is to walk round the room on your tip-toes. Do this in your bare feet and stretch up on to your toes till you feel the muscles pulling at the back of your legs. You can do it as often as you like.

Slim and supple-up ankles by doing this exercise while you are sitting at your desk or at lunch-time. Just raise and lower your heels quickly about twenty times. It doesn't take much of your time but works wonders.

Keep legs sleek 'n' smoothie by defuzzing once a week. Use a razor (but be careful when going over your shin bone) or a depilatory cream, whichever you prefer. Best time for this is after a soak in the tub, and do remember to rub in lots of hand and body lotion afterwards to keep skin velvety.

Comfy shoes for all this leg work? Stilettos and flatties are out. Shoes with heels an inch to an inch-and-a-half high are the thing. Shake a little talc into each before you set off, it's super for keeping tootsies cool and fresh.

Do all this now and you'll be ready to really step it out and swing this Christmas.

dear beauty editor . . .

I am very dark-skinned, have dark eyes and almost black hair. What colours would suit me best?

You can have the best of both worlds. Bright colours are a wow on you and some smoky pastel shades of brown and blue will also lift you into the millionaire class—lookswise.

For big date-time, you'd look stunning in turquoise, deep pink or even gold. White can sometimes look nice, but I think that if you are really dark-haired, it can be too much of a contrast.

With make-up your choice is unlimited. You can wear zingy, pink 'n' peachy lipsticks and go to town with eye make-up to add even more allure to your dark eyes.

You probably won't need to use foundation, but if you have difficulty in getting one that tones in with your skin, try Max Factor's Sun Tone. It won't drain the colour out of your face.

I have a dry skin that goes deadly white and flakes off in the winter. I've tried various creams without success.

This sounds like your circulation is at fault. Get the blood racing round your veins again by eating lots of warming foods full of vitamins (see last week's article) and iron.

Iron's the thing for keeping your blood up to par. You can stock up on iron by eating green vegetables of all kinds and, lean liver. Could be that you are a bit anaemic so pop along to your Doc. He'll be able to prescribe iron tablets for you if you are.

Nightly nourishing with Max Factor's Dry Skin Cream, 6s 3d, or Yardley's Vitamin Skin Cream, 6s 5d, should restore the moisture balance to your skin. And before you make-up, smooth in a moisturising lotion, Outdoor Girl, 2s 6d, to protect your skin during the day.

Keep soap and water away from your face. You can clean it just as well with a cleansing cream especially for dry skin. Soap 'n' water's just too harsh for you. Atkinson's Cleansing Cream is super creamy and comes in a nice-to-be-seen-on-your-dressing-table type jar, 4s 9d.

I like going dancing, love boys with sports cars and wear clothes that suit me whether they are in fashion or not, though I tend to be on the Mod side. Which perfumes would suit me best?

I was beginning to wonder whether I should pass your letter over to Cathy and Claire until I read the last sentence !

You sound like the type of girl who goes for subtle, musky and sometimes expensive perfumes. My favourites of this type are Revlon's Intimate and Yardley's Bond Street, Max Factor's Hypnotique and Coty's Emeraude.

In the millionaire class (got a rich boy friend?) there is Chanel Number Five, Nina Ricci's Capricci and Marquay's l'Elu.

To get the most out of these perfumes always keep them in a cool, dark place with the stopper tightly screwed on.

When you apply your perfume, a dab on your pulse spots, wrists, temples, throat, crook of elbows and a piece of cotton-wool, soaked in the perfume, slipped down the front of your bra will surround you in an aura of fragrance that lasts and lasts.

I use a good deodorant but I still get ugly perspiration stains on my dresses. How can I prevent this?

Some people sweat more than others and a deodorant just isn't strong enough for them. A combined anti-perspirant deodorant like Check, Sno-mist, or Stay Fresh should do the trick, though. An anti-perspirant actually prevents sweat forming for any period up to 24 hours. To make extra sure there are no tell-tale marks, make dress shields your best friends. It takes no time at all to sew these into your dresses and they are easily taken out for washing (this saves on cleaner's bills, too).

Point to remember—a deodorant, whether it is also an anti-perspirant or not, won't do its job properly if you don't keep underarms fuzz free. So make a date with your depilatory cream or razor at least once a week—after a bath is a good time.

How can I keep my hair looking neat and tidy in this weather? The wind blows it all over the place and the damp makes it straggly. Don't tell me to use lacquer as it dries my hair and gives me dandruff.

It would be great if we could just tell the weather man to give us a couple of months of spring sunshine with nothing stronger than a light breeze, but, unfortunately, we just have to do the best we can.

And that's not bad, really. I wouldn't advise anyone to use a lacquer every day, but hair sprays are entirely different. These contain lanolin and conditioners and gently hold your style in place without making it brick hard. They comb out, too.

A really blustery day? A pretty chiffon scarf (especially if it's one of those long ones from Marks & Spencer's) tied round your head with the ends floating over your shoulders looks very feminine. It's light enough not to flatten your hair out of its style, and all it needs is a quick flick through with a comb when you take the scarf off.

beauty bulletin

Heard the latest news for lashes? Max Factor have brought out a new Mascaramatic in a luxury, super-slim case. It contains lash-builder fibres and will give you luscious, long lashes in seconds.

There are three colours to choose from—black, brown and brownish-black. Luxury case costs 12s 6d, with refills at 6s 9d. A bit expensive, perhaps, but when you see the difference it makes to your lashes—mmmm!

SO YOU WANT TO BE AN ACTRESS?

Sam meets Vicky Williams, Deborah Makepeace and Stacy Dorning

I DON'T know about you lot but whenever I see young actresses on TV and films, I get a twinge of envy and wish it was me that the cameras were focused on. I'm *sure* I could act just as well, you should see the performance I put on for the Ed when I'm late in the morning! (Definitely Oscar class, the Ed).

Anyway I decided to go and see three young actresses who are making a name for themselves and find out all about it. I called in on Vicky Williams first, you can see her at the moment in the BBC TV series "Changes." She had just moved into a lovely, light airy flat which she shares in London with another actress and a nurse. I asked Vicky how she had got into acting?

"It just sort of happened really. I was at an ordinary grammar school and I was very keen on dancing. So my mother suggested that I go to the Corona Stage School, so that I'd get more ballet tuition. Gradually I found myself getting less keen on dancing and more and more keen on acting. It was as simple as that. I think it was fate!"

Did she enjoy stage school? "Yes, it was great," she said enthusiastically. "You have ordinary lessons in the morning and theatrical lessons in the afternoons. Just ordinary school with a bit of fun added to it. And there was big excitement when we did a giant cabaret production at the end of every year.

"Also of course being at a stage school gave me the opportunity to go to lots of auditions for film and TV parts that you just don't get at an ordinary school."

Vicky had three auditions in all before she got the role of Nicky, the girl suddenly transported back to mediaeval England, who goes in search of her parents. I asked her what an audition's like?

"Well," Vicky said, "you go into a big room with a lot of other girls who're after the part too, and you're all really jittery and nervous. Then you have to read a bit of the part you'd be playing so that the director and his assistants can tell what your voice is like and how much expression you put into it. Then very often they ask you to put yourself into the position of the heroine and ask what you'd do in the same circumstances! Also of course you've got to look right for the part, so there's a lot of luck in it too."

I wondered if Vicky sees herself as a big star in a few years time. "No, not at all, I'm not really interested in being a star and very famous and all that. I just want to get nice interesting parts and act as well as I can."

So she isn't ambitious? "No, I suppose not. People always say that if you're in acting you've got to be very hard and ambitious and claw your way to the top. But I don't think that's true. You can't force directors to take you on however ambitious you are, either they like you or they don't, either you're right for the part or you're not. It doesn't matter what you're like as a person, I certainly don't think I'm hard, and I wouldn't want to be."

I wondered if it had ever bothered Vicky that acting is so insecure, didn't she find the uncertainty of where the next job is coming from a bit frightening?

"Yes, I do," she said, "but if you want to act enough you put up with that. You have such highs and lows in this kind of life," she said. "When you're working, there's so much excitement and you have such fun with the people you're with; then when you're out of work you have to re-adjust again, get things back into perspective. It would be great if you just got one offer after another, but you'd be so exhausted if you did, you use so much energy when you're acting, that you'd soon crack-up. You really do need resting periods, but not too many of them!"

I asked Vicky what it was that made her want to act, when obviously there's just as many downs as ups, and when you can spend so much time doing unsuccessful auditions, putting yourself up just in order to be knocked down.

"I don't know," she said, "I think basically it's the temptation to lose yourself in different characters, to put across to an audience what the thing is all about, what the playwright wants to say. Also of course there's an excitement about acting that just nothing else has. You never know what you're going to have to do next."

Lastly, before I left Vicky, I asked her if she had any advice to give girls who would like to be actresses.

"Yes, don't think it's all glamour and fur coats because it's not. It can be a lot of fun, but it's also hard work, sometimes you're treated like dirt. And sometimes it's even dangerous, like when I was making 'Changes' I nearly drowned. I had to jump out of a barge into the water. It was an old gravel pit filled up and instead of being two foot as I thought, it had sunk about thirty foot. I was fully dressed and the weeds were practically choking me. I went under twice and I really thought this was it. If Keith, one of the actors, hadn't pulled me out in time, I don't like to think what might have happened!"

SEVENTEEN-YEAR-OLD Deborah Makepeace got her first acting part at the age of fourteen in the BBC TV series "Little Princess" while she was still a pupil at the Elmhurst Ballet School. Since then she has starred in the BBC TV series "The Chinese Puzzle," and in April you'll be able to see her as one of Queen Victoria's daughters in ATV's Edward the Seventh."

I met Deborah at her parents' home in Pinner and asked her if she enjoyed seeing herself on TV.

"I can't bear to go and see the film rushes when I'm working," she told me laughing, "in case I find I've developed a twitch or something, because then I couldn't carry on acting, I'd be worried about what I looked like the whole time. But I like seeing the series when it's finished on TV. I sit and give myself points out of ten, I think it's good to criticise yourself."

Deborah had been to "millions" of auditions before she was chosen for the "Little Princess" and she still remembers that moment as the most exciting in her life. "A thousand butterflies flew into my heart when my headmistress told me I'd got the part, it was fantastic."

Since then Deborah has started to become established as a promising young actress, but she can never feel totally secure.

"There's always a niggle at the back of your mind that it could all finish, there's lots of competition. You think you could be just a flash in the pan, but you have to be optimistic and look on the bright side or there's no point in carrying on. It can be hard being an actress, knowing you've got the talent to do the part, but being told you're too tall or too dark or too something or other. Really though, there's nothing else in the world I want to do, never has been and after all everybody's insecure to a certain extent."

I asked Deborah how she'd advise girls who really want to act but haven't been to a stage school, to get into the profession. "It's very hard to slip into acting nowadays," she said. "The best thing to do is when you leave school apply to a drama college like The Royal Academy of Dramatic Art, The Central School of Drama or the London Academy of Music and Dramatic Art. But there's a lot of competition to get into these colleges and you have to follow a three year course. That would be my advice, but I'd also say that you have to be absolutely sure you want to act, as even when you're trained there are very few openings, and for every star, there are hundreds of out of work actresses living just above the breadline!"

I FOUND seventeen-year-old actress, Stacy Dorning, just where you'd expect — with Black Beauty, the horse with whom she starred so successfully in the TV series. Although the series was finished a long time ago, Stacy still goes down to the farm at weekends where Black Beauty's kept by owner Reg.

"I really love riding now," she told me. "What I like is to come down to Reg's and stay overnight so I can get up straightaway in the morning and ride.

"But when I was auditioned for the part in the TV series I had to admit that I couldn't ride. There had been literally loads of people after the part besides me and then they called me back and said that if I was willing to learn to ride I could have the part!"

And so Stacy went away on a two-week "Crash" course to learn to ride. "Yes, 'crash' was the word," she said with a giggle looking back, "and sometimes crash was just what I did — straight off the horse."

Stacy doesn't think she'll get any more acting parts which require her to ride every day for seven months, which is what starring in Black Beauty meant, but she does hope to do more theatre. She loved playing Wendy in Peter Pan at London's Coliseum theatre over Christmas.

Unlike Vicky, Stacy didn't go to an acting school, but she did have other advantages.

"I come from an acting family but my father spent all his time trying to discourage me from being an actress. When I finally told him that that was what I was going to be he said that he certainly wasn't going to send me to drama school, and I don't regret having had to learn as I went along. I've been lucky, too, because my mother is an actress and it was her agent who spotted me for the role in Black Beauty, but I still had to prove myself. Now I'd like to work for a local rep company scrubbing floors, just to learn my craft from the bottom. I really would. Still it's very nice starring in things like Black Beauty and Peter Pan."

And for Peter Pan Stacy once again had to learn something she'd never done before . . . to fly. She had to swoop across the stage and in and out of windows high in the air with a light wire attached to her shoulders. "It was good fun but very exhausting. You ache all over, but it's a great experience flying high above the stage, almost as good as riding!"

So there you are, there's a lot more to being an actress than I'd thought. I think I'll just stick to Jackie after all. But if you're still not put off, then all I can say is, the best of luck!

A JACKIE KNIT-A-BIT PATTERN

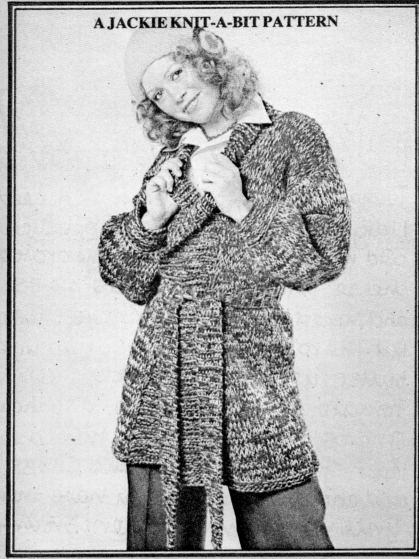

BE A BIG KNIT!

THICK, chunky jackets are all the rage for winter . . . so why not save money and knit one for yourself?

This one is a Hayfield design, exclusive to Jackie. It's really warm, easy to knit and, at approx. £6, it will cost you about ⅓ of the price of similar jackets in the shops at the moment!

You just choose the three colours from the Gaylon range you think will look nicest together (we used Bottle Green, Woodland Green and Light Grey Mix), pick up your 00 knitting needles (available from most wool shops) — and start knitting!

If you have any problems in finding Hayfield's Gaylon wool you can obtain it by mail order from:

Abbeydale Wools Ltd., Abbeydale, 8 Ilkley Road, Addingham, Yorkshire.

The cost of the wool is 12½p for a 25 gram ball, postage and packing, 20p extra.

There are 37 colours in all: Bouquet (pinky), Navy, Lipstick (red), Bottle, Sunshine, Light Beige, Royal, Japonica (cerise pink), Kingfisher, Emerald, White, Black, Gold, Rust, Butterscotch, Burnt Bronze, Mulberry, Indian Jade, Dark Grey Mix, Light Grey Mix, Woodland Green, Viola (purple), Burnt Brown, Clove Carnation (maroon), Cascade (mid-blue), Chrysanthemum (orangey-yellow), Sunbright Blue, Poppy (bright, bright red), French Navy, Aran, Cornish Blue, Mustard, Camel, Peacock Green, Lilac, Princess Blue, Burnt Orange.

JACKET

Materials: of Hayfields Gaylon D.K. 16 (17, 18, 19) balls each of A, B, C. 1 pair of 00 needles.

To Fit: 32 (34, 36, 38) in. Bust. Length: 39 in. Sleeve seam: 16½ in.

Tension: 3 sts. to 1 in. on 00 needles over st. st.

Abbreviations: st(s). stitch(es): K. Knit; st. st., stocking stitch; beg. beginning: inc., increase.

BACK

With 1 strand each of A, B, C, used together throughout and No. 00 needles, cast on 51 (54, 57, 60) sts. Work 4 rows in garter st. Change to st. st. and continue until work measures 30 (31, 32, 33) in.

Shape Shoulders: Cast off 4 (4, 4, 4) sts. at beg. of next and following row.

Cast off 4 (4, 4, 5) sts. at beg. of next and following row.

Cast off 4 (4, 5, 5) sts. at beg. of next and following row.

Cast off 4 (5, 5, 5) sts. at beg. of next and following row.

Cast off.

FRONTS

With 1 strand each of A, B, C, and No. 00 needles, cast on 34 (36, 38, 40) sts and work 4 rows in garter st. Keeping the front edge 16 (17, 18, 19) sts. in garter st. work sts. remaining in st. st. until front measures as back to shoulder shaping finishing at side edge.

Shape Shoulder: Cast off 4 (4, 4, 4) sts at beg of next row, work 1 row.

Cast off 4 (4, 4, 5) sts at beg of next row, work 1 row.

Cast off 4 (4, 5, 5) sts at beg of next row, work 1 row.

Cast off 4 (5, 5, 5) sts at beg of next row, work 1 row.

Continue on front edge sts until band measures from shoulder to centre back neck, cast off.

Work 2nd front to match reversing all shapings.

SLEEVES

With one strand each A, B, C, and No. 00 needles cast on 24 sts and work 12 rows garter st.

Next row: Inc in every st. (48 sts).

Continue in st. st. until sleeve measures 16½ in. Cast off.

BELT

With 1 strand each A, B, C, and No. 00 needles cast on 8 sts and work in garter st. until belt measures 60 in. or required length.

TO MAKE UP

Press. Join shoulder seams. Set in sleeves. Join side and sleeve seams. Press.

BACK TO NATURE... THE SWIFT FLOWING STREAM, THE HUM OF DRAGONFLIES, THE COOL SUMMER BREEZE—

WHAT MORE COULD ONE DESIRE?

HOT DOGS, HAMBURGERS, GET YER LOVELY HOT DOGS 'ERE!

PEASANTS!

14 September 1974

LET'S HAVE A Valentine PARTY

NO-O-O-O-O!

Invites

Hey! who's coming? Work out a list, with more or less equal numbers, but if possible, add a couple of extra males, too.

Look around for some zany invite cards. Seen some cr-azy ones with cartoons on the front—'bout 4d each. Or why not design your own, like the one we've done here? Send out in plenty of time.

Everyone coming? Check off on your list as each replies.

Eats

How's your budget? Set a maximum for food expenses, and keep within this. Go for plenty of simple, help-yourself fun-type eats, and arrange on a side table or dresser to look tempting and mmmmm . . . de-lish! Allow plenty of time to prepare, and have several

packets of wooden cocktail sticks for plonking in Danish open sandwiches and savouries so they're easy to pick up.

Here's the faves that will go like ten with the gang!

★ French "yardstick" bread, piled to one side in wicker basket, with a variety cheeseboard, butter, crisps, chutney and celery sticks. They can break off hunks of bread, cut wedge of cheese and . . . delish!

★ Danish open sandwiches. Base: Slice of buttered toast, roll, brown or white bread. Fillings? Anything you like. Try these:—

1. Chopped dates topped with blanched almonds.
2. Stilton cheese, with black grape and slice of mandarin orange each side.

★ Tasty eats spiked on to cocktail sticks. Have heaps of these. Fun to prepare, fun to eat and very popular with he-males! Like a cube of pineapple with wedge of cheese; sausage with wedge of tomato; prawn with button mushroom; cube of ham with green grape; cheese with gherkins.

Drinks

Soft drinks, cider and fruit punches, plus heaps of black coffee 'n' fresh cream . . . delish! Two to try? Coming up. The first is Devilled Lemon, the second, Cider Fruit Cup. Look up ye olde cook book and you'll find lots more, too!

Devilled Lemon.

Two large bottles of ginger ale,
Two small bottles of concentrated lemon juice,
Half-pint of water,
Slices of lemon, pineapple, cherry and grapes,
Few mint leaves.

Cider Fruit Cup.

Two large bottles of cider,
Bottle of tonic water,
Smallish bottle of grapefruit, orange and lemon juice,
Slices of fresh or tinned fruit,
Ice cubes.

Simple to make—just mix together well, add slices of fruit so they float on top, then several ice cubes. Let drink stand for about 15-25 minutes, and serve in tall tumblers.

Having beer? Much cheaper if you buy it by the barrel for a large party! Smallest size costs about £2-£3 (called a pin) and you order it from your local pub or off licence. Have it delivered a couple of days before, so that the sediment in the beer has time to settle. Also ask for details on hiring glasses and tankards for the evening!

Hostess Hints

. . super idea to get best beau or girlfriend to come early to give you a hand with last-minute preparations and first arrivals.

. he-males can dump coats in hall, but show girls up to your bedroom in case they want to check-up on hair-do or make-up.

. All set to make the party go? Remember, although the preparations have been organised and planned, from now on keep things casual, lighthearted — and no obvious match-making; leave that to cupid, it's his day, after all!

. eats 'n' drinks? Tell everyone just to help themselves whenever they want any food. Convince a couple of ownsome bods they'll make super barmen to help out with the drinks.

. Having a whip-round for the expense of the drinks? Fun-type way is for your boyfriend to go round with pint tankard (empty!) in hand, in which each male can plonk the cash. Early as poss in evening!

. do's that could put the damper on party fun? Gatecrashers. (Just don't let them in. Hen or stag corner-gatherings. Annoyed neighbours. (Warn them the night before that you're having a party; keep record-player turned down after twelve.) Not enough food.

. how about parents? Tell them all about the party if it's their house. If you want to persuade them to go out for the evening, why not buy them a couple of film tickets?

. ooops — drink spilt or eats trod into carpet? Don't panic! Just mop up with a cloth. S'posing it's a calamity, like the record-player breaking down? Com-promise—just tune into Luxembourg.

. the party's almost over? Serve up a hot, home-going drink like coffee or soup.

. last of the guests still hanging around? Waylay for helping with the washing-up or tidying. Do vacuum-cleaning, &c., in morning . . . Everyone gone? Big yawn . . it's been a great party . . . but now it's zzzzzz . . .

....AND IT'S LEAP-YEAR TOO.!

PART 5

After last week Myrtle saw me as her knight in shining armour—so it seems we're back together again. But I've still got to get rid of Pierre, our lodger. He's taking over the kitchen now, as well as my room in the flat!

SNAILS! HE'S COOKING SNAILS! IN OUR KITCHEN!

DISGUSTING, I CALL IT.

IT IS YOU ENGLISH WHO ARE DISGUSTING. FRIED FISH IN GREASY NEWSPAPER. PAH! YOU KNOW NOTHING ABOUT FOOD, NOTHING ABOUT WINE AND NOTHING ABOUT LOVE. GO BACK TO YOUR CRICKET AND YOUR FOOTBALL. IT IS ALL YOU KNOW. LEAVE FOOD AND WOMEN TO THE FRENCH . . . THE MEN OF EXPERIENCE.

T.P.A.O.L.J.W.T.F. L.I.A.W.T.H.S.A.H.

OR THE PATHETIC ATTEMPTS OF LEONARD J. WATKINS TO FIND LOVE IN A WORLD THAT HAS SOMETHING AGAINST HIM.

Something would have to be done about him—and fast! I was just scraping the last chip off the sports page when the idea came to me . . .

I KNOW! I'LL CHALLENGE HIM TO A DUEL!

But none of this old fashioned stuff . . .

HAH SO, VARLET! SAY YOUR PRAYERS BEFORE YOU DIE!

HAVE MERCY ON ME, KIND SIR! I SHALL DO ANYTHING FOR YOU—ANYTHING AT ALL.

No—that wasn't drastic enough for Pierre. It would have to be something which would drive him out of our flat for good.

YOU SAID THE BRITISH WERE ROTTEN COOKS. OK. I HEREBY CHALLENGE YOU TO A COOKING DUEL. WINNER GETS MYRTLE.

OH YES! IT'S A WONDERFUL IDEA!

YOU IDIOT! YOU CAN'T COOK!

PIERRE'S NICE. BUT IN A WAY, I WANT LEN TO WIN.

I'VE GOT ALL DAY TO LEARN.

IT'S EASY, RUSS, ALL I HAVE TO DO IS FIND SOME TERRIFIC RECIPE. JUST YOU WAIT. IT'LL SMELL SO DELICIOUS, THE VERY LINO WILL CURL UP OFF THE FLOOR IN ECSTACY.

SOMEHOW I DON'T LIKE THE SOUND OF ECSTATIC LINO.

GOOD BRITISH FOOD—THAT'S WHAT WE NEED. NOW LET'S THINK . . . THERE'S BEANS—BEANS OR, UM—BEANS.

I CAN'T TAKE ANY MORE. I HAVE THIS AWFUL FEELING OF IMPENDING DOOM.

Finally though, I'd decided on my menu . . .

I CANNOT BELIEVE IT. HE IS MAKING A HOLE IN THE TOAD?

I THINK IT'S A TOAD IN THE HOLE, ACTUALLY.

BUT COME TO THINK OF IT, MAYBE IT IS A HOLE IN THE TOAD. WITH LEN ANYTHING'S POSSIBLE.

FLOUR

MORE NEXT WEEK.

20 Ways ⊕ To Make Him Notice You!

1. Fall off your bike into his front garden.

2. Climb up a lamp post outside his house and start playing the bagpipes (but only if you don't mind the rest of the street and possibly the rest of the town noticing you as well!).

3. Take a crowd of mates with you everywhere; he'll think you're so popular he just has to know you!

4. Have your head shaved and wear blue lipstick — he's sure to notice you then.

5. Pretend to be the telephone exchange checking his line, and keep ringing him up. Be chatty and make the most of your chance — he's bound to guess sooner or later.

6. Wear a black eye-patch; you'll intrigue him by looking romantic and mysterious. On the other hand, you might just make him burst out laughing because you look plain stupid — but you've got to take chances.

7. Fall over his feet! And if he looks like turning nasty about it, accuse him of trying to trip you up. (Lots of romances start on a slightly aggressive note!)

8. Be bold. Embroider his name on your chest (better still, on your T-shirt — it's much less painful!).

9. Smile at him whenever you see him. Boys notice girls who notice them!

10. Rush up to him and fling your arms passionately around his neck and say "Oh, Pete, I haven't seen you for ages," when you know he's called Michael!

11. Write his name on your forehead, in eyeshadow.

12. Wear pillar-box red from head to foot. (But not if your vital statistics are 46/46/46 — he might shove a large parcel between your teeth!)

13. Break into heartbreaking tears when he's passing. He should offer his hanky and his heart!

14. Drop your shopping basket right by him in the supermarket. It's just an up-dated version of the old handkerchief trick, but it works just as well!

15. Find out his favourite colour; then have yourself dyed. Too bad if it's puce!

16. Carry a stack of books with intriguing titles like, "Swahili In Eight Lessons," "A Manual Of Poisons," "How To Cook Tripe," "My Eight Husbands," and "Keeping Gorillas." Get the right assortment and he's bound to speak to you — even if it's only out of curiosity.

17. Dance like a wild thing! (Only in the disco, of course!)

18. Take his photograph. Even if you've NEVER met, it's bound to get him curious, and then you can either be frank, "I liked the look of you, so I snapped you!" or mysterious, "Oh, it's a secret, I can't possibly say why I need your photo" or plain untruthful, "I'm a secret agent, and the government knows all about you selling secret chopsticks to the Chinese, see?"

19. Soak yourself in sexy scent and drift past him at every available opportunity. It'll get to him eventually and if he doesn't sneeze — you're OK!

20. Hire a Rolls Royce for a day — and give him a lift. It might be a bit tricky trying to explain where it's gone when you see him again, though!

Something nice or silly or both for you to do every day.

SUNDAY: Get organised — throw out all those bits of clutter hiding in nasty corners of your room. Except your old "Jackies" of course — they're always worth re-reading!

MONDAY: Start knitting — it doesn't matter what — you can think of that afterwards.

TUESDAY: Bored? Write out every single thing you've done every moment of the day. It'll probably make very boring reading, but at least it'll keep you occupied for the hours it'll take you to do.

WEDNESDAY: Plant a flower for summer. If you scatter masses of seeds around the garden, some of them must work!

THURSDAY: Choose a brand new, very unknown pop group to rave about. In six months, you'll either be able to boast you knew all about them from the very start, or feel rather silly . . .

FRIDAY: Make an effort to look smart and sophisticated — well, just this once!

SATURDAY: Dream your most wonderful, romantic day-dream. Believe that it can't fail to happen some day.

ED'S LETTER

Well, are you all sitting comfortably? Then watch out—you're sending secret messages! At least, that's what our leg feature on page 27 tells me. Apparently, the way you arrange yourself when you sit reveals the hidden secrets of your personality and not just the ladders in your tights! So don't say you haven't been warned . . .

I wonder where in fact you are reading your copy of Jackie: sitting at home, on the bus, or perhaps under the desk at school?! We're always thrilled to see one of you reading it unexpectedly - across from us on a train, or having a cup of coffee.

So if you catch someone STARING at you and your copy—have a quick check round now—it might just be one of us!

Or perhaps you read your copy in the bath. Cathy says that reading in the bath used to be her idea of bliss. However, since she's moved into a flat she's given it up. Unfortunately their loo isn't separate, and as soon as she's settled down for a long soak and a wallow with a good book, there's always someone hammering on the door in desperation.

From sitting to standing—or rather walking, and the new spring shoes. Fashion has decreed that platforms are out, and according to Alison they have been for months—she tells us that shoes are much more elegant with slender heels and T-straps. However, on the other hand (or rather foot!) loads of people just couldn't do without that extra bit of height, so our fashion special will still show you some of each.

If you're looking enviously at the super figure of the Italian model in our 'Sock It To 'Em' exercise feature—then start getting in trim right away. Next week we'll be starting a new regular series to get you in shape. It's for skinnies, slimmers and all sizes in-between! Don't miss it, will you?

Have an energetic week!

Love,
The Ed

I JUST DIDN'T THINK...

LOOKING out the window and up at the sky I can see about a million stars twinkling up there. Now they blur into one big glow as I stare at them. So I look away, and I can feel my eyes watering. I don't know whether it's tears or the effort of staring. I feel so miserable that I don't really care.

And it's all my own fault. That's what Dad says and I know he's right. He says my whole trouble is that I simply don't think — and even when I do I simply don't bother.

I've been foolish, inconsiderate and regretting it now doesn't help. But I've got nothing else to do but sit and worry over it. Because Dad's stopped my pocket money for the next month *and* refused to let me go out in the evenings.

Twenty-eight whole days without seeing the usual gang. It's a lifetime nearly. I don't see how I'm going to live through it.

And none of this would have happened if it hadn't been for Libby Sinclair's birthday. A whole crowd of us had been at the coffee bar on Saturday, when someone suggested we should celebrate Libby's seventeenth in style, because, apart / from anything else, she'd just heard that she'd passed her exams at college.

There were six of us — Libby and her boy Tom, Claire and Andy, Carole and me. I'm the youngest, but you wouldn't think so. I'm easily the tallest and biggest-built and most people take me for quite a bit older than fifteen-and-a-half. I suppose it's because of this that I've always preferred to go about with friends a few years older than myself.

So I honestly didn't give it a thought when we all trooped off down the road to the Rose and Crown. It's a pretty little

ivy-covered pub, and the river runs right past it. In the summer they put chairs and tables out on the lawn for families with children. I'd often been there with Mum and Dad when I was younger, and had a coke or lemonade, but this was the first time I'd actually been in the bar. I had a good look round as soon as we went in, because I'd often wondered what it was like.

It was just as I'd imagined — lovely low beams, dark woodwork and shiny horse brasses. It was pretty crowded and noisy like you would expect, being Saturday, so we all squeezed into the corner.

Tom, who's nearly eighteen, took charge right away and offered to go up to the bar for drinks. He asked what I'd like and I just said the first thing that came into my head: Bacardi and Coke. I'd seen it on the T.V. commercials. He looked a bit staggered but he went off anyhow and soon brought back the tray of glasses.

I took mine and sipped it, then drank it pretty quickly, because I didn't think much of the taste. Really, I preferred the Coke on its own but I wasn't going to say so and risk looking a fool in front of everyone else. Especially when they all appeared to be enjoying their drinks so much. So when Andy brought me a second one I didn't object.

There was a really glamorous woman sitting at the next table — beautiful long red dress and fantastic silver jewellery, and for some reason I was quite pleased when I heard her ask for the same drink as I had. She seemed to toss them down just as if they were lemonade, and I was fascinated. I leaned back in my chair so that it teetered on its back legs and I thought: this is really living.

I THINK we'd been there for about an hour when this policeman showed up. I didn't notice him at first, until Carole nudged me. I looked up and saw him speaking to the man behind the bar. Then he looked, almost casually, all round the pub, and his gaze eventually rested on our little group in the corner.

Even then, it didn't dawn on me. After a second or two he stared over, picked up our glasses, sniffed them and asked us how old we were. I think I said "nearly sixteen," but for some funny reason it didn't seem to come out very clearly. The words seemed to run together.

The he wrote down our names and addresses, and went back and spoke to the barman who looked pretty mad. I don't think he'd really had time to look at us before, because he'd been so busy serving people.

He came across and said something to Tom, who went a bit red and didn't answer. But he pushed his chair back and grabbed Libby's arm, and next thing I knew we were all outside and I was clutching Carole's arm because for some peculiar reason the pavement refused to stand still. One minute it was there lying straight in front of me and the next it was snaking about like a piece of wide grey ribbon.

And the kerb seemed intent on tripping me up, because I fell off it twice and only saved myself by grabbing Tom's coat. I hadn't realised that the policeman was right behind us until he caught hold of my elbow.

"I'd walk about for a bit before you go home, young lady," he told me. "Take a couple of turns round the block. Fresh air'll do you a world of good."

I tried to tell him, very seriously, that I didn't care for walking, but he didn't seem to understand what I said. He just looked at me with an odd sort of expression and what I could have sworn was a suspicion of a smile. He let go of my elbow, patted me on the shoulder, and said,

"I'll be round to see your parents in a day or two, so don't move away in the meantime."

I thought that was really funny at the time and remember how loudly I laughed.

It isn't so funny now.

I WAS lucky when I got home, because Mum and Dad had gone to the cinema and weren't back yet. I was so tired and muddled by that time that I just fell into my bed. I can't remember any more until I woke up next day with an awful headache.

I took a couple of aspirins and agreed with Mum when she said that perhaps I'd been working too hard at school. She even suggested I had the day off, and I was so pleased, because somehow I didn't want to face the others. Not just yet, anyhow.

That very evening, however, the policeman called to see Mum and Dad. I hadn't told them anything because I'd hoped he might change his mind and it would all be forgotten.

No such luck!

After the policeman had gone, Dad was absolutely furious with me. It was the first time he'd ever had the police knock on his door, he said, and it was going to be the last. He'd been too lenient with me in the past, and it wasn't going to happen again.

The lecture and shouting seemed to go on for hours, and Mum backed him up all the way. I think she was hurt more than anything else, because she always seems to have such plans for me, if and when I pass my O levels.

So here I am, stuck in my room, with nothing to do but gaze at the sky and regret everything that's happened. I won't be able to buy those new shoes I've wanted for so long but as I'm not allowed out for a month, I couldn't wear them anywhere anyway. But the worst, the very worst, is not being allowed out with the gang. Not being part of what's going on. Not even *knowing* what's going on.

As I lean my elbows on the window-sill, a star suddenly shoots right across the heavens. That's supposed to be lucky — a falling star.

I hope it's going to be, for me. I know I don't deserve it, but I feel I could do with some good luck right now . . .

Dear Cathy & Claire

WHEN *JACKIE'S* **CATHY & CLAIRE PROBLEM PAGES** crop up in conversation with females of a certain age, their eyes either mist over with nostalgia or they blush furiously – because they remember writing to Cathy & Claire themselves …

When a new acquaintance heard that I had once done a stint as Cathy & Claire during the early Seventies, she burst into tears and said that their reply to her problem (when she was fourteen) had been so important to her that she had written back to let them know how much they had helped. She refused, however, to reveal to me exactly what her dilemma had been!

The Cathy & Claire page was the hot favourite in the magazine and the one to which most readers turned first, often crowded round the magazine with their mates. The publisher, DC Thomson, had a strict moral code and topics such as sex were taboo. The page dealt with weighty issues such as fancying boys, falling out with your best mate (always over a boy, of course) and your dad telling you had to be home by 10.30 – or else.

It would have come as a shock to the troubled teens who wrote to Cathy & Claire that the agony aunt duo weren't real people and that the mountains of letters received each day were handled by members of the *Jackie* staff, who nevertheless took the task very seriously.

It was a far more innocent era in many ways and no matter how trivial some of the problems might seem today, the editors realised how important they were to the teenage girls who were anxiously waiting for a reply. In many cases, those who wrote in felt that they had no one else to turn to and we were well aware of the courage it had probably taken for them to put pen to paper in the first place.

There were very few magazine helplines or counselling resources for teens before the 1990s, and readers often told us that they felt they couldn't talk to their mums, or even their friends, about the vexing question of how to handle their first kiss, chat up a boy they fancied, or pour their hearts out about the boyfriend who didn't seem to care … There was a huge responsibility to try and give helpful and honest advice and set the girls' minds to rest. The queries covered everything from crushes on pop stars to bad-hair days and whether or not having to wear glasses or teeth braces might mean they would never find a boyfriend.

There's no doubt that the dating game was a lot less straightforward before the age of mobile phones and Facebook. Girls would be upset because the object of their desires hadn't replied to their letters, or that Gran was vetting his phone calls. Some readers even complained that their parents were "too mean" to have a phone in the house.

It was also long before the age of computers and the *Jackie* staff didn't even have a typewriter each. We would pass our written replies to the office typist – whose own typewriter wasn't even electric – for our words of wisdom to be transferred to letter-headed paper and despatched with all speed to the waiting, angst-ridden readers, many of whom simply wanted reassurance that their worries were "normal" and that they wouldn't be the first – or the last – to agonise about their spots, lovebites or how to dress for discos. That's if they could persuade Dad to let them go in the first place. One letter, which now would seem more suited to a parish magazine, asked a vexing question along the lines of: "I've been invited to my boyfriend's parents' house for the first time. I don't want to go because I'm frightened I'll spill tea or something – and should I offer to help with the dishes afterwards?"

Few readers betrayed any desire to be regarded as feminists. Their world revolved round finding a "fella" and seeking "true love" and, in many cases, what they really needed was a big injection of self-confidence.

It wasn't unusual for some letters to be pages long and include half a dozen diverse problems at once, but we had to be up to the challenge of making sure all the reader's concerns were addressed. ▶

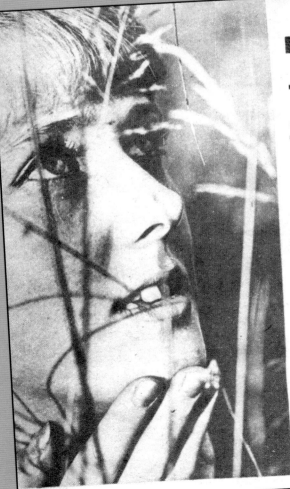

THERE MUST BE A REASON WHY

Dear C. and C.,

My boy—or should I say my ex— is
He wrote me recently, saying he d
any more.

Everyone—including our families—
on my birthday, so Bill said he wasn't b
said to let him know the reason I'd li
that public.

I don't know what to do.

Ignore him. The public don't have to
the truth and let Bill tell whatever he
fellow who takes himself this seriously
heart for anyone else.

IS HE NORMAL?

DEAR CATHY & CLAIRE – I'm worried about my brother, who is twenty. He used to be fairly outgoing and went about on a motorbike with a crowd of lads, though now he says it was only to be like them. Recently he sold it and bought a pedal bike instead, and he uses that to get about all the time now.

He's now only got one or two close friends, and he doesn't seem to go out with girls. I'm scared he's turning a bit feminine. I get on really well with him and would be glad of your advice.

Forget it! You're creating a problem out of absolutely nothing here, and if you weren't genuinely concerned about your brother, we'd be getting quite annoyed with you!

Boys don't have to be all butch and follow in the "traditional" masculine roles to be normal, you know. Far more normal, as far as we can see it, to have enough of a mind of your own to break away from being one of the crowd and suiting yourself instead. We think it's great your brother's got the confidence to go his own way, and he sounds like the kind of friend most girls would be glad to have. So stop worrying and enjoy him for what he is — an individual who's great fun to have around!

HE DOESN'T NOTICE ME

DEAR CATHY & CLAIRE – I'm absolutely nuts about a boy two years above me at school. I don't know him to talk to or anything, and have to worship him from afar, as it were, because he just doesn't know I'm alive.

I've had my fair share of boyfriends in my year, and my friends say I should stop mooning over someone I can probably never have, but I can't just forget all about him. What can I do to make him notice me?

While you're at school, a couple of years age difference can seem an awful lot, and if this boy happens to think of your year collectively as a lot of kids, there's not an awful lot you can do about it.

Out of school, though, isn't there a youth club or disco he goes to regularly, one that you could go to as well, where you might stand more chance of being noticed? Don't you have any friends involved with his crowd that could organise a party you could both go to, as things could take off from there? At the moment, though, remember that you hardly know him — so be prepared that he might be one big yawn to talk to . . .

HOW CAN I GET HIM BACK?

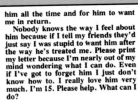

DEAR CATHY & CLAIRE—I expect you've heard this a hundred times before, but here goes. You see, five months ago I went with a boy, Alan, who I liked very much. After a month he chucked me. I was really upset. Then a few weeks ago he asked me out again.

After only a week he chucked me again. I still like him very much and sometimes see him and speak to him. But that's not enough. I want to be near him all the time and for him to want me in return.

Nobody knows the way I feel about him because if I tell my friends they'd just say I was stupid to want him after the way he's treated me. Please print my letter because I'm nearly out of my mind wondering what I can do. Even if I've got to forget him I just don't know how to. I really love him very much. I'm 15. Please help. What can I do?

Sadly, love, there's not a lot you can do. You can't *make* Alan fall in love with you again, but, on the other hand, you can't forget him, either. We suppose it's not much comfort to know that practically every single person in the world has gone, or will go, through what you're going through right now? Honestly. It happens to everyone at some time or another, and, hard as it may sound, the only thing to do is grin and bear it and wait for time to heal the hurt.

In time, you *will* stop thinking about Alan. Really. You may not believe it now, but we promise you, in two or three months, you'll wonder what all ...

THE CATHY AND CLAIRE PAGE

NO, MY DARLING DAUGHTER!

— that's the verdict on her boy

Dear C. and C.,

I am 17 and have been dating since I was 15. My parents, to give them their due, have always been very understanding and helpful. And I can honestly say I've never abused any of my privileges.

Now I feel boys of my own age a bit boring. I like older fellows. In fact, my present steady is 21—and a walking dream!

Dad feels I should go out only with boys my own age. He says older boys are too fast and smooth-talking for " a young girl like me!"

Mum, I think, secretly sides with me, but doesn't want to show it.

What's your opinion of this set-up?

We're with you! A bright, sensible girl of 17 isn't likely to stay interested in a boy of her own age. In any case, it's usually the 17-year-olds who are fast. An older boy has more respect for his girl.

We hope your mum and dad will relent. We'd stake a month's wages on you being sensible, so there!

Dear C. and C.,

Recently, I started going out with a boy who is studying music. He takes me to highbrow concerts and, although I quite enjoy them, I always feel a drag because I can't discuss them intelligently afterwards. I'm afraid he'll think me stupid and lose interest.

If the boy is really interested in YOU, he won't be too worried about your knowledge of music, as long as you enjoy it.

Claire suggests taking him along to a real swingin' jazz club some night. Maybe he'll go for that as much as the Bach 'n' Beethoven and your problem will be over.

Dear C. and C.,

I have been invited to a cocktail party, but when I drink my eyes get blurred and can't see straight— even wearing my glasses.

Stick to Coke—unless the place is electrically heated. With alcohol you might make a spectacle of yourself after a couple of glasses.

Dear C. and C.,

My boyfriend and I recently saw a fellow pushing his girl around in a restaurant.

Bill refused to go to the rescue. In fact, he hustled me away from the spot.

I think Bill's a coward. Am I right?

No. Never butt in on a private fight. It was up to the restaurant owner to help the girl.

Dear C. and C.,

Stan has asked me to spend a Sunday with his family. I enjoy going out with Stan, but I'm not in love with him and feel that " meeting the family " is a bit on the serious side. What d'you think?

We think you're counting your chickens! Going to a guy's house doesn't make you his future wife. Treat this invitation like any other. Go if you feel like it. Otherwise, don't.

Dear C. and C.,

For three years I've gone steady with a boy and I was certain we were altar-bound. Then he confessed he was mildly infatuated with a very attractive girl in his office. He asked my permission to take her out a few times to get her " out of his system." I was shattered!

Three weeks passed without a word from him. Then I received two dozen red roses with the enclosed card, " It's you I love."

I love him, but what assurance do I have that something like this won't happen again?

If you love him, forget the past. Start the romance anew. A good second beginning could lead to a happy ending.

THE CATHY & CLAIRE PAGE

We can't promise the perfect solution, but we'll do our best. If you're stuck with a problem and you can't see the way out, write to us at this address: Cathy & Claire, Jackie, 12 Fetter Lane, Fleet Street, London EC4A 1BL. Please remember to enclose an S.A.E.

DEAR CATHY & CLAIRE — My problem is that when my mother goes into town to shop, she sometimes buys me clothes. You know, skirts, jumpers and that sort of thing. Lately this has been happening more often, as we're due to go on a late holiday.

When I come home from school, she has these things all laid out for me to see. Sometimes I like them, but more often I find them old-fashioned. I really wouldn't be seen dead in some of them, except around the house, but how can I tell her this without hurting her feelings? She says I should be grateful for all the things I get, and I suppose I am lucky because I do get quite a lot.

The trouble is that I don't want to upset her, so I just say that I like them and then of course she believes me, and makes me wear them. My friends are always on at me for not being fashion-conscious, but I am really, if only I could get the chance!

Well, we reckon it's time for you to do a bit of window-shopping! Your mother seems to be kind, very generous, and wants you to be well-dressed. The only thing is that she's got 'sensible taste' in clothes as opposed to knowing what's really fashionable. So why don't you give her some help by telling her exactly what you'd like? But do this tactfully, so that she won't be offended.

Perhaps you could go along with her, on some of her shopping expeditions. She'd probably appreciate the company, and an extra pair of hands to carry the shopping! Then, when you see something you fancy, you could tell her that you liked it. We're not saying that she'd buy it for you — but at least she'd have an idea of your taste in clothes.

Alternatively, you could go round the shops after school or on a Saturday and see just what's in stock. Then, when you get home, you could just mention about that beautiful blouse you saw in the boutique, or that lovely jumper in Marks & Spencer . . . But remember not to be too demanding or outrageous in your choice of clothes. Show her that you realise you're lucky to have such a generous mum, (cos you are, you know!) and soon you should have a reasonable wardrobe — and a great relationship with your mum!

When serious issues such as bullying arose, we would always urge the reader (who invariably said they couldn't tell their parents) to enlist the help of a responsible adult such as a teacher or an older relative. It also helped that a number of typical teenage concerns would also be tackled in the pages of "Readers' True Experiences", picture stories and, later, photo stories.

Readers' problems made no references at all to drugs and very few mentioned alcohol. Most of the readers were part of "conventional" families. Stepfamilies were rare and one reader wrote that she was embarrassed, and taunted at school, because her sister was an unmarried mother.

We had a selection of "standard" responses to more light-hearted queries such as: "I fancy a boy I see on the bus every morning. How can I make him notice me?" Standard reply: "Smile and say hello". One plea for reassurance read: "I brushed past a boy on the bus. We had our cloths on (sic). Could I be pregnant?" There wasn't a standard letter for that one. There was also a series of help leaflets written by professionals, covering frequently asked questions, which we included with our replying letters.

The letters on the problem page of the magazine were chosen and edited to cover as wide a range as possible of the burning issues that beset the readers. At one point, in its heyday, *Jackie*'s print run reached nearly 1.5 million copies and it was quite daunting to visit the building where the presses were rolling and to realise just how many readers could be relying on the advice of "Cathy & Claire".

Medical and psychological problems such as depression were referred to a qualified doctor who would write a personal reply on our behalf. The terror of teenage pregnancy was distressingly illustrated when a desperate reader sent a urine sample together with her letter.

In 1974, the National Health Service made the contraceptive pill free on prescription, and so under editor Nina Myskow the magazine introduced a "Dear Doctor" column, which covered what were termed as "below the waist issues" but which would be considered very tame today.

"Medical" problems also covered an appeal from a reader whose mother was concerned about her daughter having her ears pierced. What would that mother have made of today's multiple piercings and tattoos? However, the advice that was given is still as sound today: If you are going to have your ears pierced, make sure the deed is done by someone reputable and follow the advice for hygiene care afterwards.

Dealing with the volume of correspondence was an ongoing task – just as we felt we were making progress in answering the current pile of post, the mail girl would stagger into the *Jackie* office twice a day, pushing a two-tiered shopping trolley contraption, stuffed to the brim with yet more letters from anguished readers. Many were anonymous, but we fulfilled our promise that every letter with a stamped, addressed envelope would receive a personal reply. It wasn't unusual to get more than 100 letters in one day and we realised the importance of making sure each one was sent a prompt response.

It was generally a question of commonsense when replying and

She Won't Believe I Love Him

DEAR CATHY & CLAIRE — I've been going out with Dave for two years, since I was fourteen, so it's fairly obvious to me, at any rate, that we're serious about each other. Dave wants us to get engaged soon, but when I told my mother this she got very angry and said it's just teenage infatuation and we don't know what life's all about. She did say I can go on seeing Dave, but said she doesn't want to hear any more about an engagement.

But we *want* to get engaged. What can we do?

Quite frankly love, although you think your mother's being a bit harsh, we can understand how she must feel. You're not a little girl any more, but you're still her daughter and she'll always want what's best for you.

She wants you to get the most out of life, to enjoy yourself and have fun while you've still got the chance. She probably thinks that an engagement is as total a commitment as marriage and your fun will be restricted once you've taken this step.

It's up to you, love, to prove her wrong. You can show her that you'll still be enjoying yourself even though you're engaged. In fact, you should be happier, and having more fun, with your fiance there to share all the good times. She certainly doesn't seem to object to Dave, as she doesn't mind you going on seeing him.

Make her see that your life from now on is not going to be drastically changed, and that you're not going to be burdened for a long time yet by the financial and other problems which can often arise with young newlyweds.

In this way, your mother should realise that an engagement is all you really want and what will make you happiest.

Just one thing, though — remember that an engagement *is* a promise to marry — nothing more or less. Your mother realises this — but she's not too convinced that you do.

So before you do anything, have a good, long, think about the true meaning of, "an engagement". You might find your mother knows best, after all . . .

it certainly helped that most of us weren't much older than the readers ourselves. Although we might not have shared some of their torment – "I can't sleep at night for thinking about David Cassidy. I have to meet him – even just once!" or "I'm a Bay City Rollers fan but my boyfriend likes Led Zeppelin and he makes me listen to them" – we could still relate to the majority of problems the typical reader faced.

One of the most gratifying parts of the job was getting feedback from readers thanking us and telling us that we had solved their problem.

Although *Jackie* was aimed at 12–16-year-old girls, we knew from their letters that sisters – and brothers, too, although they never would have admitted it – weren't averse to taking a sneaky peek at the magazine as soon as it was delivered, even though they knew they would be in for it if sis found her copy had been tampered with before she had had chance to get her hands on it.

Looking back at the problem pages now, it's not only a trip down memory lane, it's also hard to believe how much times have moved on – and that isn't just reflected in the written words. Cathy & Claire's page included photographs, posed by models, all sporting the alarming fashions of the Seventies – and the Eighties weren't much better. But they were the same clothes that the readers – and most of the *Jackie* staff – wore too and could identify with: platform soles, midi-skirts, crocheted mini dresses, dungarees. And let's not go down the male angle with tank tops, flares and dodgy caps à la Donny Osmond …

Someone should have phoned the fashion police, but we all thought we were cutting edge at the time.

The innocent era of Cathy & Claire may seem a world away by today's standards as girls grow up much faster and have access to so much more information, but Twitter and Facebook reveal that teenagers still anguish over boyfriends, falling out with their mates and doing battle with their parents.

Some things never change …

Hilary Bowman

My doctor has told me that I have scabies. I'd like to know what this means, as I don't understand what it is or how I managed to get it.

I don't know what to do and I'm getting very depressed as I'm scared to go near people, although I've been given a lotion called Quellada to treat it. How long will it take to go away? Please help me.

Scabies is caused by an insect which can travel from one person to another where there is close contact. It is very contagious and it often spreads to other members of the family and to close friends. The female insect burrows into the skin and leaves her eggs which hatch out after about three or four days.

After the eggs hatch this produces intense itching of the skin which is always worse at night. Scratching tends to spread the infection but it is completely curable with the lotion you have been given. If it's used as directed, it kills the mite and once the cause of the rash is gone, your skin will no longer itch, you'll stop scratching and any rash will disappear.

Do be careful, though, to change your clothes and bedlinen to prevent reinfecting yourself, and watch out whom you come into contact with so that you don't pick up this irritating problem again.

THEY SAY WE'RE TOO YOUNG!

DEAR CATHY & CLAIRE — My boyfriend and I are both fourteen, and everyone says we're too young to be really in love, but we are. Or we were, anyway, till he began ignoring me at school when he's with his mates. Yet he says he'll never chuck me.

A girl he used to go out with keeps flirting with him and I know she wants him back. He doesn't seem to realise what she's doing. I've always said I'll never chuck him, either, but I'm beginning to have second thoughts. I'm very confused.

We think that perhaps you're beginning to realise what's meant by being too young for real love. Because at fourteen, no matter how strong your emotions, they are liable to change without warning, and even without any real reason. Now that you feel you might lose your boyfriend, you're unsure whether to fight for him or finish with him first, so no wonder you're feeling mixed up!

The only answer is to keep your cool, and take everything — especially this relationship — nice and easy. There's no point, and nothing to gain, in getting uptight. Try to be relaxed and more casual, try not to expect too much from a relationship and that way you'll stand less chance of being let down.

If you feel you're being badly treated in this relationship, then get out. The break-up may not be pleasant to begin with, but at least you'll become aware that without him the world won't collapse, and there will be other boys.

DEAR CATHY & CLAIRE — I have a problem which I am very worried about, and cannot do anything about myself, so I'm writing to you for help.

At school, I dread Maths lessons because of my teacher, who is middle-aged and married. The trouble is, he keeps asking me if I want any help with my work or if I understand things and he says that if I don't, I've to go and see him privately. And he's always putting his arm on my shoulder when he tells me these things.

I always say I understand the lessons, because I'm afraid of what he'll do if I say I need help. But I really don't understand Maths and I'm falling far behind in my work, just because of him.

My friends all think he's a nice man and that I'm just being silly, but it's really getting me down. Please help.

Well . . . this is always a very difficult problem and is doubly hard to solve when we don't know the people involved. So all we can do, really, is try and make a judgement on the basis of your letter. OK?

Right — you say your friends don't find this teacher's actions off-putting. In fact, they like him. So — is it possible that you dislike him and maybe overreact to him because you can't do Maths and are transferring some of the blame onto him? And you kno... there's not much point...

I DON'T TRUST MY TEACHER!

Really try with Maths, and, as you ... rest of the class,

FIRST DATE!

DEAR CATHY & CLAIRE – It's my first date next Saturday, and I'm going mad with worry! There's just so many things to think about and I'm so scared I mess it all up or do something disastrously wrong.

I mean, what shall I wear, how much make-up should I put on, should I buy something new or what? We're supposed to be going to the pictures, but then one of the boys in our class is having a party and I think we might go on to that. I'm in such a panic I almost feel like not going!

The best thing to be on a first date is as natural and relaxed as possible — that might seem impossible right now, but with a bit of forward planning, and by making a conscious effort to calm down a bit, you might even start to look forward to your date!

Whatever you choose to wear, make sure it suits you, and that you're comfortable in it. It is tempting to rush out and buy something new, but this isn't really a good idea. Remember, whatever you wear, however old it may seem to you, it's going to be new to your boyfriend. You rarely feel very comfortable or relaxed in new clothes, anyway, so stick to something you already know suits you. Trousers and a more dressy top would be fine for what you're planning to do, we think — with a fairly warm jacket, and shoes you *can* walk in.

Make sure your hair is clean and shiny, but don't try anything new or dramatic with your make-up — just think what a shock the poor guy would get if you turned up looking completely different from the way you are at school.

The same goes for the way you act too — remember, he fancied you enough to make a date, so just be yourself, and we're sure you'll enjoy the evening very much indeed.

I DON'T AGREE

DEAR CATHY & CLAIRE — In a recent issue, you published a letter from a fourteen-year-old girl who thought she might be pregnant. In your advice, I thought you were terribly bigoted, irresponsible and dangerous, and I disagree with what you said.

You told her to abstain from sex in future, which is the decent answer, fair enough, but it's hardly realistic. I think it's a fair assumption she'll continue to have sex, if she's not pregnant, but you don't even mention contraception. Surely it would have been far more sensible to outline the dangers of underage sex — disease, prosecution of the male, etc. — than to go on in your self-righteous way, almost regardless of present day pressures and behaviour.

I'm writing because I hate to see anyone impose on another person's freedom. I'm 17 and male.

We're always glad to hear another point of view, and see a reaction to our replies, but in your anger you have overlooked one very important fact, and that is that we force our advice on no-one — the girl in question wrote to us asking for help.

We answered as we thought best in her case and we stand by it. Unfortunately, space on our page is limited but if readers enclose an s.a.e. when they write to us, we do, of course, go into greater detail and give addresses, send leaflets, etc., where helpful.

We don't expect everyone to agree with what we say, because there are far too many points of view — and, yes, freedom of thought — for that. Just as there is always more than one side to a story, so there is always more than one way of looking at a problem. In our answers, we give what *we* believe to be the best and most practical advice for each particular case — it may not always be what you would want to hear or what you would want to have to do, but the way out of a bad situation is never pleasant, even if the result will be good.

The Cathy 'n' Claire PAGE

Hi there! I'm Cathy

And I'm Claire

If our pictures make us look oh-so-chuffed, they're right —and you must forgive us. The fact is that the Ed (bless his size eight Chelsea boots) has given us a job we're head-over-heels about. Answering problems sent in by you, the readers.

We never thought a room of our own could give us such a kick! And <u>two</u> phones!

All we need is a pile of knotty problems and we'll be in biz. If something's bothering you, why not write to us? Two heads are better than one!

To launch the page, we put our heads together and wrote down all the problems we'd shared with our friends. Was their worry then, your one now?

Here's a selection, and don't forget, let's be hearing from you.

Cathy And Claire

Dear C. and C.,
My poser? Simple. I want a boy friend. Although I'm considered pretty, fun and sometimes witty, it's no go. I just can't find anyone eligible. Help, please!

Solution? Easy. Get with a swish hairdo and a snazzy dress, slosh on lots of perfume and go where the boys are.

P.S.—Looking appealing will catch him, but it's a girl's charm and lively personality which will really floor an unsuspecting male!

Dear C. and C.,
I love to go on picnics. Thing is, if my boy sees an insect, I practically have to unstick him from the highest branches of the nearest tree.
I'm not a crawlie-lover myself, but this is ridiculous. What can you do with a man like mine?

Colour him yellow!

Dear C. and C.,
My boy friend creates when I tell him I have to be in early on week nights, Dad's orders! What do you think? (By the way, we're not given a deadline weekends.)

Play along with Dad's wishes! He wants you to have your beauty sleep so you're lively and bright. Explain to night-owl boy friend—firmly! And if he still moans? Tell him either to play along or get lost . . .

Dear C. and C.,
We're going Youth-Hostelling this year, but haven't much idea about the average charges.

Youth-Hostelling is fun, exciting and very cheap! Average charges are—each night you stay, 2s-3s according to your age; supper, 2s 6d to 4s; breakfast, 2s 6d; and packed lunch of sandwiches, 1s 6d. If you need to hire a sleeping bag, it costs 1s.

Dear C. and C.,
Liz and I have been pals for years, but now I've a steady boy friend. She feels out of things and hints on joining up with Dave and I in a threesome. What do you think?

Taboo. Instead, why not dig out a spare male and team up as a foursome?

Dear C. and C.,
He's gorgeous—he's super —he's fab! He's the boy I see every morning on the way to work. All he says is a friendly "Hello." How can I get to know him?

Sounds promising. Next time you see him (so long as he isn't dashing off 'cos he's late) add a casual remark to your "Hello." Make sure it's something he has to stop and give an answer to, even if it's just about the weather. If he's really keen, he'll take things up from there.

Dear C. and C.,
Four of us are plann to go to France for holiday this year. We all speak fairly good Fre but we don't know m about the customs. Can help? Also, where do get passports?

Gee, lucky you! Main t you'll notice is that the are fab, but for more det drop a line to—Fre Embassy (Tourists' Enquir 51 Bedford Square, Lon W.C.1.

To get your passport, dr line or call at your Ministry of Labour offices.

Dear C. and C.,
My boy friend insists meeting me inside pictures, as it saves eit of us having to wait arou I'm getting cheesed o this. Can I change him

Yeah, for another boy! one's a confirmed meanie. him the "So long" line.

Dear C. and C.,
A friend and I have j moved into a flat and w to throw a party n Saturday. There's a upstairs we'd like to inv but we're only on "Hell terms. How should we about asking him?

Write a short note, gi all the lowdown, then sli through his letter-box. way, if necessary, he refuse without embarrassm

Love lines
by PAUL HART

I give my heart, my soul, my love to you, my heart for you alone to care and keep,
I give my soul into your hands to soothe, and tenderly caress that I may sleep
The whole night through, an angel by my side, who keeps me safe from sinful thoughts or word,
And dries my tears and heals my broken pride, that I may live a man who walks with God.
I give my love to you that you may find the magic of the breathless kiss of spring,
The surge of joy to feel your lips on mine, the craziness to hold my hand and sing,
And shout, and laugh together, as when walking
busy streets we cause bored eyes to pop,
And stare, and start dull tongues a-talking
at sight of love convention could not stop.

THE CATHY & CLAIRE PAGE

DEAR CATHY & CLAIRE — I went out with Tom for about two months and I became very fond of him. Then he finished with me and I was upset for a long time.

Well, about eight months later, just as I thought I'd got over it and started going out with other boys, I met him again at a party. I was with him all evening and I realised I was in love with him.

About a week later he came down to our local disco for the first time, and talked to me, but not very much. Later he danced with another girl and I felt very jealous and upset. He only danced with him once, and I still think he likes me, only perhaps he's a little shy or is trying to make me jealous. I don't think he realises I like him so much. Please help me, I'm depressed. I'm 15, by the way, and he's 18.

Well, we reckon you're doing all you can, and if he wants to do anything about it, it's up to him from now on!

From the sound of things, we'd say (at the risk of being depressing) that Tom just isn't ready to involve himself too deeply, 'cos if he was, let's face it, he would have carried on the relationship he had with you eight months ago.

Don't worry, there's not much more you can do to let him know you're crazy about him, save rushing at him and declaring your love, which we bet you'll agree would be a bit daft! You're around when he is, at parties and discos — you're there to talk to, and we think he *must* know you like him. So you'll just have to leave it to him! Showing a bit of interest in other boys wouldn't be a bad idea, either — could be that's what re-started his interest in you this time. We think that's the line you should be taking!

DEAR CATHY & CLAIRE — My friend and I have a great problem. We are both fourteen and we go to boarding school. The problem is that in the holidays we don't get to meet anyone.

It's no good saying we should go out together as we live a long way from each other and we don't have a chance to meet.

Please help us — we're desperate!

Well, your school friend isn't the only other person in the world! What about all your old mates in your home town before you went to boarding school? What about friends-of-parents with girls your age?

And what about all the social group activities you could join in with when you're at home?

Tennis clubs, swimming, local church youth clubs — go to your library, they'll probably have all sorts of information and it's likely it'll be displayed on notice boards so you won't even have to ask!

Honestly though, you'll have to make a bit of effort, but try everything and anything. There's plenty going on without you sitting moaning because this one particular friend isn't with you!

DEAR CATHY & CLAIRE — I'd been friends with Andy for quite a few weeks before he asked me out. I really like him and my mum and dad met him and don't mind me going out with him, so I feel great about that.

But one evening when he walked me home, he put his arm round me and then he kissed me. After this I felt very guilty and as though I wanted to finish with him, but I like him a lot and I'm afraid I'll hurt his feelings, because he's always saying how much he likes me. I'm 13 and Andy's 15. Please help me.

It is shyness, in a funny sort of way, that's making you feel like this, and we reckon that's a very natural thing in the early stages of a relationship. You're pretty young and probably not used to actually going out with someone, but as you do feel more used to being with Andy it'll seem quite natural for him to give you a kiss when he sees you home.

There's no need to feel guilty about it at all, because it's an expression of your friendship, and if you finished with him because you felt awkward and shy, you'd most likely be very sad about it afterwards. You probably feel your relationship's a more binding thing than it was because of this, and this is making you cautious and afraid, but basically you and Andy are friends, do like each other, and we think you'd be wrong to run away from it.

DEAR CATHY & CLAIRE — Please help me. My problem is that my friend gets all the boys. I'm not shy but I usually finish up playing gooseberry to my friend and her new boyfriend. What can I do?

Ask your friend to ask her boyfriend to ask a friend! Then you can make up a foursome, and you won't feel out of things, and you could meet a great new boyfriend!

That might be one way out — another would be just to stop going out with both of them together. Say "No, thank you," and get going by yourself, or with another friend, to anywhere you might meet someone of your own.

Could be, you know, the reason why you lose out when the two of you are together is that your friend's a little bit more pushy than you are, so that makes you hang in the background. If that's so, you'll be better by yourself, 'cos you won't have a competition and then you won't worry yourself all the time about your friend getting a boyfriend and you not.

So get out on your own, make the effort, and say goodbye to gooseberry-itis!

We can't promise the perfect solution, but we'll do our best. If you're stuck with a problem and you can't see the way out, write to us at this address: Cathy & Claire, Jackie, 185 Fleet Street, London EC4A 2HS. Please remember to enclose an S.A.E.

DEAR CATHY & CLAIRE — For the past couple of years, my friend and I have fancied a boy two years older than us. Just recently, though, we've started to be really good friends with him.

He's mentioned to his friends that he likes us, but it never goes further than that. We were both prepared to give each other the chance, if ever he did ask one of us out. But he never has done!

We've seen him at clubs and discos, and he always seems very shy there, especially towards other people.

Please could you give us some advice on how to be more than just friends?

It seems to us as though this boy needs your friendship more than anything else at the moment! We really don't think there's much point wishing for an imaginary something else, when you've all got quite a lot going here and now. If you've got a friendship, that's the best thing of all, firstly because we don't think he's ready for anything else at the moment and secondly because anything else would cause lots of complications!

It's all very well to say that you and your friend are willing to give each other the chance, but we reckon that's easier said than done.

Don't you think you'd be a tiny bit jealous if it was your friend who started going out with him regularly and getting much closer to him? Or, say you developed a boy-and-girlfriend relationship and things went wrong, we think you'd soon be wishing you were just good friends again.

Honestly, it's far easier all round the way it is! Some shy boys get through to girls much better on this basis and we don't think you should feel it's a limiting relationship. Real friendship and no complications — think how lucky you are!

DEAR CATHY & CLAIRE — I've been going out with Malcolm for about a month now. I know that might not sound long to you, but to me it's like for ever. He's seventeen and I'm fourteen and he's fantastic.

The problem is, I only get to see him at discos, because he lives in another town and it costs a lot of money for him to come to my town by bus.

I usually ring him up to tell him when the discos are on, but when I told him about one last Saturday night, he said he couldn't come because none of his friends were going, and anyway he didn't have enough money. But the week before we'd been to a really expensive disco, and he had enough money for that so I couldn't understand why he suddenly used that excuse.

I was practically in tears, I was so upset about it. Please, please try to solve my problem. I'm still going out with Malcolm and I still love him, but every time I ask him to come over he tells me not to get too serious about him.

Well, then, don't! We can't put it any other way than that, because you'll be wasting your time and getting loads more depressed if you do. Of course often you don't even mind getting upset and in a state because you're so crazy about someone, but then there comes a time when you wonder why you've been wasting your life. So it all depends how much of it you're prepared to waste, at the moment, by thinking about — and getting depressed over — Malcolm.

We're not telling you to forget him — we know you can't do that with someone you really care about and want to be with. What we're saying is that you should stop wanting him exclusively — go to the disco with your girl friends for a change: go out with anyone else you can, wherever and whenever you can. But stop depending on Malcolm because if he doesn't want to get involved, you're beating your head against a brick wall.

So take your mind off him even a little — and, in time, he might even change his.

DEAR CATHY & CLAIRE — I'm finding it very difficult to get over my last boyfriend. The reason for this is that I see his sister at work every day and she keeps giving me letters from him, asking me to go out with him again.

I really don't want to and I'm trying my best to forget him. But it's no good if he keeps writing to me.

Ignore the letters, as you obviously did him! And isn't it far easier to throw away a letter than get rid of someone who keeps coming round and seeing you? He's not there in person, so count yourself lucky that you've only got a bit of notepaper to dispose of!

We reckon it'll be even easier if you don't open them, just drop them in the bin before you give yourself a chance to think about them. If you let his sister see you doing it, too, she might just get the message across to him. Have you tried simply not accepting them from her, too? Another point in your favour is that the letters are by personal messenger, so you've got the advantage of being able to say "No, thanks — I don't want them!" and just leaving her holding them.

You see — it's not that difficult. A bit more of the willpower you used when you first decided not to go out with him, and you should soon be over it — this is only the tail end of a tricky situation.

SHOULD I ASK HER OUT?

DEAR CATHY & CLAIRE — Since other boys have written to you about their problems, I thought you might be able to help me. There's this girl, you see, who I like very much.

I've got over the worst stage, actually letting her know I want to go out with her, but she didn't want to know. It was a real disappointment for me at first and I thought I'd get over it, but the feeling of wanting her keeps coming back. I've tried to forget her and mix with other girls but no-one else can take her place.

The other night I saw her at a disco and she looked so good that the minute I saw her I wanted to be with her. I wanted to ask her for a dance, but I was so frightened she would tell me to go away and make me feel a fool. So I spent the evening with another girl, but every time I looked over to where she was sitting she was watching me.

Do you think that although she said "No" the first time, she might be interested in me now, and what would you advise me to do to get to know her better?

Try again! We know there's an enormous risk to your pride, and you must be prepared for feeling as if you want to crawl into a hole in the ground if she does reject you a second time!

But really, you won't get anywhere unless you do approach her again, will you? And since she's obviously very definitely what you want, you'll only sit around thinking about her and wondering whether to ask her again — so go on, just do it!

We've an idea, too, that *if* she makes it clear she's not interested (and she wouldn't have been casting glances your way, we don't think, if she hadn't been asking you to say something!) that could be the thing to put you off! After all while there's still a bit of chance, you will pine for her; but we bet there's a point where you'll just stop being bothered, and face the truth.

So find out what it is, now!

Printed and published by D. C. Thomson & Co., Ltd., 185 Fleet Street, London, EC4A 2HS.

Jackie~SLADE

MARVELLOUS MUSTARD!

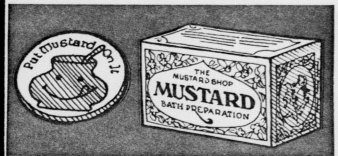

We're mad about mustard! . . . and we're sure you are too. Not just a lovely great dollop of it on a hot dog, but mustard in baths, on badges, on mugs, aprons, posters . . . all over the place!

You see, we've discovered "The Mustard Shop," an amazing shop in Norwich which sells all sorts of mustard goodies. They run a mail order service, so you can order what you want through the post.

For example, the bath mustard costs only 35p plus 20p postage and packing — mustard baths are very soothing and refreshing, and don't smell in the least like hot dogs!

Or what about a "put mustard on it" badge for 22 pence (plus 20p postage and packing)?

A leaflet of the goods available can be obtained from: The Mustard Shop, 3 Bridewell Alley, Norwich, NOR 02H. Please remember to enclose a S.A.E. when writing for a leaflet.

ANIMAL MAGIC!

If you're interested in helping animals — and the World Wildlife Fund in particular — you'll be interested in their new gift catalogue. It's packed full of mail order gifts, many of which feature the lovable Panda which is the Fund's symbol. If you'd like a catalogue, write to W.W.F. Trading Ltd., Panda House, 29 Greville Street, London EC1N 8AX.

PATCHWORK

SHINE A LIGHT!

A great new idea from Boots is this disposable torch — yes, disposable! Designed in hardwearing plastic, in a choice of six shades including apple green and red, it costs only 55 pence.

It lasts for ages and ages — and when it finally runs out — you just buy another one! At that price you can afford it! The torch is compact and neat, and is a really useful thing to have — no more fumbling about trying to get your key in the lock in the middle of the night! The torch is available from most Boots' branches.

A JACKIE RECIPE — Roll Up!

Here's a really unusual taste sensation — it has to be tried out to be appreciated!

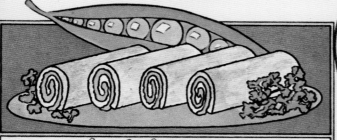

Green Pea Sandwiches.
You need brown bread, cooked peas, sour cream, salt, pepper and butter. Cut the crusts off the bread and butter them. Mash together peas, a little sour cream, salt and pepper to taste. Spread onto buttered bread and roll up. This looks very pretty!

CRAFTY COATHANGERS!

Coathangers — let's face it — are not the most interesting of objects. But with a little bit of imagination and some Copydex glue, you can cheer up a coathanger in no time at all.

For example, the hanger on the top is covered in foam first and then in material, so it's great for clothes you want to take special care of, as the foam padding acts as a cushion against wear and tear.

You can decorate coathangers in all sorts of ways — like with coils of string, on the orange one, or a felt train, for a child, on the blue one, or with pretty lace material, as in the bottom coathanger.

YOUR PATCH

A PLACE FOR EVERYTHING

SPINNING A YARN . . .

A novel craft idea from Hallmark is that of yarn pictures — simply and effectively made from their "Yarn Gift Tie," stuck onto cardboard with glue. This comes in six bright and cheerful colours, including red, yellow and turquoise, and costs only 10p for a card of 4 metres length (which is 4.37 yards for muddleheads who haven't gone metric yet!)

It's amazing how easily you can form pictures with the yarn when you start — flowers, houses, faces, abstracts — you could have your own art gallery in your bedroom in no time at all!

You'll find Hallmark "Yarn Gift Tie" at most stationers.

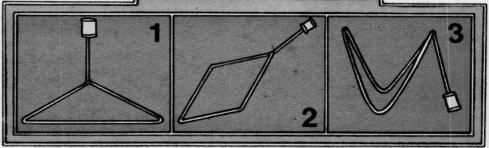

And talking of coathangers — I'm sure you often wonder how on earth you can keep your copies of Jackie tidy, yet handy at the same time. Well, reader Tessa Newman, of East Grinstead, Sussex, has sent us in a terrific idea for a magazine rack, simply made from a metal coathanger! Here's how:-
1. Straighten out the hook of the coathanger and stick it into a brightly painted cotton reel.
2. Pull the hanger into a diamond shape.
3. Fold it in half and bend the straight piece of wire — with cotton reel on it — down to form a stand.
And that's it! One attractive, super-efficient "Jackie" holder!
Teresa wins £1 for her idea — if you'd like to win one too, why not send in your ideas to Your Patch today? They can be things to make, sew, cook, knit — anything at all which you think might interest other readers. So get busy! The address is:- "Your Patch," Patchwork, "Jackie," 185 Fleet Street, London EC4A 2HS.

Patchwork

MISS PRINT!

Mass-produced clothes, while easily available, have one problem — you tend to end up looking like one of a thousand identical twins! But there's no reason for any

"Jackie" reader to worry about that!

Not only can you follow the ideas in So Far Sew Good every week, but this week — at no extra cost (ta-ra!) we're going to tell you how to design your own T-shirt.

Here's all you do:
1. Take a plain white T-shirt and iron it.
2. Choose your design — maybe a cartoon character from a children's book or your own name, drawn on a large sheet of cardboard to the size you want. Trace the design onto a piece of tracing paper with a heavy black felt tip pen, so that the design will show through.
3. Place your design inside the T-shirt and secure it to the front with pins. Then using a soft pencil, draw the design onto your T-shirt.
4. Place a sheet of plastic in the T-shirt to prevent dye seeping through to the back.
5. Prepare your chosen colour of fabric dye according to the instructions.
6. Then simply paint on your design with a paintbrush, allowing each separate colour to dry before applying any other shades.
7. When the T-shirt is completely dry (about 6 hrs) rinse it in cold water, then wash normally and allow to dry.

And that's it! Have fun!

SHAVINGS SAVING!

We were totally amazed when reader Michele Shemming of Pinner, Middlesex, sent in her idea — amazed that anything as boring as old pencil shavings could be made into something as attractive as her lovely flower picture, shown here! Yet that's exactly what it's made from — pencil shavings carefully formed in the shape of a

flower, complete with coloured petals, leaves and stalk, and stuck onto cardboard with glue. So why not kick off the year by learning to make them for yourself? They're easy to do, and look tremendous, as you can see.

Clever Michele wins £1 — so can you, if you have any interesting ideas you'd like to tell us about. The address is, "Your Patch," Patchwork, "Jackie," 186 Fleet Street, London, EC4A 2HS.

BAGS MORE FOR EVERYONE!

What do you do when your handbags are all too small for your bits and pieces? Panic? Start carrying a suitcase around with you everywhere?

Not if you're a "Jackie" reader! You rush round to Boots to see their great new collection of "Jolly Bags" — handy corduroy or canvas bags which are the right size for stuffing all your stuff inside!

Starting from the back, with this roomy corduroy zip-top holdall in navy/red, dark brown/beige or rust/luggage. Style No: TN409. Price: £6.79.

On the left a super canvas bag with detachable shoulder strap and zipped centre section, Style No: 667200. Price: £4.95. In red/navy, blue/black, black/yellow and natural/yellow.

Sitting pretty in the centre, a neat corduroy holdall bag with two handy buckled front pockets. Colours: Rust/luggage, green/dark brown, all brown. Style No.: TN402. Price: £4.86.

And last but not least, on the right a canvas shoulder bag with five pockets and centre zipped section. Style No.: 661700. Price: £4.95. Colours: Beige/brown, navy/red and all brown.

DEAR DIARY . . .

Resolve to keep a diary in 1975 — and it doesn't *have* to be an intimate, day-to-day "true confessions" type of thing, you know!

Diaries can be invaluable if you're a slimmer, student, motorist, keep-fit fanatic, cook, — or just about anyone else you can think of! They're an instant source of information beforehand, and a lasting record of memorable events afterwards!

Boots have a huge selection — but hurry, cos they're selling fast! They're really well worth spending some of your Christmas money on — and this time next year you'll be able to look back on the year's great events!

HERE IS THE NEWS . . .

Of course, there's no need to wait till 1976 to find out what the next twelve months have in store for you — if you put a little trust in the stars!

At the incredibly low price of only 7p, "Old Moore's Almanack" is really one of the most amazing and interesting books you could find. Published annually, it's crammed full of predictions for 1975 — ranging from royalty to racing! Past predictions have proved to be uncannily accurate, so can you afford to be without the book which holds (maybe!) the secrets of 1975?

It's available from most major bookstores now.

CHICKEN AND ALMOND SOUP

Resolve to try out new taste sensations in 1975 — after all, you don't know what anything's like until you've sampled it! You shouldn't need any encouragement for this one, though, 'cos it tastes just as delicious as it sounds.

Chicken and almond soup.
½ onion, chopped, a handful of split almonds, a little parsley, a tin of chicken soup. Fry the almonds, onion and the parsley for a few minutes in butter, then add the chicken soup and heat through.

BEST FOOT FORWARD!

Resolve, this year, to make full and best use of one of the cheapest and best services available to young people — the Youth Hostels Association.

A year's membership is well under £1, and as a member, you can trot off any time you want for a long weekend — or a fortnight, or a month! — at an incredibly low cost. There are over 320 hostels throughout Britain, so whether you're trying to put as much space between yourself and home as possible, or just want to go out of town for a few days, there should be one for you!

The idea is to take along your own sleeping bag and food — they'll provide the bed and the kitchen!

Most hostels are open all the year round, so you can take off more or less where you want, when you want. Furthermore, if you're under 15 and can persuade both your parents to join the Youth Hostels Special "Family" schemes, you'll be able to join the Y.H.A. free.

Youth Hostelling is a super way of meeting new friends, and having great times with old ones, at a minimal cost. So don't miss out on the fun in 1975! Write for details to the Youth Hostels Association, Trevalyan House, 8 St. Stephen's Hill, St Alban's, Herts, AL1 2DY. But *please* enclose an S.A.E!

What's the difference between a Wallflower and a Peach?

THE ANSWER LIES IN THE *Perfume*

That gorgeous hunk you have your eye on will notice you—and how!—if you surround yourself in a mist of dreamy perfume. We don't mean you to pour a bottle over your head. Notabitofit! Successful girls are subtle! Here's how it's done . . .

Beauty begins in the bath. Team-up your bath-oil, talc and cologne with your fave perfume and have fragrance wherever you go!

WHY has perfume such a devastating effect male-wise? Simply because it's very, very feminine and has a mysterious way of reflecting a girl's personality . . . of bringing back happy memories . . . of dreamy romance and just being in love . . .

There are dozens of lovely perfumes to choose from, yet only one is just for you. So pick your perfume to team-up with your personality. Here are some to choose from.

YOU LIKE . . .

. . . watching bike scrambles, joining in a car rally, cheering on your boyfriend when he's playing football, cycling, rambling, long walks down country lanes with the wind in your hair? A refreshing yet light-hearted perfume would suit your practical, out-door girl personality—Paris, French Moss, Tweed, Passport, Blue Grass, or Yardley's Lavender.

. . . gay, zippy parties, dancing, having lots of fun at the fair with the crowd, dozens of admirers, flirting light-heartedly with adoring males? Your perfume is appealing, magnetic like your personality—Hypnotique, L'Aimant, Goya's No. 5, Midnight, or Intimate.

. . . or dream about going out with slick-looking males to swish dinner-dates or shows, fast sporty-looking cars, sailing, and striking clothes? For you, with your stunning girl of the world air, a perfume such as—

Oriental Chypre, Flair, Entice, Lady Manhattan, Primitif, or Viva!

. . . flowers, especially roses and violets, tiny-waisted dresses, bikinis, just one steady boyfriend to look after you, romantic films and books, broiderie anglaise and soft 'n' simple hair-dos? A sweet, feminine, delicate perfume would play-up your sincere and appealing personality — Love Affair, Heavenly, Apple Blossom, Jonquille, Muguet Des Bois, or In Love.

. . . sketching, designing and making your own clothes, huge antique rings, suede coats, classical and mainstream music, and tall, quiet-thinking males? For you, a musky, spicy fragrance with off-beat appeal to match your artistic personality—Meteor, Electrique, Sandalwood, Toledo, Emeraude, or Aquamarine.

TRY BEFORE YOU BUY!

Most mod-in-mood perfume manufacturers have small trial-size bottles of their perfumes, designed to hold just enough for a first-time try-out. You'll find these in special display holders at the beauty counter.

Never test more than three perfumes at a time, as the fragrances will become confused with each other.

Don't sniff straight from the bottle. Instead, dab a little on the inside of your wrist. Wait a few seconds for the true " tone " of the

perfume to come out, then smell its fragrance.

Like it?

Once you've chosen your perfume, it's a lovely idea to gradually buy all your bath-beauty aids in the same fragrance. Bath-oil, soap, talc, cologne and body lotion. Hair-spray, too. Some cosmetic houses make them to match their perfumes.

Just the greatest to make an even prettier you, wrapped in a romantic cloud of dreamy fragrance. But go easy. Keep to talc plus toilet water or cologne for daytime, and the much-stronger-fragrance perfume for night-time dates.

ONCE YOU'VE BOUGHT YOUR PERFUME, USE IT OFTEN!

Say " So long " to the line that a dab behind your ears is all you need! If your perfume isn't already in spray form, buy a small spray-bottle and fill it, a little at a time, with your perfume.

Sprays on in a fine mist—quicker to use this way. Long lasting, too! So you can afford apply it lavishly, especially on temples (super if you've an ex tallish boyfriend!), nape of neck, pulse spots of wrists and cr of elbows.

PERFUME POINTERS

Don't apply perfume to clothes, as apart from it stai it quickly goes stale.

Refresh perfume as often as do your normal make-up, carry a tiny bottle around in handbag—always!

Never stand perfume bottle strong light or heat, as the f rance will quickly evaporate go stale.

After you've used your perfum cologne, always check that tiny plug fits tightly, and the is screwed on securely!

Jackie *Jackie* *Jackie* *Jacki*

CHAMPAGNE all round! Today sees the birth of the bonnie, bouncing, colourful baby girl we've christened Jackie. It's a day of celebration for us . . . and, we hope, for you, too.

Each week Jackie will show you how to be subtle 'n' skilful with all the latest cosmetics. You'll see lots of new, zany, zippy things to wear. The biggest, brightest, and best full-colour pin-ups. And all the inside info about the top pops. In fact, EVERYTHING you really live for!

Oh . . . and let's have a look at that horoscope under Jackie's birthdate on page 23. "FLIRTIN' TIME AND LOTS OF FUN ON THE WAY FOR THE GADABOUT GIRL." Sounds pretty promising, huh?

We hope you'll make a date with Jackie . . . and the rest of the gang . . . every week. See you!

Jackie *Jackie* *Jackie* *Jacki*

SCOTLAND THE RAVE

You'd be mistaken if you thought that the only music to come out of the Highlands was the sound of bagpipes! Haven't you noticed? There are lots of really good Scottish groups in the charts these days. To mention just a few names, there are the Bay City Rollers, Pilot, the Average White Band, and a host of individual musicians who play for other well-known bands.

As everyone knows, the Scots are a proud nation. And it could be that they're prouder than ever at the moment, because of all the talent they're producing on the music scene. But what about the boys in the bands, themselves? Are they proud of being Scots? Well, we've been asking a few of them to find out their own opinions on Scotland . . .

YOU may not realise it, but Wings too, are great fans of Scotland. Paul and Linda own a farm in Campbeltown, right at the tip of Argyllshire, and like to spend as much time there as they possibly can.

Linda explained that their lives were not filled with all the glamour and excitement that people imagined.

"Basically, Paul and I are down-to-earth types and we enjoy the simple family life," she said. "That's why we like to retreat to our farm as often as we can – to lead a quiet life with the kids.

"We like our lives to be as uncomplicated as possible, and the best place we've found to achieve this is up in Scotland. It's really peaceful there."

And to further strengthen their Scottish alliance, the McCartneys last year recruited a new guitarist – Jimmy McCulloch, who is of course a Scot. (What else could he be with a name like that?!)

This gives them another reason to be thankful for all the time they've spent in Scotland – because now they can understand his accent!

L. to R.: Eric, Woody, Alan, Les, Derek.

THINK of the Bay City Rollers, and immediately you think of Scotland too. The boys really look the part of a Scottish band, dressed up as they usually are, in tartans. But surprisingly enough, when I spoke to them, they confessed that they weren't *terribly* patriotic.

"When you travel around the world a bit, you tend to lose that sort of feeling about Scotland," explained Woody. "You get interested in the customs of all the places you visit, and you realise other countries have a lot to offer too!

"It's good to be proud of your own heritage – but I think you should always appreciate other places as well."

"But there's no place in the world that can beat the Scottish scenery," put in Eric. "My favourite part of Scotland is the really wild countryside in the north-west. There's nothing to beat that."

The boys really enjoy all the travelling they've done since they became so popular. They love visiting London and all the other English cities – but only visiting them! If there's anywhere they want to be when they're a little bit tired of touring, it's Scotland.

"And we'll never move away from it," said Alan firmly. "We'll always remain based in Scotland, because we love it and that's that! We lived in Edinburgh all our lives, and all our really good friends are still there.

"Besides, we've just bought our own houses in the hills outside Edinburgh, so we're not likely to move now!"

One of the Rollers' trademarks is of course, all the tartan they wear. But, oddly enough, they insist that they don't wear it because they're from Scotland!

"We just wear it because we like it!" said Alan. "It's different and it's really bright and colourful.

"We're all fairly fashion-conscious, and have started designing our own clothes – jerkin suits with tartan down the sides and down the trousers. Red tartan is our favourite because it looks especially good on stage."

What about kilts, I wondered. Hadn't they ever worn them?

"Oh yeah," laughed Les, "I can remember quite a few embarrassing moments when I was really small, wearing a kilt! I used to have the whole outfit – complete with sporran!

" I didn't particularly enjoy wearing it then – but my mum made me!"

And although the Rollers did enjoy dressing up in kilts once again, just for our photo, they say that they won't be making it a regular stage outfit. It's far too chilly around the knees!

THE newest triumph for Scot Rock is the Average White Band who came from the Dundee area in Scotland. Actually, they're not average at all — the name is just a typical Scots joke! And although they are white, they do have a very funky, black sound.

Although "Pick Up The Pieces" was their first hit here in Britain, the boys have been a big name in America for some time now, and they were recently top of both the US single and album charts at the same time!

It may seem strange that a Scottish band should have to go so far afield to find success, but that's exactly what happened to the Average Whites. For a long time, they didn't receive any recognition in Scotland, and that's one of the reasons why they've decided to forsake their homeland for America.

"We've decided to live in America for a least a year," Alan Gorrie, the group's lead singer told me.

"It's not that we don't love Scotland – we certainly do, and we'll really miss it. It's just that it's very frustrating when you work hard for a long time, as we did in Scotland, and all your efforts go unnoticed. We appreciate America, but we love Scotland."

WE'RE really cheating a bit by including Rod Stewart on this page, because he's actually only half-Scots. But, as you'll have gathered from the way he surrounds himself with tartan, he's very proud of that half!

Like a lot of Scotsmen, Rod is particularly patriotic when it comes to the country's national sport – football, of course!

Rod is the Scottish team's number one supporter, and he's been known to travel thousands of miles just to see one of their matches!

"I'd go anywhere to see Scotland play," said Rod. "I hate missing them. As far as I'm concerned, no other country has a team to touch Scotland's. They're the greatest!"

Rod singing on a recent T V Show with Maggie Bell who is, would you believe, yet another Scottish talent!

L. to R. Stuart, Billy, Ian, Dave.

BILLY CONNOLLY is a Scots star with a difference! He started out singing in a folk group called the Humblebums, along with Gerry Rafferty who incidentally, is now with Stealers Wheel, another famous Scottish group!

But Billy gradually came to realise that his speaking was more popular than his singing! He's a very funny person, and the stories he told between songs had everyone in stitches. Nowadays, Billy combines both his talents onstage – with great success.

Although he's only just becoming known elsewhere in Britain (his album "Cop Yer Whack For This" and the single from it, "The Welly Boot Song" have both been big hits) Billy, or "The Big Yin" as he's known in Scotland, has been a favourite in his own country for ages now!

Although Billy constantly makes fun of Scotland and the Scottish people, he's really very patriotic at heart.

"There's no one like us," he says in his broad Glaswegian accent. "The Scots are the warmest, friendliest and most generous folk in the world. Contrary to the ridiculous public opinion which makes us out to be meanies!

"The Scottish sense of humour is second to none – who else can laugh at themselves so freely? Sure, we've got faults, but we know we've got them, and we can laugh about it. Scotland's definitely a place of great cheer.

"And don't believe what they say about cities like Glasgow being slum areas. Sure they are – but they're beautiful in their own way – they've got character and feeling. And it's the Glasgow people who give it that character."

WITH their "Magic" rise to fame, Pilot have now become well established in the pop scene. Like the Bay City Rollers, they come from Edinburgh, and like the Rollers, they like to return home whenever they get the chance.

"It's a really picturesque city," Dave Paton told me. "In fact, it's a twin to Athens, being built as it is, on seven hills! And some of the architecture is marvellous; there are lots of buildings of great historical interest. It may sound boring to Sassenachs, but it's fascinating just to walk around Edinburgh, there's lots of cultural stimulus, especially when the big festival is on. Plenty of life and excitement then!

"But when you want peace and quiet, you can still get it easily. In London you can drive for miles without hitting any open land, whereas in Edinburgh, ten minutes' drive takes you out into fields and open country. Great!"

Stuart Tosh, the group's drummer, has a slightly different opinion.

"Yes, Scotland is unspoilt and quiet – too quiet! For night life, London wins hands down.

"You see, with Edinburgh, in fact with Scotland generally, it seems that the social life just stops at ten o'clock in the evenings. That's when the pubs close and there's nothing much else to do!"

Guitarist Ian Bairnson, however, thinks differently about Edinburgh. You see, he comes from the Shetland Isles and compared with there, Edinburgh is a real hive of activity!

"It's so remote where I come from, that even the sheep are good company!" he laughed. "In fact, it's due to my quiet upbringing that I've learned to play the guitar in my own style. I had to teach myself because, living on such a small island, I never heard anyone else playing music apart from bagpipes!"

It's obvious that they're fond of Scotland, but are Pilot proud of being Scottish!?

"You bet!" said Dave. "Scots are really proud of being Scottish – it's hereditary. I inherit my love of Scotland from my dad – who's so patriotic he even has tartan wallpaper! In fact, if I have time to read, I like to learn about Scottish history, and it really doesn't bore me! You can't get much prouder of being a Scot than that!"

This week's big excitement was definitely the day I got a brand new, shiny tape recorder!

As you've probably realised by now, most of the people in here are convinced that they're potential stars, just waiting to be discovered.

So, naturally, they all wanted to have their talents immortalised on tape!

The result is that I now have a whole tape filled with lots of exciting things — like Alan humming "The Old Grey Whistle Test" theme, Dorothy doing her favourite tap dance, which makes the sound of a train coming out of the station, Cheryl singing "Land Of Hope And Glory" and Alison reciting some limericks — all of them unrepeatable! I tell you — "New Faces" has got nothing on us!

Pete

ARROW, ARROW!

Oh boy!

When you're in a top pop group, you have to be prepared for anything — as 10CC found out when they were in Glasgow a few weeks ago!

One sunny day, Graham Gouldman and Kevin Godley went for a walk in Kelvin Park — and found themselves being joined by a Boys' Brigade march heading for the bandstand in the middle of the park. Once at the bandstand, they were handed songsheets, and soon they were happily joining in with a sing-song!

Kevin and Graham's part in the singing, however, came to a sudden end when some of the boys began to recognise their famous companions. Kevin and Graham decided that perhaps it was time to leave — before they found themselves being trampled on by hundreds of Boys' Brigaders!

Arrow Alan Merrill says that, although he's been involved in music for quite a long time now, he's still amazed at the loyalty of his fans! "For instance," he told me, "there are some girls who come round regularly to our manager's office. Sometimes they take Friday afternoons off school (tut, tut!) and just sit outside and listen to us rehearsing downstairs.

L. to R.: Paul, Alan, Jake.

"I recognise some of them now, because I've seen them over and over again, and every time, they've asked us for our autographs! I reckon they must have about seventy autographs by now! But seriously, we love seeing them there. We just can't believe how good they are to us!"

Bjorn Lucky!

Abba are, of course, one of the most popular groups in Britain at the moment. But over in their home country, Sweden, they're even more successful!

"Benny and I have a record company," Bjorn told me, "and we produce other artists as well as ourselves. I enjoy working with other people and bringing on their talent.

"I hope, also, that there will be a time when someone comes up to us and says, 'Why don't you write a song for me?' — somebody already well-known, I mean. That would be fantastic!

"There might come a time when we wouldn't continue with Abba, or even singing ourselves. But I'd never consider giving up music altogether. I'd always stay in it — some way or another!"

Up From Down Under!

Hush are already Australia's top group — and they're hoping that soon, they'll be just as well known here in Britain!

The boys have already released one single in this country, "Glad All Over," and they're due to fly in for a visit in the near future. And one person who just can't wait for that trip is lead singer Keith Lamb!

"Although the others were all born in Australia, I'm actually English," Keith explained. "As a child, I lived in Norwich, which as you can probably imagine, isn't exactly exciting! So as soon as I left school, I went down to London to work.

"One day, I was walking past Australia House, and something made me decide to go in — and the next thing I knew, I was on my way down under! I remember arriving in Sydney, and thinking, 'What am I *doing* here'!"

Luckily though, Keith soon grew to like Australia, and he's never regretted moving there. But he admits he still misses Britain.

"I've told the other three all about how great it is," he said, "and so now they're just as keen as I am to come so they can see it for themselves!"

L. to R. Les Gock, Keith Lamb, 'Smiley' Pailthorpe, Rick Lum.

BACK...

As you probably know, Rod Stewart recently deserted the California sunshine to come home to Britain for a while — and, of course, his beautiful girlfriend, Britt Ekland, came too! (Hard luck, girls!)

Rod and Britt had been looking forward to coming back to England for a long time, and when they finally got here, the first thing the happy couple did was to go on a sightseeing tour of London!

And Rod's verdict on the city? "It hasn't changed a bit!" he laughed.

...HOME!

Another star who recently made his homecoming was the new, extra slim-line David Bowie!

David's arrival, however, was a bit different from Rod's, because as you perhaps know, he's one of those people who hate flying. So instead of Heathrow Airport, David made his triumphal return to Victoria Railway Station!

And as soon as his chartered train came into the platform, David got into a waiting Mercedes, and stood up to wave to the 500 fans, who'd come along to show him that, despite his long exile from Britain, he's just as popular now as he ever was!

POP PUZZLE

Speaking of David Bowie, this week's puzzle is all about him! But first, here are the answers to last week's puzzle. Those old records were made by the following groups:
1) **Rollers**
2) **Mud**
3) **Slik**
4) **Slade**
5) **Osmonds**

Did you know them?

And now, here's this week's puzzle. All you have to do is put these photos of David Bowie in order, from the oldest to the most recent.

Have a go — and as always, I'll tell you the answer next week!

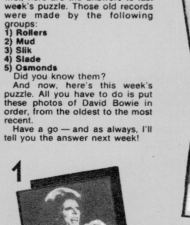

HOW ROMANTIC ARE YOU?

WELL? Is February 14 the most important day of your life? Or do you think it's just the day after February 13 and you can't see what all the fuss is about? Either way, try our quiz and find out how romantic you *really* are. You could be surprised!

Choose your alternatives to find out what sort of Valentine girl you are

a

b

c

1. Which Valentine heart do you like best?
- (a) Red Victorian-type heart with gold-embossed pattern and bordered around the edges with lovely old lace.
- (b) Plain old-gold heart on background of oriental or Indian traditional pattern.
- (c) Large exploding heart, with beams of light and stars shooting from it in all directions.
- (d) Drawing of a real biological human heart with words "thump, thump!" emanating from it.
- (e) Picture of solid gold heart jewelled with diamonds, rubies, emeralds, etc.
- (f) Heart drawing with modern psychedelic designs.

2. What kind of Valentine card would you most like to receive?
- (a) A very romantic flowery one, with the words: "To the one I love with all my heart."
- (b) A classical madonna-like girl's face with the words: "All my love."
- (c) A very modern angel with a flirty expression and the words: "You're no angel — but I love you!"
- (d) A madly cute, zany face and the words: "To funny face!"
- (e) A picture of a beauty queen in crown and robes and the words: "To the most beautiful girl in the world."
- (f) A sun-tanned, laughing girl's face and the words: "To my sunshine girl."

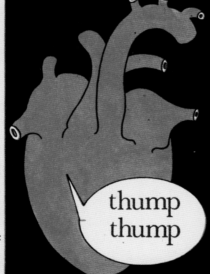

thump thump

d

e

3. These are the printed messages inside six Valentine cards. Which one would you choose to send to your boyfriend?
- (a) "To my love, my life, my whole world."
- (b) "My heart and soul are yours."
- (c) "To my best boyfriend — the other 364 don't mean a *thing* to me — honest!"
- (d) "I'm sending you a Valentine cos you're such an ugly old mug, no-one *else* will!"
- (e) "My love for you is as deep as the seas and as strong as the mighty mountains."
- (f) "To the best boy in the whole world — from the girl who loves you."

4. Which Valentine serenade would you prefer?
- (a) Romeo singing with all his heart underneath your balcony.
- (b) A solitary violinist, looking terribly soulful and absorbed.
- (c) A Spanish guitarist.
- (d) David Essex.
- (e) A sexy singer in a really smooth suit.
- (f) A cowboy sitting on a fence with his guitar.

f

5. Which anonymous Valentine card would you most like to be sent from someone who admires and loves you from afar?
- (a) A card crammed with hearts and flowers in lovely pastel shades.
- (b) A classical-type painting of a Greek goddess.
- (c) A drawing of six boys with bouquets, all down on their knees in front of one beautiful girl.
- (d) A funny cartoon-style cupid shooting arrows.
- (e) A picture of a huge bouquet of orchids.
- (f) A picture of a brick wall with graffiti-type heart and arrows chalked on it.

6. Which card would you choose for your Valentine, if you wanted to suit it to his character?
- (a) A knight in shining armour, sword in hand.
- (b) The famous statue of, "The Thinker."
- (c) A loveable-looking boy with a wicked expression but a halo around his head.
- (d) A clown.
- (e) A dramatic picture of a mysterious cloaked figure in a mask.
- (f) A friendly-looking boy on a motor bike?

7. Which Valentine card do you think would suit *your* character best?
- (a) A beautiful Cinderella-like princess with golden ringlets.
- (b) A ballet dancer in a graceful pose.
- (c) A wild, barefooted gypsy girl.
- (d) A mad, zany girl floating up into the sky, holding onto a bunch of balloons.
- (e) A girl in a long 30's type dress, reclining on a sofa.
- (f) A healthy-looking out-door girl.

8. Which Valentine couple appeals to you most?
- (a) A couple in evening dress by a moon-light fountain.
- (b) A couple holding hands beside an ancient temple.
- (c) A couple dancing at a lively party.
- (d) A madly happy couple jumping for joy on a trampoline.
- (e) A couple on stage, enacting a dramatic love-scene.
- (f) A couple running hand in hand along the surf on a deserted beach.

Now count which letter you scored most of — and turn to the conclusions on page 34.

Up The Ladder To The Top!

THE SECRET of success is to choose the job that's right for you. This week, in the final part of our careers series, we aim to help you do just that! Our special career ladder ought to help you work out the kind of job you might be suited to. As well as that, we've added some information on one or two jobs you might not have thought of!

THE JOB FOR YOU	WHAT YOU DO	THE QUALIFICATIONS	GENERAL INFORMATION
ANIMAL NURSING AUXILIARY	Help the vet in his surgery, hold animals during treatment, look after instruments, prepare medicines, assist during operations.	You must be 17 and have 4 O-levels with English Language and science subject or maths. You must be an animal lover and you ought not to be too squeamish!	Training is on the job with day or block release courses. To enrol for training you must be employed with a vet or hospital approved by the Royal College of Veterinary Surgeons.
THE ARMED FORCES — THE WOMEN'S ROYAL ARMY CORPS (WRAC)	As a non-commissioned servicewoman, you'll be trained in a skill (cooking, driving, hairdressing, secretarial work, radar operation, physical training instruction and so on), and you'll generally help in the defence of Queen and country!	A lot of self-discipline and the ability to work in a team. An active interest in an outdoor sport is desirable. Minimum age is 17. You must be physically fit. No GCEs are required.	The other 2 branches of the Armed Forces are the Women's Royal Air Force (WRAF) and Women's Royal Naval Service (WRNS). All offer an interesting, varied life and the opportunity to learn a useful skill or trade which can come in handy once you're back in civvies!
BANKING	You move steadily round the various departments, learning all the basic operations. Juniors start by dealing with payments, collecting cheques and so on.	4 to 5 O-levels, including English and a numerate subject. A clear, logical mind and a definite feeling for figures, together with accuracy.	Training is on the job. You work part-time for the National Certificate of Business Studies. After that (or if you already have 2 A levels), you study for the HNC/HND in Business

THERE are hundreds of jobs for you to choose from but, unfortunately, it's impossible for us to tell you about all of them. So, instead of trying to find out about all the different kinds of jobs, think about yourself, the things you like and exactly what it is you want out of life and take it from there...

THE CREATIVE YOU

... enjoys using your imagination to the full ... dislikes dull routine ... is best of all at non-practical subjects such as art ... is enthusiastic and full of flair.

THE JOB FOR YOU Interior Hairdresser, Journalist, Chef. Beauty Designer, Fashion Designer, Photo-Designer, Window Dresser, Consultant, Artist, Advertising grapher.

Job	What you do	Qualifications	Training
CATERING	...services, in a hotel, restaurant, school, hospital or airline. You plan menus, order food, budget, and supervise staff.	...ambition and the ability to work hard are just as important. Many people work their way up from waiting or cooking, learning skills on the job and combining this with part-time courses until they move into management.	You can take a 4-year full-time course in cooking/catering for the City & Guilds Certificate. Hotel groups such as Trust House Forte and Grand Metropolitan run 4 to 5-year management apprenticeship schemes for school leavers.
COMPUTER OPERATOR	You control each batch of work through the computer, checking input and output, making sure the computer is functioning with maximum efficiency.	5 O-levels — most employers expect these to include English and maths.	You can train on the job, going on day release at a college of further education for a Royal Society of Arts Certificate in Computer Operating or enter a trainee scheme with one of the computer manufacturing companies.
DENTAL SURGERY ASSISTANT	Record-keeping, mixing, fillings, handling instruments, helping with X-rays, looking after patients before and after treatment and so on.	Minimum age for training is between 16 and 19. For the training course, a few GCE O-level passes are necessary, preferably in English and biology or another science.	Training is on the job and should be supplemented by a part-time course at a college of further education. There are also full-time training courses at the various dental hospitals.
HAIRDRESSER	You shampoo, cut, set, perm and tint hair. Most hairdressers eventually specialise as tinters or stylists.	No particular entry qualifications for a college course, except you should be over 16 and have a good standard of education.	You can be apprenticed for 3 years to a salon, studying part-time for the City & Guilds Certificate: take a 2-year full-time course at a technical college or take a 6 to 9-month course at a private hairdresser school.
HOME ECONOMIST	You advise and demonstrate for manufacturers of domestic equipment, for food marketing boards and for gas and electrical industries.	You must be 16 and have 4 O-levels or CSEs Grade 1.	You can take a 2-year full-time course leading to a job as demonstrator, recipe developer, etc., leading to a Certificate in Home Economics.
ENGINEERING	Engineers make motor cars, cookers, hospital equipment — you name it — and even the things they don't make depend on machines designed by engineers! The Engineering Industry Training Board is begging girls to come into the industry, and even offers special technician courses.	Above average ability in mathematics, physics and other relevant sciences. To qualify for a degree course at university or polytechnic you must have either 2 A levels in maths or another science, preferably physics, or chemistry if you're going to do chemical engineering; or an ONC/D in approved subjects and at least 4 O-levels including maths and a science subject.	Engineering offers you enormous scope and it is one of the few expanding industries left. Aeronautical Engineers design, produce and test all types of aircraft. Agricultural Engineers design equipment and machinery. Chemical Engineers transform chemical processes into commercial products. Other types include Civil, Gas, Marine, Electronic and Highway, to name just a few.
NURSERY NURSE	Your look after babies and young children under seven. Nursery nurses also work for a family as a nanny, or in holiday camps or aboard liners.	Minimum age for training is 16. Minimum qualifications required are 2 O-levels. You must be fond of children and have lots of stamina!	Work is in day nurseries run by the local authority, residential nurseries for children in care, hospitals and private homes. There are a variety of courses (mostly 2-year) which you can take at colleges of further education.
POLICEWOMAN	Basically, it's your task to maintain law and order and generally keep the peace!	Good health, a liking for the outdoors, the ability to work in a team. Minimum age: 18½; minimum height: 5 ft. 4 ins. If you have less than 4 O-levels, you must take an entrance exam.	After 2 years on the beat, you can specialise in traffic work, river police, mounted police, dog-handling, Special Branch, or CID.
PHARMACY TECHNICIAN	You work under supervision of a qualified pharmacist, helping to make up prescriptions.	3 GCEs/CSEs Grade 1, including chemistry.	Training is on the job, with 2 years' day release evening classes at college.
TRAVEL & TOURISM	You start as an office clerk, learning to do paperwork, arranging and booking tours. You may then be promoted to counter selling and arranging tours and holidays. Senior operators go abroad to try out different holidays and facilities.	A high degree of accuracy, and a minimum of 4 O-levels. Knowledge of a language is an advantage. You should be outgoing and adaptable.	Most people train on the job while taking evening classes or a correspondence course for the examination of the Institute of Travel & Tourism.
PHYSIOTHERAPIST	You help treat patients suffering from injury or disease by means of exercise, massage and so on.	5 GCEs including at least 1 at A level, and English and a science subject.	You take a 3-year course of full-time training leading to the qualification of Member of the Chartered Society of Physiotherapy.
RETAILING AND DISTRIBUTION	You can start as a school leaver with few qualifications and work behind the counter in a big store — then, if you're willing and work hard, you could be in a top job as a buyer or department manager by your mid-twenties.	You need physical stamina. A few O-level passes or CSEs Grade 1 are a useful minimum qualification because they enable you to get on to a good training scheme.	The best stores allow you to take part-time day release courses in various types of distribution, as well as their internal training programmes. Make sure that there are training schemes available before you apply for work in a big store, and make it clear you want to be considered for them.
SECRETARIAL WORK	Anything from copy typing, to being someone's personal secretary, handling their correspondence, arranging their schedule and so on.	If you do a commercial course at school, you'll be able to find a job as a clerk or typist. You can also do a 1 to 2-year business course at college.	The job you get depends on a lot of things — your skills, education and willingness to accept responsibility. There are a wide range of training courses at colleges of further education and some universities.

THE HELPFUL YOU

- ...enjoys being with other people and makes allowances for people and doesn't let their tantrums upset you
- ...is fit and healthy, patient and sympathetic
- ...is best of all at lending a shoulder to cry on.
- ...is kind to animals and to people!

THE JOB FOR YOU: Nursery Nurse, Social Worker, Health Visitor, Doctor, Vet, Teacher, Stable Lass, Dental Hygienist, Nanny, Speech Therapist, Kennel Maid.

THE ORGANISED YOU

- ...is neat, tidy and efficient
- ...is good at taking care of details
- ...has a strong sense of responsibility and hates letting people down
- ...is best of all at tying up loose ends and coming up with commonsense solutions.

THE JOB FOR YOU: Typist, Secretary, Personal Accountant, Librarian, Computer Operator, Civil Servant, Pharmacist, Data Preparation Operator, Bank Clerk.

THE OUTDOORSY YOU

- ...enjoys playing or watching things like sport
- ...has interests that include walking, cycling, tennis, swimming, climbing, etc.
- ...isn't too keen on prolonged study
- ...is tough and resilient and can keep your cool even when you're tired, cold or wet.

THE JOB FOR YOU: Navy, Merchant Navy, Forestry Commission, Police Force, Agriculture, Armed Forces, Horticulture, Jockey, Gym Gardening, and Landscape Gardener, Riding Instructor, Teacher, Athlete.

THE PRACTICAL YOU

- ...enjoys working with your hands.
- ...loves working with machinery, do-it-yourself, working with tools
- ...loves working on practical projects such as cookery, crafts
- ...is best of all at practical subjects
- ...is calm, methodical and patient.

THE JOB FOR YOU: Dental Technician, Engineer, Animal Nurse, Dentist, Dental Technician, Pattern Cutter, Textile Technician, Machinist, Landscape Gardener.

THE TALKATIVE YOU

- ...loves meeting new people
- ...has a pleasant manner and appearance and gets along
- ...has the gift of the gab and is outgoing with people from all walks of life
- ...is friendly, helpful and outgoing.

THE JOB FOR YOU: Sales Assistant in a department store, Sales Rep, Travel Courier, Broadcaster, Receptionist, Telephone Operator, Public Relations Officer, Air Hostess.

Take to the sands in a perfect mix of creams in denim, linen, wool and raffia . . .

THE CREAM SCENE!

Cream waistcoat, £29.99 and beads, £9.99, both from Oasis. Cream shirt, £19.99, from Warehouse. Cream crepe flares, £29.99, from Miss Selfridge. Cream raffia platforms, £27.99, from Miss Selfridge.

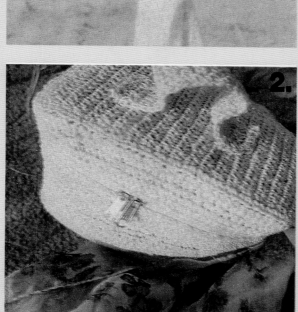

1. Linen shirt, **£39.99,** from Oasis. Cream denim waistcoat, **£19.99,** from Miss Selfridge. Cream denim flares, **£21.99,** from Snob. Print scarf, **£5.99,** from Warehouse.

2. Cream crochet bag from a selection at Oasis. Scarf, **£5.99,** from Warehouse.

3. Cream raffia shoes, **£27.99,** from Miss Selfridge. Beads, from a selection at Oasis.

4. Cream dress, **£27.99,** from Warehouse. Cream waistcoat, **£12.99** and cardigan, **£29.99,** both from Snob. Cream raffia shoes, **£27.99,** from Miss Selfridge.

MEET ME ON THE CORNER...

IT MUST BE SOME KIND OF PUBLICITY STUNT.

NAW. I'LL BET IT'S CANDID CAMERA.

MAYBE IF I JUST ACT NATURALLY THEY'LL ALL GO AWAY! THING IS HOW D'YOU ACT NATURALLY HOLDIN' A CAMEL?

YOU DON'T BELIEVE THIS, EH? THAT I CAN BE STANDING IN THE MIDDLE OF THE ROAD WITH A CAMEL? WELL, NEITHER DO I, REALLY!

I was beginning to collect quite a crowd.

WHAT'S HAPPENING?

DUNNO. I THINK THEY MUST BE MAKING A FILM.

A FILM? IS STEVE McQUEEN IN IT?

YOU GOT ME INTO THIS. IT'S YOUR FAULT EVERYBODY'S STARING AT ME!

DON'T BLAME ME, DEAR! I'M JUST STANDING HERE MINDING ME OWN BUSINESS, SMILING ENIGMATICALLY...AS CAMELS DO!

NOW THEN, NOW THEN, WHAT'S ALL THIS 'ERE?

OH NO...THE LAW! THAT'S ALL I NEED.

AHEM...I'M AFRAID YOU'LL HAVE TO MOVE ALONG, MISS.

BUT WE'RE NOT DOING ANYTHING! WE'RE JUST STANDING HERE. AND ANYWAY, THERE'S NO LAW AGAINST STANDING ON A STREET CORNER WITH A CAMEL, IS THERE?

BLIMEY—COME TO THINK OF IT, I DON'T KNOW IF THERE IS OR NOT. MAYBE I OUGHT TO CALL THE SERGEANT...

WHY DON'T YOU GET YOURSELF A NICE BUDGIE FOR A PET, DEAR? THEY DON'T COST AS MUCH TO FEED, I BET.

AHA! CAUSING A DISTURBANCE IN A PUBLIC PLACE! THAT OUGHT TO COVER IT. I THINK I BETTER HAVE YOUR NAME AND ADDRESS, MISS.

OH, ALL RIGHT THEN. IT'S JUDI FRASER, 15 CANNON AVENUE.

As if I wasn't in enough trouble—My boyfriend Alec had to go and turn up right at that minute.

JUDI! WHAT THE HECK ARE YOU UP TO NOW?

OH...ER...HI, ALEC. BET YOU CAN'T SPOT THE OBVIOUS MISTAKE. HA, HA... EH...HMM!

patchwork

The language of flowers

Did you know that two thousand years ago, flowers were used to carry messages in Eastern countries because few people could read or write?

Gradually, the custom spread to England, and even now flowers are sometimes given for a reason — to mean something very special.

Here's a list to help you make up your own flower messages. Watch what you're saying, though, some of the meanings can be quite odd!

Almond Blossom — Hope and sweetness. **Anemones** — "I may leave you soon." **Asters** — "I will think about it." **Bluebells** — Constancy. **Bramble Flowers** — "I envy you." **Buttercups** — "I am behaving childishly." **Camellias** — "Beauty is your only attraction." **Red Carnations** — "Alas, my poor heart." **Striped Carnations** — "I intend to refuse you." **Celandines** — There are joys to come. **White Clovers** — "Think of me." **Daffodils** — "You are high in my regard." **Dahlias** — "I am yours for ever." **Daisies** — "I will think it over." **Everlasting — like plants** — "I will never forget." **Forget-Me-Nots** — Remember your true love always. **Foxgloves** — "I am sorry for you." **Harebells** — Grief. **Heliotropes** — "I think I love you." **Honeysuckle** — "We are secure in love."

Hyacinths — "I am well and cheerful." **Iris** — "A message will arrive soon." **Jasmine** — "You are an amiable person." **Jonquil** — "I desire a return of affection." **King Cups** — "My ambition is to find wealth." **Larkspurs** — "Read what is written in my heart." **Lilies** — "I am pure and modest." **Lavender blossom** — "This is the beginning of our love." **White lilac** — "You are too young and innocent." **Marigolds** — Anxiety and despair. **Meadow-sweet** — "You rule my heart." **Narcissi** — "I think highly of myself." **Nasturtiums** — "I will serve my country first." **Pansies** — "Think of me continually." **Peonies** — "Your beauty lies in the heart." **Pinks** — "My love is pure and ardent." **Roses** — True love. **Rosemary** — Remembrance. **Shamrocks** — "I am in a light-hearted mood." **Sunflowers** — "I adore you." **Sweetpeas** — "Yours are delicate pleasures." **Snowdrops** — "You bring me hope." **Tulips** — "I love you madly." **Verbena** — "I am sensitive to your charms." **Violets** — "I think you are too modest." **Wallflowers** — "I will be faithful always." **Water-lilies** — "I am pure in heart." **Wild Roses** — Simplicity.

Well, here's hoping your next bouquet isn't made up of buttercups and marigolds!

COLLECTING FOR FUN: BOTTLES DON'T BOTTLE IT UP!

Do you realise that a hundred or so years ago people used far more bottles than we do today? They had no throwaway paper and plastic packs then! But now, "bottle clubs" are springing up all over the country to help collectors dig up the fascinating bottles the Victorians threw away. But you don't have to dig — you can buy them.

Why collect bottles? Because the oldest ones weren't made by machine — they were blown from a blob of hot glass like a big bubble. So each bottle was slightly different. It might be a bit lopsided or have long air bubbles trapped in the glass — "tears," the experts call them.

And bottle colours were much nicer then. Medicine bottles were a lovely deep royal blue. Beer bottles were almost black glass — with a fat ring of glass round the lip, known as a "blob top"!

"Codd" bottles are fun to find. They used to hold fizzy drinks. There's a marble trapped in the neck to keep the gas in — so each bottle rattles! Ginger beer bottles weren't made of glass, they were made of stoneware. Collectors love their printed labels in the shape of a fish, insect, animal or a long written advert for the maker.

Ginger beer bottles are usually a cream or rust colour. But the top may be a different shade, and green tops are rarest of all. Ginger beer bottles cost from about £1.

You can date a bottle by the seams down the side, the marks on the bottom, and the shape of the lip. For more information write to: The British Bottle Collectors Club, "Greenacres," Church Road, Black Notley, Braintree, Essex. But please send a stamped self-addressed envelope.

Two blob top bottles with a raised "embossed" pattern in the glass.

GROW YOUR OWN!

Everyone knows how useful lemons are — for shining your hair, softening hands and elbows, quenching your thirst, and helping you control your sweet tooth when on a diet.

But fresh lemons are expensive — and a lemon tree would be an absolute luxury!

Now, however, thanks to P.L.J., you can grow your own lemon tree for a fraction of the cost of buying one — and have a lot more fun, too!

There's no need to have a greenhouse or even a garden, in order to grow a lemon tree. Just follow the instructions on the pack, and you can't go wrong! Within two years, your efforts will be rewarded by a sturdy little plant with glossy leaves, fragrant white flowers and perfect fruit — mmm!

Your lemon tree will cost you just £1.95, and you'll find details on the "special offer" P.L.J. bottles now.

YOU CAN MAKE IT

Enamel jewellery like this looks great, but is usually much too expensive to buy. But we'll let you into a secret — it's not really enamel at all! In fact, it's all done by "Sellotape" Coloured Cloth Tape!

Want to know how to make this super, professional - looking jewellery? It's easy really, just take a piece of strong cardboard (approx. 2 inches square is a good size for a brooch or hairslide, but you can make it bigger or smaller if you want). Now cover the whole piece of cardboard in "Sellotape" Coloured Cloth Tape in your basic colour (you can choose from red, black, white, blue, yellow and brown).

Decide upon the design you want (flower, bird, or whatever) and draw on its outline with pen. Then just build up your design by adding pieces of different coloured cloth tape on top to form petals, wings, etc.

Cut round the outline carefully, leaving a "frame" of the base colour round the edges if you want.

Finish off by fastening on a safety pin or hairslide to the back with a small piece of cloth tape.

If you want a nice, bright finish, paint your jewellery with clear nail polish.

"Sellotape" coloured cloth tape costs just 17p a roll, so you get lots of jewellery for very little money. Sounds like a bargain to us!

HOW TO . . .

1 . . . stop varnish bottles jamming up. Wipe the outside of the bottle clean with a tissue, then wipe lightly with Vaseline. Wipe the inside of the lid. Replace lid, and store the bottle upright always.

2 . . . mend a ripped nail. Cut a small scrap from the thin end, (without bandage on it) of a transparent band-aid. Stick this over the nail, holding the torn bit in place, and you can paint over it with nail varnish if you like. Lasts up to a week.

3 . . . mend a belt with a tear on your favourite hole! Get a short length of strong fabric, thin leather or even heavy-duty tape, the same colour as the belt, and glue it with Copydex. Let it get tacky. Press out the belt as flat as possible, and glue the inside. When tacky, press the tape on the inside of the belt. Leave to dry under a weight. Then re-pierce the hole. It may also help to undo the buckle and adjust, to bring the tear to the next hole in line, then re-close the buckle end.

Give us a smiler!

We've combined "Your Patch" and the recipe this week. We don't normally, but "Jackie" reader Elizabeth Cook sent in such a super recipe as her "your patch" idea that we just couldn't resist it!

Elizabeth from Ayr, is very fond of making these delicious "Smilers" as she calls them. She says they're just right for chilly October days, and we're not arguing!

To make "Smilers," start by cutting thick slices from a French loaf and toasting on one side only. Now cover the other side with slices of Cheddar cheese, and make the face by adding chutney "hair," pickled onion "eyes", a chopped chives "nose," and a tomato "mouth." Grill gently until the cheese bubbles, and serve immediately.

Having tried them ourselves, we warn you that you'll soon be back for second helpings! They're also good for parties, keeping kid brothers and sisters quiet, or for a late-night supper in bed!

Elizabeth wins £1 for her idea, and if you'd like to try your luck, send in your ideas to "Your Patch," "Jackie," 185 Fleet Street, London EC4A 2HS. "Your Patch" doesn't have to be a recipe by the way, it can be any idea at all that you've thought up yourself. So get busy!

David Essex Jackie

Jackie DUSTY

HARRY GOODWIN HAS VERY FOND MEMORIES OF *JACKIE*, but working for a teenage girls' magazine wasn't something he ever dreamed he would do.

Harry was born in Manchester in 1924 and his first job was working in his dad's bookmaking business. He gained experience as an untrained photographer in the RAF during the Second World War, and when he returned to Manchester, he made photography his full-time job. In the early days of his career he worked on the beauty pageant and boxing circuits.

Harry's connection with the pop world took off big style with the iconic BBC show *Top of the Pops*. He photographed pop stars from all over the world, from the very first show in 1964 until 1973. Throughout his career, Harry's took thousands of photographs of hundreds of famous faces, including Elton John, the Bee Gees and Rod Stewart.

Harry remembers *Jackie* as a "clean" magazine and loved working with the team. "I loved it," he says. "Everyone was so nice, even the lady on the switchboard was lovely."

And he wasn't alone in his fondness for the title as the teen idols loved it, too. He remembers, "All the pop stars I met wanted to be in *Jackie* magazine."

Harry has a real soft spot for Scotland and enjoyed his visits to Dundee where *Jackie* was created by the editorial team at DC Thomson. He's never been interested in driving and always travelled by train, always choosing to stay in the nearby seaside town of Arbroath where he enjoyed the fresh fish, washed down with his favourite tipple – cups of tea.

Harry admits to being a sports fanatic and is particularly mad about football and boxing. He's a great mate of the former Manchester United manager Sir Alex Ferguson. Sir Alex has attended several of Harry's photographic exhibitions and thinks he's "an amazing man".

Jackie ROY ORBISON

Jackie GEORGE

Jackie GEORGE BEST

A STORY

The exhibition of his *Tops of the Pops* photographs at the Victoria & Albert Museum in London received a fantastic reception and was viewed by over 100,000 visitors. He also has a permanent exhibition of his work, which was opened by Yoko Ono, at John Lennon Airport in Liverpool. Harry first photographed The Beatles way back in 1963 at the Apollo Theatre in Manchester and he enjoyed a close relationship with the band.

Celebrities can be notoriously difficult to work with, but Harry says he never had a problem. He had his own way of dealing with tricky situations. "Certain pop stars could be a bit awkward, but I could always handle it. I never had a hard time with any of the stars. There could be awkward moments, but I always won them round. Johnnie Stewart who was the original producer of *Top of the Pops* would say, 'As soon as Harry gets in the room they love him straightaway.'"

He had a great relationship with Sir Elton John. "I got on well with Elton and he liked me as well."

He admits to having his favourites and Harry is a particular fan of the Bee Gees. "The Bee Gees are my favourite band. I think Robin had the best voice – it comes over the best of the lot."

He remembers his *Jackie* days as being fun times. "It was marvellous. I used to wind Lulu up. I used to say, 'Sandie Shaw is better than you' and I used to say the same thing to Sandie Shaw about Lulu! But it was all good-natured."

Technically, photography has moved on in a major way. Back in the *Jackie* days, before digital images and instant messaging, Harry sent his photographs to the magazine as transparencies or prints.

At the ripe old age of 89 years young, Harry is still hard at work. "Nobody believes how old I am!" he says and it's easy to understand their confusion when you look at this fit man who completely belies his age. Retirement isn't part of his vocabulary as he contemplates putting his life story in print and more exhibitions of his amazing images. Harry's upbeat, positive attitude is reflected in his legendary catchphrase … "Keep smiling!"

And that's the true secret of his success.

Irene K Duncan

Jackie PIN-UP JOHN LENNON

Jackie Suzi Quatro

JACKIE
PINUP

Shot: **Ulf Magnusson/**
Idols

TAKE

THAT

COUNTDOWN TO THAT
big dat

Big date on Saturday nigh
Want to look your best? I'll be
do . . . and you can.
All it takes is a little
planning and organisation.

We at Jackie have drawn up The Big Date Survival Plan to help you leave the house radiant, beautiful and relaxed.

And for those of you who haven't had a week's notice for this meeting with the boy of your dreams, there's the ACTION STATIONS PLAN . . . counting 30 minutes to go, 29 minutes 55 seconds . . . 28 minutes 16 seconds . . . help!

THE BIG DATE ▼SURVIVAL PLAN▼

►►► COUNTDOWN 4 DAYS TO big d. day...

Preparations for this biggie start four or five days beforehand when you should buy anything new you'd like to wear.

This gives you time enough to try it on at home a few times, decide you like it and feel comfortable with it, take it back to the shop if you're not happy with it. If you're not wearing anything new, check that your planned outfit is clean and doesn't need sewing, etc.

Sort out accessories now, too, and take time to select cosmetics and make-up to go with the colours of the outfit. If you're going to experiment do it now, not on the night!

If you're planning a new hairstyle, do it now, too. But you need to feel comfortable and happy about yourself, so if in doubt about whether to have your hair cut or not, *don't*. Remember he asked you out because he likes the way you look, so there's no need to change yourself drastically.

►►►► COUNTDOWN 1 DAY TO big d. day...

Give yourself the works on Friday night. This will take some of the pressure off Saturday and leave you free to enjoy yourself. A facial, and defuzzing session if you usually shave your legs, etc. should be done now.

For the facial, boil a kettle, and whilst it's boiling, cleanse your face, neck and throat. Pour the hot water into a bowl and putting a towel over your head, put your face over the bowl. If you have oily skin, stay under for five minutes; dry skin, seven minutes; and if you have combination skin, six minutes. Don't put your face too close to the water, though; there's no need to come up bright red and panting!

If you have any blackheads, now is the time to remove them. Cover your fingers with a tissue and apply pressure on either side of the blackhead. The pores are soft, so it should pop out easily. If it doesn't, don't squeeze hard, you'll only cause scarring. Try to avoid using your nails for the same reason.

Now apply your favourite facepack, pop some cucumber slices or used teabags over your eyes to revitalise them, lie down for 15 minutes and listen to your favourite records.

After washing off the face mask, splash your face 25 times with cold water to tighten up the pores. Apply moisturiser, using small light circular motions over the skin with your fingers. Be especially careful you don't drag the skin around the eyes, as the skin around this area is especially thin and sensitive.

Avoid wearing make-up until tomorrow.

DE-FUZZ The next thing to do is to treat the skin that's going to be on show. If you're wearing a sleeveless top, shave your underarms. If you're not going to wear any tights you might want to shave your legs. Now is the time to do all of these things.

PEDICURE While you're at it you could also give yourself a pedicure. Soak your feet in warm soapy water, put a little baby oil in the water to soften the skin. After 3 minutes rub off hard skin with a pumice stone.

Dry your feet carefully then apply moisturiser.

Try to avoid wearing shoes all evening and exercise your feet by walking around barefoot.

Just before you go to bed, iron your clothes for tomorrow night, polish your shoes and set everything out, ready to wear.

ZZZ . . . Ensure a good night's sleep by having a warm soothing bath. Use a loofah to scrub any areas of hard skin, then after drying yourself off, apply moisturiser, especially on your legs. Have an early night, but no extra, extra long-lie-ins tomorrow. Too much sleep can make your face puffy, and because lying down for long periods makes it difficult for excess fluid to drain away from your face, you can end up with a headache. 9-10 hours sleep is enough for anyone.

COUNTDOWN
▸▸▸▸▸▸▸▸▸▸▸
big d. day IS HERE!

Before you even get out of bed, start the day like a cat-s-t-r-e-t-c-h! It's said that a good stretch first thing in the morning adds an extra five minutes to your day, and you never know, it could mean those five minutes tonight on your doorstep saying goodnight . . .

Before breakfast put on your favourite L.P. or exercise record if you've got one and do 15 minutes stretching and bending.

Have a light breakfast, something like fresh orange juice, two rashers of grilled bacon, slice of tomato and 1 slice of wholemeal toast; *or* muesli, and 1 slice of wholemeal toast and a thin layer of butter; *or* 1 poached or boiled egg with 2 slices of wholemeal toast.

Go out with your friends today, go swimming or shopping in town, do something totally unconnected with your Big Date, anything to take your mind off *him* and feeling nervous.

Get Ready Steadily

It's 2 hours before the Big Date, and it's time to get ready. Have a shower, wash or bath and wash your hair. You don't need to worry about doing anything extra special as you did it all last night!

Have something light to eat now, butterflies or giant bats in the stomach might not make you feel like it, but do try and have something, even if it's only some soup.

Now blow-dry your hair, apply some setting lotion or mousse if it needs extra hold. Go and give your teeth a brush. Use a minty mouth wash for extra freshness.

Use a hairband to hold your hair back from your face as you put on your make-up.

If in doubt, too little make-up is better than too much, so don't overdo it.

A little spot concealer, mascara and lip gloss are the favourites of a good make-up.

A few minutes to spare? Put on your fave record and have a little bop, it'll put colour in your cheeks and give you that sought after natural glow!

Zero Hour—He's ▼ Here! ▼

Time to go! Check you've got hairbrush, money, paper tissues, a little make-up, perfume, and house keys in your handbag, take a deep breath and head on down the stairs. Take a look at him, smile and say, "Hi! Are you ready? Let's go!"

THE 30 MINUTE ACTION STATION PLAN

Enlist the help of any spare Mums, sisters, brothers and Dads (bribery may be useful) to polish shoes, iron clothes, find handbag, vacate bathroom, lend you hair mousse, etc., etc. You need all the help you can get at times like this!

● Shower, or wash quickly all over, there's no time for a bath.
● Apply moisturiser all over your body.
● Give your teeth a quick brush then INTO THE BEDROOM.
● If your hair's greasy, sprinkle talcum powder on it then brush it through to get rid of any excess 'white'. Or tie a scarf round your head in a fashionable turban style, this looks very attractive and hides the lank locks beautifully.
● If your hair's clean but still needs a 'revamp', quickly apply some mousse to those areas that need extra body and blow-dry them into shape.
● Now for some make-up, start with your eyes first, because, at least if you don't have time for anything else, you know you'll still look good.
● If you've got two pairs of tights but both pairs are ripped or snarled in one leg, cut that leg off at the thigh, save the other leg and knicker section, do the same with the other pair then wear both knicker sections with one leg each, a new pair of tights, voilà! (This can even work if the tights are different colours, one blue leg and one red leg is fashionable this year!)
● Quickly pull on something clean and ironed, squirt some perfume round your wrists, take a deep breath and smile! There! You're ready!

FAST FORWARD
FLOELLA

SCREEN SCENE

WE first met zany actress Floella Benjamin at a Press launch for the comedy series **Fast Forward**, in which she stars with Joanna Monro, Nick Wilton and Andrew Secombe. She looked great in her bright red dress, hat and beads — so we told her so!

She laughed. "Would you believe the whole outfit only cost about £5? I'm a great believer in second-hand shops, picking up bargains and dressing clothes up with nice accessories. I love the colour, too — bright colours make other people happy, and I think that's important.

"I also like dressing my hair up. I usually wear loads of beads and things; today it's ribbons and sequins. As for my earrings — well, they're Polo mints. I don't believe in expensive things! You get about ten Polo mints in a packet so these earrings work out really cheap. And they've got an added advantage — you can eat them if you start feeling a bit peckish . . ."

Floella was born in Jamaica, one of six children, and came to England when she was six years old.

"Mum and Dad, two of my brothers and a sister all live near me," she told us. "Then one brother lives in America and my other sister is a concert pianist in Hong Kong.

"After I left school, I went to work in a bank, which was safe but boring. Then I saw an advert for singers and dancers for the stage show Hair. The trouble was, they expected everyone to take their clothes off (blush), which I wasn't prepared to do. I told the casting director so, and surprisingly they gave me a part. Then I did things like The Black Mikado, and Jesus Christ Superstar.

"Then? Well, I went on into TV, and did some drama and comedy. I was in Angels, The Gentle Touch and Mixed Blessings, among other things."

Floella also worked as a presenter on the children's programmes Play School and Play Away. She has written a joke book called "Fall About With Flo" and an activity book, "Floella's Fun Book," both for children.

"Silly jokes are very much a part of Fast Forward, too. The director, Robert Smith, has been all over the country, visiting schools to record kids telling their own jokes. I think it's one of the best parts of the show."

It would seem that Floella's hardly had a moment to herself, but she still finds time to do charity work, working with underprivileged and handicapped children. "I believe in being kind to people. That way I'll always have a clear conscience.

"I like talking to people, too. If I see someone who looks nice, I'll tell them so. Once the ice is broken, people chat away to you — and as you may have gathered, I never stop talking!"

Right now, Floella is writing a West Indian cookery book, to be published later this year; she's making a wildlife programme for the BBC and plans to become a producer.

"I just see something I think I might like and then go off and do it. I believe in fate — that things happen to you. And I think that if you want to do something badly enough all you have to do is tell yourself you can do it. And you will. I've proved that time and time again!"

Barry
Manilow

Jackie

I WAS TOO SHY TO TELL HIM

A S I set out for a walk with my dog, the evening air is filled with the promise of Spring. It's a perfect evening for walking — and I'm not the only one to think so.

As I walk towards the park, there's a couple coming towards me; a boy and a girl, so wrapped up in each other that they're scarcely aware of the rest of the world.

And as they pass, I think sadly, that could be Paul and me, if only I wasn't so shy . . .

I've known Paul for about two months now, ever since my friend Diane persuaded me to go to the youth club with her. I'd been reluctant to go at first, knowing how I always feel shy and awkward among strangers.

"We won't know anybody," I kept saying to Diane when she suggested going. "We'll be all alone and no one'll talk to us."

In the end she'd got a bit angry with me. "Don't be so silly, Diane," she said impatiently. "Of course they'll talk to us. We'll just have to make an effort, that's all."

I tried once more to explain how I felt, but it was no use. Diane couldn't understand. She had two brothers and a sister, so she was used to having other people around all the time. But I was an only child.

Most of the people I met out of school were older people, friends of my parents, and they always managed to make my shyness a lot worse, by saying tactless things like, "Aren't you quiet? You're not like your parents." And that was guaranteed to make me blush scarlet and not say another word till they left.

No one seems to understand that I need to know someone quite a long time before I can talk to them easily. I have to be sure that they like me. I can't just make conversation with anyone the way Diane can. With boys I'm even worse — and the fact that I go to an all-girls' school doesn't exactly help.

T HAT first visit to the youth club was a great ordeal for me. I found out beforehand what Diane planned to wear, so that I'd be sure of wearing the right thing myself, and I asked her to come round for me, in case I decided to change at the last minute.

When she arrived, she tried hard to convince me that I looked all right, but even so, as we got to the door of the club, I wanted to turn round and go back home. I could hear music and voices, talking and laughing. My knees turned to jelly and I just knew I wouldn't be able to say anything. But Diane had already caught hold of my arm, so I had to follow her inside.

At first I just stood there, not speaking, not moving away from Diane. But she seemed quite at home. She soon saw a boy she knew and dragged me over to be introduced to him.

As we walked across, my mind was full of all sorts of clever and witty things to say to him, but the moment he smiled and said hello, my shyness overcame me. The words stuck in my throat and I just stood there, blushing stupidly and feeling as though everyone was staring at me.

The same thing happened a little later, when Paul introduced himself. He was so goodlooking that my heart raced crazily as he spoke to us.

"You're new here, aren't you?" he said in a friendly way, speaking to both of us, but looking at me.

I wanted so much to say something bright, something to make him laugh, something that might impress him. But the words wouldn't come. I could only mumble yes and nod my head and go crimson, while Diane started to talk to him quite happily.

But even though I'd scarcely said half a dozen words to him, knowing Paul would be there was the encouragement I needed to keep going to the youth club every week.

We got to know a few more girls there and I soon found I could talk to them quite easily, without feeling shy. But the minute Paul came up and smiled or said hello, I'd just fall apart. I'd start blushing and stuttering and feel so stupid that I just wanted the floor to open and swallow me . . .

T HEN this week, Paul said he'd walk home with Diane and me since he lives in our direction. Half of me was happy, because Diane had told me she thought Paul fancied me a bit, but the other half was terrified.

All went well at first though. Diane kept talking and I just said yes and no in the appropriate places. Then we got to Diane's house and she went in, leaving the two of us alone.

And that's when the panic started. Paul tried so hard to get me to talk and I just couldn't say a word as my awful shyness came over me again.

I expected him to give up trying then, the way the other boys had done when they'd realised how quiet I was. But Paul was different.

When we got to my gate, he asked if he could see me again.

"At the youth club?" I asked stupidly.

He shook his head. "No, there's a film on in town that I thought you might like to see. We could go on Saturday."

And I wanted so very much to say yes, but he was standing there, looking at me, waiting for an answer and I suppose I just panicked.

"I'm not sure," I heard myself mumbling. "I might be busy . . ."

He looked kind of hurt then, but there was nothing I could do, nothing I could say. What could I say? *"I'm sorry, of course I want to go with you. I don't know what made me say that."* I could never say something like that. Not in a million years!

So instead, I just stood there looking miserable. Maybe he sensed what I was thinking though, because he didn't turn and walk away like I expected. Instead, he said gently, "Look. I'm on the phone, so maybe you could give me a ring if you change your mind?"

And he wrote a number down for me on a piece of paper and I put it in my handbag.

That was on Tuesday. Since then I've changed my mind a thousand times. I've gone to the phone, then not dared to ring. And now it's Friday, and I've got to decide . . .

And suddenly I remember the couple I saw on my walk. I remember how happy they looked together, and I realise Paul and I could be like that too. It's up to me to conquer my shyness . . .

So I'll go to the youth club tonight, and if he's there, I'll go up to him and tell him, "Yes, Paul. I'd like to go to the pictures tomorrow."

Because, for all I know, he's maybe just as nervous as I am . . .

True Confessions

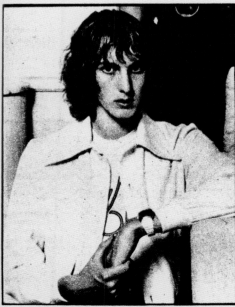

Eddie Jobson
(Roxy Music)

My idea of beauty	SUNSET
My favourite flower	CARNATION
My favourite colour	RED
My favourite place	IN FRONT OF THE FIRE
My closest friend	MARIA
My greatest happiness	MAKING PEOPLE HAPPY
My greatest misery	SEEING PEOPLE SAD
My favourite amusement	LAUGHING
My favourite residence	SUNSET TOWERS — HOLLYWOOD
My favourite song and composer	"GOODBYE YELLOW BRICK ROAD" — ELTON
My favourite hero/heroine in real life	NONE
My favourite animal	KITTEN
My favourite names	—
My present state of mind	CONTENT
My motto	NONE
My signature	*E. Jobson*

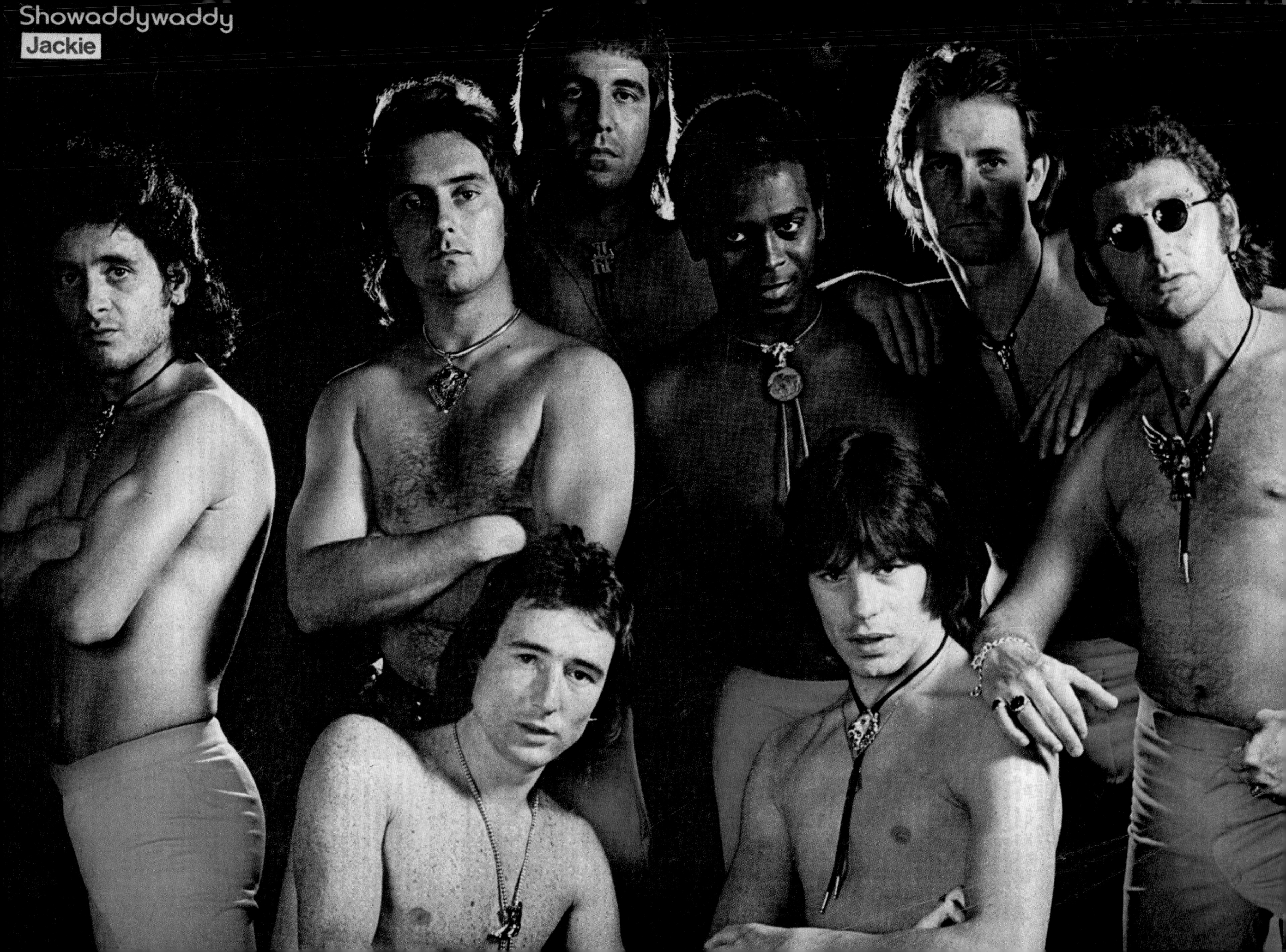
Showaddywaddy
Jackie

The Cathy and Claire Page

DEAR CATHY & CLAIRE — My boyfriend is so possessive it's unbelievable. He even gets angry if I *talk* to another boy.

I'm not a flirt but I do like a bit of freedom and I know quite a few boys who are just friends.

He's really beginning to make me feel tied down.

What do you think I should do?

Well, to be quite honest, it doesn't sound as if you're all that keen about continuing your relationship with your boyfriend. You're already getting a bit fed up of being tied down and being restricted all the time so maybe you'd be happier making a clean break and finishing things?

It sounds as if your boy's pretty keen on you so it would be fairer to him in the long run if you told him that you didn't feel ready to be so tied down.

Tell him honestly how you feel and, although he's likely to be hurt at first, we hope you'll still be able to be friends.

DEAR CATHY & CLAIRE — About two months ago I got a Saturday job in a supermarket and now I find it's ruining my whole weekend. I can't go out late on Friday or else I'd be too tired to go to work and by the time I get home from work on a Saturday I'm too tired to go out that night!

Have you any suggestions how I can get round this problem?

Oh, the things we have to give up to earn money! Seriously, though, this *is* quite a problem. Could you maybe try getting a job that was a bit less tiring? Or one that was nearer your home?

Maybe you're not really suited to supermarket work. It *is* very tiring — spending all day packing shelves etc. Why don't you try doing some other part-time job that would bring in some extra cash? You could try baby-sitting during the week, or you could wash cars or something similar at the weekend. You may find this suits you better.

We hope you find something. After all, having a good weekend is important, and you shouldn't have to miss out on all the fun.

We can't promise the perfect solution, but we'll do our best. If you're stuck with a problem and you can't see the way out, write to us at this address: Cathy & Claire, Jackie, 185 Fleet Street, London EC4A 2HS. Please remember to enclose an S.A.E.

DEAR CATHY & CLAIRE — A girl I don't know very well invited me to go to a party with her one Saturday night not long ago.

My parents were a bit dubious, but they said I could go as long as they came for me in the car before midnight.

Well, I went to the party and to cut a long story short, the party wasn't my kind of party at all. There was a lot of drink and rough people and things got a bit out of hand. I decided to leave before I got involved and this boy, who I quite fancied, said he'd take me home.

We'd to wait ages for a bus and by the time I'd got home my parents had left to pick me up.

They went to the door of the party and asked where I was and they saw what sort of party it was. When they found out I wasn't there, they came home and they were very angry. I tried to explain to them what had happened but they don't believe me. They think I went off somewhere with Steve (the boy that took me home).

Now they won't let me out and I want to see Steve again. How can I make them understand I was only doing the thing I thought was best and that I wasn't up to anything they'd disapprove of?

Your parents are very likely acting in this way because they got a fright. They probably were very shocked when they saw what sort of party it was and they may feel you *knew* that it was going to be like this and deliberately deceived them.

Now that things have calmed down a bit, though, we think you should try talking to your parents again. Explain to them that you didn't know what sort of party it was going to be and you did what you thought was best. We're sure they can't really fault you for that.

They're likely to be a bit stricter about the parties you go to in future, but at least they'll be letting you go!

DEAR CATHY & CLAIRE — I'm really unhappy and I just don't know what to do. You see, my uncle, who's a manager, got me a job in this firm. I've been working there for four months now and I really hate it! The work is really boring and the girls resent me because my uncle is the boss.

I don't know how to tell my parents or my uncle that I want to leave.

What do you think I should do?

Well, we think you should try and last out another two months in this job. Then you'll have been there six months and we think that's long enough to have given it a fair trial.

After that, start looking for a new job you think will be more interesting for you. Then tell your parents about how unhappy you are at work. Explain to them that it's very awkward having your uncle as your boss and tell them that the other girls resent this. Show them the new jobs you're going to apply for and tell them you think you'd be better suited to these.

Perhaps they'll have a word with your uncle. It's likely he's realised you're not very happy where you are, and we're sure he'll agree you have given the job a fair chance.

Try not to worry and we're sure things will work out.

DEAR CATHY & CLAIRE — I know this isn't really a situation I should be complaining about, but our school dance is being held a few weeks from now and two different boys have asked me to go with them.

I know you'll say I should go with the one who asked me first and I suppose I should but I don't fancy him as much as the other one.

When Peter rang (the first one) I said yes. Then two days later Marty rang and I had to say I couldn't go with him as someone else had asked me first. He just said I could change my mind and let him know if I wanted to go with him.

Well, I do! I've fancied Marty for ages and he's never shown any interest before. I just don't know what to do. I hate to miss this chance with Marty but I'd hate to hurt Peter as he's a really nice person.

What do you think I should do?

Well, you must make up your mind about this. You know if you *do* go to the dance with Marty, Peter's going to be very hurt and he's unlikely to forgive you easily. The "correct" thing would be to go with Peter, but when you like Marty so much, the "correct" thing isn't always easy to do.

If you decide to go with Marty, remember you'll have to tell Peter and that will be very difficult.

We think the best thing to do would be to explain to Marty about the situation you're in. Tell him that you really want to go to the dance with him but you feel that it would be a bit unfair on Peter.

If Marty's keen, he'll more then likely understand and ask you out again, so don't worry about this too much. We're sure things will work out fine for you.

DEAR CATHY & CLAIRE — I'm really beginning to worry. I seem to spend all my time thinking about my appearance. I'm forever looking in the mirror to check my hair or look at my face.

I think I must be really vain or something.

How can I stop myself from being so worried about what I look like? Surely it doesn't matter that much?

Well, we agree. looks certainly aren't the most important thing in life but there's nothing wrong with *caring* what you look like — and that doesn't necessarily mean you're vain. You must try not to let this become an obsession, though. Worrying about your looks is really a basic feeling of insecurity and you're obviously very self-conscious.

So try to have a little more confidence in yourself as a person, and you'll find you won't feel the need to be checking up on what you look like all the time.

DEAR CATHY & CLAIRE — My boyfriend is very argumentative and quick-tempered and this is beginning to annoy me.

Honestly, we can't go anywhere without him starting a discussion about politics, football, or something else I don't know anything about. He's always picking fights with people and I get really fed up of this. He seems to spend all his time ignoring me when we're out.

How do I go about changing him?

Well, we doubt if you'll ever be able to change him, but a few gentle hints might make him a bit more considerate when he's in your company. Tell him you're fed up with all the arguments he has with people, and tell him you're bored with the never-ending discussions you can't join in with. This will probably give him quite a shock, but shock treatment might work!

If things don't improve, the next time he starts discussing something and causing arguments, don't just stand there feeling stupid — go away, and talk to someone else who's more interesting! If he's keen about you, he won't like that very much. When he asks you why you went away just say something like, "You were being boring!" That may sound a bit cruel but he sounds as if he's pretty thick-skinned.

If, after all this, he *still* causes fights when you're there . . . well, you'll just have to find yourself a more attentive boyfriend.

I'M NOT GOOD ENOUGH FOR HIM!

DEAR CATHY & CLAIRE — I've known Billy for a long time and before I started to go out with him he was well known in our area as a flirt.

He's really good-looking and he's got a great personality. Nearly everyone I know fancies him and people are always telling me how lucky I am. If only they knew!

I know it's silly of me but I just can't believe I'm good enough for him. I spend nearly all the time worrying that he's going to go off with someone else.

It's stupid of me because I'm pretty sure he's never done anything behind my back and he's really good to me.

I just can't seem to get this through my head, though, however hard I try. I'm even beginning to wonder if all this is worth it. I'm so sure I'm going to get hurt.

I think Billy knows I feel this way and so far he's put up with me. I try not to be distrustful but I can't help it. I'm really reserved because of all this and I never seem to be able to relax and show him how much I like him.

What can I do to overcome this stupid feeling of insecurity?

You've summed up your problem in the last sentence — insecurity. You can't believe things can possibly be as good as they are.

But they can be! And they are! We know it's difficult for you, but you've just got to convince yourself that Billy's going out with you because he likes you and because he *wants* to go out with you. After all, he'd be pretty weird if he went out with someone he didn't like, wouldn't he?

If you like, and if you think it would help, you could tell Billy what's wrong. No doubt he'll understand and assure you you've nothing at all to worry about. But — a word of warning — once he's assured you he really *does* like you, don't mention the subject again. Otherwise you're in danger of becoming a bit of a nag.

So relax, enjoy yourself, tell yourself Billy likes you and we're sure you'll get over this feeling of insecurity. And as for getting hurt. Well, we can't tell you whether you're going to get hurt or not. You may end up hurting Billy, he may end up hurting you; we don't know. But what we *do* know is that you shouldn't let the fear of what *might* happen scare you into making yourself miserable now. O K?

Printed and published by D. C. Thomson & Co., Ltd., 185 Fleet Street, London, EC4A 2HS.

T-TIME

TIME for T-shirts to make you feel on top of the world. T-shirts to team with your favourite jeans or long cotton skirts for super summer evenings.

Short-sleeved T-shirt with square neck and white collar and cuffs, from Shar Cleod.
Style No.: 14/213. Price: £3.30. Fabric: Cotton. Colours: Navy, red, green, yellow. Sizes: Small, medium, large.

V-neck, button-through T-shirt with short sleeves and super stripy design, from Stirling Cooper.
Style No.: BL70. Price: £2.95. Fabric: Cotton. Colours: Assorted. Sizes: 1 to 3.

Stripy vest from Marks and Spencer.
Style No.: 4536. Price: 79p. Fabric: Combed cotton. Colours: Navy/white, green/white, red/white. Sizes: 32 to 36.

Halter top with lace trim, from Nicki Ferrari.
Style No.: 8119. Price: £2.70. Fabric: Cotton/Polynosic. Colours: Pink, white, blue, cream. Sizes: Small, medium, large.

Crisp, bright stripy T-shirt with short sleeves and v-neck, from Nicki Ferrari.
Style No.: 8049. Price: £2.40. Fabric: Cotton/Polynosic. Colours: Green, navy with white stripe. Sizes: Small, medium, large.

Unusual, long-sleeved T-shirt with stripy collar and cuffs and gathering at the neck, from Nicki Ferrari.
Style No.: 8118. Price: £3.75. Fabric: Cotton/Polynosic. Colours: Green, yellow, red, blue, pale blue, pink. Sizes: Small, medium, large.

Racing car T-shirt with pointed collar and cut away shoulders, from John Craig.
Style No.: 14/280. Price: £4.20. Fabric: Cotton towelling. Colours: Brown, green, red. Sizes: Small, medium, large.

Super, sexy T-shirt with long sleeves and ringed front, from John Craig.
Style No.: N116P. Price: £2.40. Fabric: Cotton. Colours: Assorted. Sizes: Small, medium, large.

Button-through, vest top with flowery design, from John Craig.
Style No.: V/3004/3158. Price: £2.60. Colours: Assorted. Fabric: Cotton. Sizes: Small, medium, large.

Button-through T-shirt with long sleeves and button-down pockets, from Bellmans.
Style No.: 7236/06. Price: £2.99. Fabric: 100% cotton. Colours: Ivory, yellow, navy, turquoise. Sizes: Medium.

Gatsby-look T-shirt with round neck and long sleeves, from John Craig.
Style No.: C970. Price: £3.10. Fabric: Cotton. Colours: Assorted. Sizes: Small, medium, large.

Wild West T-shirt with round neck and long sleeves, from John Craig.
Style No.: C415. Price: £2.80. Fabric: Cotton. Colours: Assorted. Sizes: Small, medium, large.

WHERE TO FIND THEM

Stirling Cooper T-shirt from Ronnie Stirling, 94 Old Bond Street, London, W.1.; Peter Robinson; Owen Owen branches. Shar Cleod T-shirt from Angella, Oxford Street, London, W.1.; Brown Muff, Bradford; Unit 6, Guildford; Jane, Bath; Arrival, Henley-on-Thames. Marks & Spencer T-shirt from major branches. John Craig T-shirts from Peter Robinson and branches; Snob, Golders Green; Debenhams Stores; Just Looking, Kings Road, London, S.W.3. Nicki Ferrari T-shirts from Miss Selfridge and branches; Chelsea Girl; Joan Barrie of Manchester and branches; Marshall & Snelgrove, Oxford Street, London, W.1.
All prices approximate.

A Jackie Special on a Very Special Person.

Everybody sends their mother a card on Mother's Day (don't they? It's this Sunday in case you'd forgotten!), and tries to be especially nice. But what about the rest of the year . . .? Well, we're forced to admit it — we all take our mums a bit for granted. And to really UNDERSTAND the complex person who is "just me mum," means going a lot deeper than merely the casual acceptance of having her around!

So with her very own day coming up, we decided to ask you, some of our favourite pop stars and ourselves, the deceptively simple question, What is a mum? And this is what we came up with . . . A Mum Is . . .

SOMEONE WHO LOVES YOU

And if you're inclined to shrug that off as a bit obvious — think again. There are MILLIONS of people in the world, and only a very, very few who love you!

You can't afford to under-estimate the importance of any love that's directed your way! And don't forget that your mum's love is without any strings at all — she knows all her offspring's faults, and yet she loves you just the same. She doesn't want anything in return, except genuine affection.

Most of us use our mother's love in the most shameless way, to be quite frank.

MAJDA FRELIK, Yugoslavia (16)
❝A mum is more than just a friend to you, she will always help you when nobody else can. She is somebody that you can always rely on. When I have friends round, my mother always tactfully leaves the room so that she doesn't get in the way, but I'd much prefer it if she stayed and joined in, because to me there is no generation gap.❞

We can't help it — it comes naturally to every baby! But as we get older, it's up to us to realise that just because our mum's love is always there, and because she can't STOP loving us, even if she wanted to, however badly we treat her, we owe it to her to stop taking her love for granted!

Start thinking about it. Often, you'll find you assume your mother does things for you, or acts in a certain way, because it's her job to run the home and look after you, nothing more. Try imagining that her place was filled by a paid housekeeper! You'll discover that your mum does all kinds of things "extra" to the essential work — and why? Not for the pay, that's a cert! It has to be . . . because she loves you.

More than that . . .

ALAN MERRILL (Arrows)
❝To me Mother is a blonde figure on a stage, because my mother, Helen Merrill, is a Jazz singer and when I was a kid I was always away at boarding school and so I didn't see a lot of her, but when I did she was usually on a stage. So my impression of a mother is a great white Goddess on a stage.❞

MIKI ANTHONY
❝A mum is the one person that you can really rely on to give you love. Whenever you have a problem you can turn to her for advice. A lot of kids complain about their parents, but once they leave home they find they learn to appreciate them far more, and realise that both a mum and a dad will never let you down.❞

SHE UNDERSTANDS YOU . . .

She should! She's been studying you for quite a few years — and she understands your faults better than anyone else. Maybe she even recognises some of them in herself!

But that doesn't mean she's being critical — she loves you and accepts you the way you are, but because she wants great things for you, she also wants to help you overcome your faults. It can often seem that a mum is forever pointing out your faults because she enjoys nagging and picking on you, but if you ask yourself WHY she's prepared to make herself unpopular by ticking you off, you'll find that she's trying to improve YOU, so that YOUR life will eventually be happier and more successful.

GAIL HENDERSON (14) Newtown, Gt. Yarmouth.
❝A mum should have never-ending love for her family and should never single out one child as her favourite. I think a mum should make sure that she can spare a little time each day to listen and talk to her family about things that matter to them.❞

You see, she understands you, maybe better than you do yourself. And you'll come to a happier relationship if you can accept the fact that she knows your faults and still loves you. You don't have to be with her like you are with outsiders. You don't need to cover up, to pretend, or to try to make out you're nicer than you are!

So accept her understanding for what it is — be frank with her — it'll pay off.

She's someone you DON'T have to hide from, because . . .

SHE WANTS TO PROTECT YOU!

This can be the most maddening thing of all — because you don't WANT to be protected!

But it'll help if you remember that this is an important part of a mother's instinct — a mother's most important duty is to guard her offspring from all hazards. The best mums also realise that if you cotton-wool a person too much, they'll never be able to stand on their own feet, so they do try to "let go" bit by bit as you get older.

But habits are hard to break — haven't you ever tried to give up something, like nail-biting or eating sweets? So have some consideration, then, for the mum who's torn in two between her strong natural urge to protect you, and the knowledge that you have to start making your own decisions now!

ANNE CZARNOWSKI (13) London SE3.
❝A mother is a person who should be easy to talk to and confide in. My mum clothes and feeds us and encourages us to save our pocket money, but will always help us financially if we need it.❞

Incidentally, if you look at situations from this angle, you'll often find the solutions — and a lot more pleasantly than arguing it out in rows. If she's over-protective, it's not because she doesn't want you to have fun, enjoy yourself, spend money, and it's not because she doesn't trust you. What she doesn't trust is other people — and she's probably been around long enough to find out the hard way that there are plenty of people around who'll deliberately hurt you for their own fun, who'll let you down, cheat on you, and break your heart.

How you can help yourself is to recognise the dangers — be prepared to protect YOURSELF — and let her know you're taking care. So, if you prove to her that you're able to look after yourself, she'll relax and feel she needn't be quite so watchful!

But she'll probably always be someone who . . .

RUSSELL MAEL (Sparks)
❝A mum, or mom as she is called in the USA, is the only female who ensures that your socks are clean while at the same time permitting you to see other women.❞

ROGER TAYLOR (Queen)
❝The essential qualities of a mum are a good sense of humour, enduring patience and practical capabilities. A woman shouldn't let the fact that she's a mother ruin her appearance; just because she's married and got kids she should still concentrate on making herself attractive. A mum shouldn't spend all her time being a mum, she should make sure that she has plenty of time to 'live', entertain, and enjoy herself.❞

WORRIES ABOUT YOU!

And isn't it nice to know someone DO worry? It can seem a bore, when a worry mum means you maybe have to catch earlier bus home from the dance than you really like . . . or when you have to pho home to check if you can stay on at the pa that's stretching itself into the small hours

But plenty of girls who thought comple independence was the answer, have fou out the hard way that when you're alone, when you've cut yourself off fr your family, knowing NOBODY cares i frightening fact that's hard to live with.

CELIA YE-MYINT (15) Lee, London SE12.
❝I think a mother should be fairly strict else we'd lose our respect for her. My moth worries if I'm home late and always like know where I am going. I think it's nice know she takes so much care and would upset me if she wasn't so concerne about my movements.❞

So, even as you move towards y independence, be grateful for the ties bind you to your home. You'll learn, if don't already, that loving someone is all roses. The minute you really care a boy, you're concerned about him, an he's in trouble, you'll worry over him. Y understand, then, the way a mum feels . but don't wait until it's too late, and you cut the ties between you. Try to apprec NOW that her worry isn't a mean way stopping your fun — all she wants reassurance!

She's earned that much consideration after all, she's the one who . . .

WORKS FOR YOU

Most of us hate household chores. COULD enjoy plunging into a sinkfu greasy dishes, the boring sameness tidying a bedroom or peeling heaps of sp the sheer hard work of cleaning a floor?

But there's one person who has to Mum. She's the one with a real 24-hour a job! Ever REALLY given a thought the amount of work there is in the ho and the fairness of the way it's shared yourself — who totters to your aid ... you have a bilious attack at 3 a.m.? ... many people in your house use the ... and who cleans it? If mum hasn't ... outside job, maybe it seems that ..., cleaning, washing, etc., is just her ... earning her living. O.K., but like ... workers, she shouldn't be expected ... more than a regular number of ... on the job! Try working out how ... people you'd need to employ if you ...'T have a mum!

... BROWN (17) Newcastle-on-Tyne.
... love both my mum and dad equally ... have great respect for them. My mother ... herself out regularly each Sunday ... help me learn something new domesti- ... and as I have recently got engaged, ... fiance is very grateful to her for my ... don Bleu lessons!

... 'll find things work much better if ... eat her with a little consideration. She ... bly quite happily cooks and cleans ... u — though they moan about it, most ... enjoy feeling wanted, and don't really ... when their children are independent ... ave home! But her chores will come a ... sier if you give some thought to the ... ou treat her, and she'll be more than ... ul for your co-operation.

... PHIPPS (Glitterband)
... think my mum is great. A mother has ... to be really feminine and quite ... stly when you're a boy your ideal ... an is your mother, and as you start ... g girls out you tend to compare them ... r. Also, your mum makes a lot of ... ices for you, whether you realise ... the time or not.

... ngs like, turning clothes the right ... out before putting them out to be ... ed. Putting things back where you ... them, if you've been amusing yourself ... cooking session or have been using the ... n for your own private hobbies. ... g sure that if you do a job around the ..., you don't make two more in the ... ss, such as doing some washing up but ... g the sink clogged with tea leaves!

... PAUL
... o me, my mum's perfect. I don't ... any faults in her, she's probably got ... ad, just like everybody else, but I ... see them, so to me she's faultless!

LINDA BLAIR (Sixteen year old star of The Exorcist.)
My mom and me get on great because she understands that I'm not a kid anymore. That means she lets me dress up in some tight jeans, and clothes that don't look like they come from the "children's department!" A mom should always remember what it's like to be young.

And remember too, that though she works for you happily for 99% of the time, it's hardly fair for one person to take on ALL the chores when there are others who share the use of the house. When you DO tackle chores, do it with a good heart — add a smile, not a grudging look! Maybe after doing the shopping, you could put the things away — if you go to the launderette, you could fold the stuff or hang it to dry when you get back.

ANDREW SEARL (14) Eltham, London SE9.
A mother looks after you and helps to keep you looking neat and tidy. She always encourages you to entertain your friends and will always buy the necessary food and stuff to help things along, but in return you should respect her and assist her whenever possible.

Because if your mum feels that you appreciate what she does, and try to help when you can with a good heart, she won't turn into . . .

A NAGGER!

If you claim you have a nagging mum, it's as good as owning up to being a lazy, selfish member of the family! Not fair on you? Well, there ARE mums who nag simply for the sake of it, but they are VERY rare — and most of those get that way because their families are so unco-operative!

So, for your own sake, look at the situation afresh. If you're on the wrong end of a good nagging, ask yourself if you could beat her to it next time! If you know that sooner or later you have to get around to doing a certain chore, then do yourself a favour by getting it done and over with, promptly. That cuts out the possibility of nagging. If you get nagged because you genuinely have a poor memory, get a nice big jotter, and write things down, and check the pad regularly for things that may have slipped your mind.

HARVEY ELLISON (Glitterband)
Unfortunately I lost my mum when I was 12, so I really miss not having her around. So really it's difficult for me to say what I reckon are the qualities of a mother. All I do know is any kid who has lost his mum realises just how much he has lost.

PETER McDONALD (15) Bexley, Kent.
My mum's very lenient and lets me make up my own mind about most things but not to the extent of letting me take advantage. She's always concerned that I get my homework done first and then allows me as much freedom as I want. My mum's great!

Nagging often starts when you've grown older, need more freedom and tend to break the rules that were set when you were much younger. So, instead of simply breaking the rules and making trouble for yourself, a fair, calm discussion often helps a mum to see things differently. You may not get ALL you ask for — but if you compromise, you'll both win . . . and the nagging should stop.

Because, of course, nobody really enjoys nagging . . . and what a Mum wants most of all is for you to accept her for what she sets out to be . . .

RAY MITCHELL (14) Liverpool.
A mum is a female who comes into my bedroom in the morning forcing me to wake up and go to school. A mum repairs my clothes when I ruin them playing football. A mum expects you to be nice to your horrid little sister and her horrible little friends. I love my mum.

YOUR VERY BEST FRIEND

Treated right, a mum can be just that. Tick off the qualities you expect from a first-class friendship, and though you'll probably find most girls you know *don't* come up to this standard, your mum can!

After all — she's LOYAL — she wouldn't dish dirt about you with somebody else or suddenly drop you cold and start making a fuss about somebody else's daughter!

She's HONEST — you can ask her what she thinks, and she'll tell you! It may hurt your pride occasionally, but you know she doesn't say things to deliberately wreck your self-confidence or to put you off someone because she's hoping to get off with that person herself!

SUZI QUATRO
My mother is Hungarian and my father's Italian — a funny mixture! I had a pretty happy childhood and got on quite well with my mother — not brilliantly, but not bad — I was always the rebellious one, so I suppose I gave her a lot of trouble. Now we're apart for such a lot of time we get on much better. She's very religious — a strong Catholic — and if she cares for somebody she'll say a prayer for them. We're not over-close, but she's a good lady.

IAN GARDNER, Edinburgh.
I'm an only child and as I no longer have a father I'm possibly more close to my mother than most boys of my age. We get on fantastically well and she treats me more like a friend than a son, and I think that this kind of relationship with your parents is very important.

She's RELIABLE — she'll still be your loving mum in ten years' time . . . can you say the same about any other friendship with real certainty?

She's HELPFUL — she may moan, but she's about the only person you can rely on to help you out of a jam, whatever it is! Even good friends may jib at being asked to give up their own spare time to help YOU . . . specially if it's your own carelessness that has got you into a mess!

MARIE OSMOND
As I'm the only girl in our family I'm very close to my mum. In fact it's quite uncanny how our tastes are exactly the same and Mom says I look the same as, she did when she was young! If I ever have any problems she's the first person I go to. Once I was asked who's the most beautiful woman in the world, I said, "My mom" and I meant it. I've learnt so much from her — we both love cooking and dressmaking, we also love going shopping together — we always seem to buy an incredible amount and always end up taking extra trunks home!

She's GENEROUS — maybe she can't afford always to be as generous with actual money as she would like, but she's generous with the important things, like her time, her affection, her patience. There's not much you could ask a mum for that she'd refuse without a really good reason — friends tend to be more self-centred!

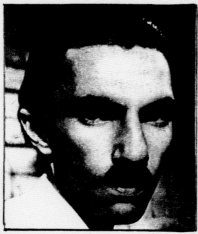

RON MAEL (Sparks)
A mum is very similar to a dad in that both are the same spelt forwards or backwards!

And if you still can't think of your mum as a "best friend" — maybe it's because the fun has gone out of the relationship. Fun??? Who are we kidding! But it COULD be fun . . . if you both work at it. Meaning, that you take the trouble to share jokes — that when you get home, you don't just turn off the liveliness and personality that makes you popular with friends, only showing a grouchy face to the family! Having fun together means working it so that you and your mum can have time off together occasionally — even if it means helping with the chores so you can relax later. She won't be much fun if she's working non-stop with never a second to spare!

In fact, the best advice we can possibly give you is forget she's your mum — treat her instead as if she were any other human being, with a certain amount of considera-tion, affection, respect for her point of view — even if you think she's wrong.

And then, quite soon, you'll find out for yourself what a mum is . . . and you'll be very, very glad you've got one!

OILY SKIN

OILY skins benefit greatly from face packs and there are loads of lovely ones to make or to buy if you haven't got much time. No turning your noses up at the ones to make, either, they're all tried and tested and include loads of pure ingredients that can do wonders for your skin!

Have A Lemon Mask
A lemon mask will lighten and brighten your skin and will even help to bleach a fading suntan (that's a tip to remember for when summer's over!). Lemon masks are usually for oily skin although this one is suitable for normal skin as well.

Squeeze half a lemon and mix the juice with the yolk of one egg. Return the mixture to the empty lemon half so that oils from the skin can be absorbed. Leave it to stand for about two hours if you've got the time and then spread the mixture on to your skin, avoiding the delicate area around your eyes. Leave for 15 minutes and then sponge away with warm water and apply a light film of moisturiser afterwards.

Lemon packs to buy are, Lemon in the Boots 17 Country Clear range, 10p, or Lem-Pak Beauty Mask, also 10p.

Have An Apple Mask
An apple mask will help to reduce the flow of oil from greasy sections of the skin like around the nose and chin — and can help to reduce the tendency for spots in these areas.

All you do is grate a little cooking apple and apply to the greasy areas . . . you'll have to lie down for this (obviously) or the apple will fall off! Strawberry, tomato, orange or grapefruit slices are all good alternatives and have the same effect.

Have An Egg Mask
Make up an egg mask to clean and revitalise oily skin.

Mix one egg with two teaspoons of lemon, orange or grapefruit juice or with a piece of cucumber about an inch long, grated. Spread the mask on to your face and allow it to act for 15 minutes before washing off with warm water.

Other masks to buy for oily skins are Boots No.7 Mud Face Pack, 43p, Boots 17 Mint Pack in the Country Clear range, 10p a sachet, Innoxa 41, 8p a sachet, Anne French Glow 5 Mask, about 10p, or try Rimmel's Oatmeal Beauty Pack, about 18p a tube.

NORMAL TO DRY SKIN

A GENTLE face pack should leave a normal or dry skin feeling clean and fresh but certainly not taut and stiff. Remember that all face packs will be slightly drying so be sure to choose a mild one if your skin is dry.

Have A Milk Mask
Milk is very soothing and a good cleanser as well.

Make your own milk mask by mixing a piece of fresh baker's yeast (about the size of a walnut) with enough milk to form a thick cream. Spread the mixture very thinly on to your face and neck avoiding eyes and mouth. Leave on for about 10 minutes, then wash away with warm water.

Have A Porridge Mask
This is another kind of milk mask, but this time with porridge oats.

Heat two tablespoons of porridge oats in a little milk to make a soft "porridge." Add three teaspoons of rosewater (from most chemists) and when the mixture has cooled to just warm, spread it over face and neck. Leave on for about 15 minutes and then sponge off with lukewarm water.

Have An Egg Mask
Make an egg mask to cleanse and dry skin.

Mix the yolk of an egg with a few drops of olive oil and spread on to face and neck. Rinse off with warm water after about 15 minutes.

Packs to buy are Boots 17 Peach Mask in the Country Clear range, 10p a sachet, Christy's Lanoline Beauty Mask, 10p a sachet, Boots No. 7 Egg and Milk mask for dry skin, 14p a sachet, Yeast Pac Beauty Mask, 9½p.

THOSE are the two main categories, but there are other masks such as Almay's Deep Mist Gentle Mask, 80p, for sensitive skin, and Innoxa's White Mask Facial about 8p, which is great for refining large pores.

Make yourself a delicious yogurt and herb pack to lighten and clear the skin and help to close up large pores. Mix three tablespoons of plain yogurt with some very finely chopped mint or fresh sage, apply the pack and leave it on for about 15 minutes before washing off with warm water.

If you have an Elder Flower tree in your garden or nearby you can make a pack that is said to tone down freckles and brighten the skin. Mix chopped Elder Flowers (*not* berries) with enough plain yogurt to make a spreadable paste and allow the mixture to stand for about an hour. Spread on to face and neck and wash off with warm water after about 15 minutes.

Finally, how about a stewed lettuce mask for softening rough or "orange peel" skin? Take some lettuce leaves (the limp ones that aren't any good for a salad) and stew them for a little while with a little water until they're soft and limp. Strain, and when cool, press the lettuce pack on to your face and neck-remove after 10 or 15 minutes. This pack is really mild and can be used as often as three times a week.

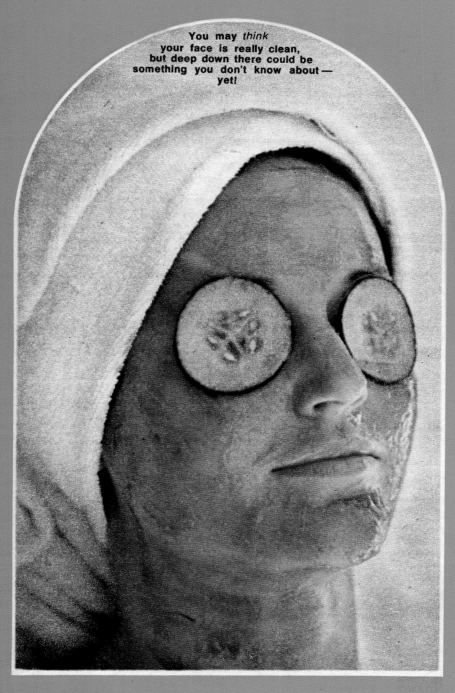

You may think your face is really clean, but deep down there could be something you don't know about — yet!

BEAUTY BOX

DOWN UNDER

EVER tried a face pack? They're great fun to use and can make loads of difference to your skin. You can buy them or try your hand at making your own . . . consider stewed lettuce on your face, for instance, or porridge oats and milk!

So what's the point of a face mask? Well, it could bring roses to pale, wan cheeks, it could lighten and brighten a sallow, dingy skin, temporarily tighten up enlarged pores and generally deep-cleanse your whole face. A face mask can also help to dry an oily skin, moisten and soften a dry skin and banish unwanted blackheads!

The wrong pack for your particular skin-type can do more harm than good, though, so make sure you don't use a pack for oily skin if yours is dry, or vice versa.

Many people make the mistake of thinking that a good wash or cleanse, tone and moisturise routine has just the same effect as a face pack. Not true! A face pack actually draws dirt and grime to the surface, because all those little glands in your face are working extra hard to try to help get rid of the mask which is covering your face and stopping air from getting to it!

It's obvious that you shouldn't use a face pack too often if you've got a dry skin . . . you'd be removing far too much of what little moisture there is in your skin to start with! Once every two weeks will be plenty, and do try to make sure that the pack is specially made for dry skin. Oily-skins *need* deep cleansing often, on the other hand, so a pack twice a week wouldn't be too much.

All prices approximate

SUNNY SIDES UP!

SEE yourself basking in beautiful bikinis; stretched out on the golden sand, lounging about at the local pool or just lying on the lawn.

Whatever you do, you're going to need a new bikini or two, and the best time to buy them is now . . . so water you waiting for?

1. Super new bikini from Dorothy Perkins. The bottom is elasticated and the top has halter and back ties.
   Style No.: 1704. Price:£2.99. Fabric: Cotton. Colours: Mauve, red, navy, lime. Sizes: 10 to 14.

2. Two bikinis in one . . . reversible bikini from Dorothy Perkins. The bottom has bows at the sides and the top has halter and back ties.
   Style No.: 1713. Price £2.99. Fabric: Cotton/vincel. Colours: Lime/black, red/navy, brown/beige. Sizes: 10 to 14.

3. Pretty bikini from Brettles, with plain bottom and tie-front top with halter neck.
   Style No.: 6042. Price: £3.99. Fabric: Crimplene Jersey. Colours: Turquoise, brown or red prints. Sizes: 10 to 16.

4. Super, striped bikini with halter and back ties and horizontally striped bottom, from Dorothy Perkins.
   Style No.: 1700. Price: £2.50. Fabric: Cotton. Colours: Navy, red, brown, lime. Sizes: Small, medium, large.

5. Floral print bikini from Silhouette. Top has a metal catch at the front and halter tie.
   Style No.: S641. Price: Approx. £6.50. Fabric: Lycra tricot. Colours: Blue/orange, orange/brown, pink/mauve. Sizes: 10 to 14.

6. Flattering, denim-look bikini with tiny straps and halter neck, from Palmer's Swimwear.
   Style No.: GH7069. Price: £3.50. Fabric: 100% cotton. Colours: Blue only. Sizes: 10 to 16.

7. Bandeau top bikini from Dorothy Perkins. The top is elasticated at the front, ties at the back and has detachable halter straps, the bottom is elasticated.
   Style No.: 1729. Price: £4.99. Fabric: Cotton. Colours: Black or navy print. Sizes: 10 to 14.

8. Pretty, toning bikini with back catch and adjustable straps which can be attached to the back strap or made into a halter, from Marks & Spencer.
   Style No.: 1175/3308. Price: £2.99. Fabric: Nylon/lycra tricot. Colours: Green/yellow, purple/pink, brown/orange. Sizes: 10 to 14.

WHERE TO FIND THEM

Dorothy Perkins bikinis from all branches. Brettles bikini from Waterloo House Ltd., 98 Lower Marsh, Waterloo, London S.E.1.; Irene, 427 Oldham Road, Rochdale; Mason, High Street, Dumbarton. Marks & Spencer bikini from a range at most stores. Palmer's bikini by post from Quality Post Ltd., Dept. 62/482, Granville Street, Worsley, Manchester M28 5RA. The price of the bikini includes postage and packing. Silhouette bikini from Barker's, London W.8.; John Lewis, London W.1.; Dickins & Jones, Regent Street, London W.1.; Daly's of Glasgow; Co-op, Plymouth; Rackham's, Birmingham; Keddies, Southend; Isaac Walton, Newcastle; Enquiries to Silhouette, 84-86 Baker Street, London W1M 2AU.

ALL PRICES APPROXIMATE.

GOOD FOR MUM

A lot of people moan about their mums quite a bit, but how would they feel if they had no mum to nag about?

They don't realise how lucky they are. They have their mums to help solve their problems, someone waiting for them at home after school or work, their meals ready for them, and most of their washing done for them.

We lost our mum three years ago, and I do quite a bit of housework and cooking, and look after my two brothers.

If I had one wish, it would be that my mum would come walking through the front door again.

Yvonne Cozens,
Lancing,
Sussex.

PETER PAN?

I thought I'd write and tell you how great I think young kids are. A few days ago, I was talking to Steve, a small friend of mine who is the grand old age of five, and I asked him what he wanted to be when he grew up. Normally kids spend all their time wishing they were grown up, while the "grown ups" wish they were younger, so I was very surprised to hear him say sadly, "I don't want to grow up."

I think he's got the right idea, don't you? Enjoy life and don't worry about the future; it catches up with you too quickly!!

Julia Parratt,
Salisbury,
Wiltshire.

DANCE IT AWAY

Many people complain about tidying bedrooms, but I've found a good way to get down to this horrible chore! Turn on the radio and find some really lively music. Start dancing, and as you float by, put everything away.

Further advantages are that you gain a happy mum, and lose some weight!

G. Robinson,
St Albans,
Hertfordshire.

SLIMMER'S DREAM

If only I could try to slim,
And keep away from that bread bin;
Put the biscuits on the shelf
And try to discipline myself.
I'd cook and smell those tasty chips
And then I'd look towards my hips.
To cream cakes offered I'd say "No!"
And crisps would be the next to go.
I'll always try to stick to lettuce,
And get into a size twelve dress.
But I'm afraid it's just a whim —
Do I *really* want to slim?"

Theresa Cullen,
Wigan,
Lancashire.

money savers

If you have an almost empty bottle of nail varnish which has become thick, put a few drops of acetone (nail varnish remover) in the bottle and shake well. This makes the varnish useable again and saves money on getting a new bottle.

Jacky Radbourne,
Warwickshire.

YOUR letters

It's been a cream cake week this week; what with two birthdays in the office and other minor celebrations like finding flats and it being Friday afternoon, we've been munching contentedly every tea-time. Not much originality among this lot though — you just know Pam's going to pick a custard tart, Alison's long been associated with cream doughnuts, and the Ed. unfailingly goes for cream-oozing vanilla slices. I'm the only one to try something different every time!

Watching the eating processes is better than the circus, too — tongues running along the creamy bit of eclairs, puff pastries taken layer by layer, and Ingrid *has* been known to demolish a cream bun in two bites — and then pretend it was never there at all!

Carry on writing — interesting, funny, original letters are worth celebrating, too — the address is Sam at Jackie, 185 Fleet Street, London EC4A 2HS. If I print your letter, you'll win £1, and if it's the Star Letter of the week you can choose from a Boots 17 Make-Up Kit, a Pifco Go-Girl Hairdryer, a £4 record voucher or £4 in cash. And remember — all letters must be original.

A REAL GAS!

A rather embarrassing thing happened to me a short while ago — though looking back it seems very funny now.

I dashed out of school in my customary graceless manner at the end of the day, and almost fell into a hole which some workmen had just dug outside the school. In reply to the workmens' suppressed guffaws, I asked them if they were digging for gold. One of them answered "No, love, gas" — only due to his accent, and the noise of the drill, I thought he'd said "guess"! "Water?" said I intelligently; "No — gas," replied he. "Er-Electricity?" asked I, somewhat less hopefully. "No, gas," he said more emphatically. "Um, well what on earth are you digging for, then?" I asked brightly. Say no more! Was my face red as I skulked round the corner to escape their unsuppressed laughter!!

Jenny Siddall,
Gt. Abington,
Cambridgeshire.

This week's star letter wins £4 in cash.

LOVE AT LAST SIGHT?

I would like to tell you about how I met my boyfriend.

One Friday night, our gang got together and went down to the monthly disco. As soon as I entered, I saw him. He was sitting all alone in the corner. As time went on, I noticed he was staring at me more and more and soon he asked me to dance. I thought it was love at first sight, but not quite so!

It wasn't until he was walking me home that we realised we worked at the same place. We must have passed each other hundreds of times, but never given each other a second glance!

David Essex Fan,
North Lancing,
Sussex.

(Now, if they had a few low lights and some records going at work . . . – Sam)

MAKING A SPLASH

After browsing through some magazines the other day, I came to the conclusion that this summer's beachwear is absolutely ridiculous.

Don't get the idea that I'm some kind of old-fashioned eccentric who expects everyone to be walking around with leggings down to their knees and necklines up near their chins, either. I just think that most swimsuits are too scanty for comfort — for example, look at those bikinis held together with little strings at the sides! These costumes are fine if you want to lie on the sand all day, looking like a model girl, but when you get someone like me who loves splashing about, you want something you feel confident and look good in, not something you're worried is going to fall off at any moment!

So what about it, costume designers?

Carollyn Porter,
Suffolk.

MAKING CONTACT

A letter to all you specs wearers.

For eight years I have had to wear glasses — but no more! I've taken the plunge and got contact lenses. They are, I must admit, rather expensive, but if you're a student or are still at school, you may find an optician who will give you a student discount.

So shop around if you're thinking of investing in a pair of these marvellous inventions! They do take some getting used to, but it's really worth the effort, and you could find that they're just what you need to boost your confidence!

Ruth Taylor,
Beeston,
Notts.

BIRDS WHO'VE FLOWN

Although I've the best family a girl could wish for, I decided to leave home and share a flat with three other girls. Life away from home wasn't easy by any means, and I often felt like giving it all up, but we all stuck it out together despite quarrels and differences. On reflection I think each one of us has learnt the real meaning of self-respect and independence and, most important, how to give and take, share and care.

But I would not advise any other "Jackie" readers to do the same as me unless they are determined to face the hard "rubs" of independence instead of the soft sponging off their parents.

Are there any other "Jackie" readers who would add anything on this important subject of "freedom," I wonder?

Abbey Redmayne,
Fife,
Scotland.

STARS IN YOUR EYES

Further to the letter in a recent "Jackie" about pop stars saying what kind of girls they go for, I'd like to make a comment.

I've often seen girls read descriptions of their idol's perfect girl, then do everything they can to change to fit the bill. Hair suddenly becomes short and curly, jeans change to long skirts, make-up is strained to its limits to alter whole face shapes.

Why don't they consider just being themselves? After all, someone somewhere is the right person for you — just as you are; and he'll be a star in your eyes, anyway!

Jackie Reader,
Warley,
W. Midlands.

WELL—VARNISHED

I've just got to tell all you "Jackie" readers about my brainwave.

I suggest you start using nail varnish — but not just on your nails: it's super for painting other things, too.

A couple of ideas I've carried out are collecting and painting shells and making beautiful little mosaic patterns with them, and painting bottles which then make great ornaments.

So get down to your chemist's and buy up all those cut-price discontinued colours — and get your imagination working!

David Essex Fan,
Bootle,
Liverpool.

teenscope

for the week beginning Saturday, July 12

CANCER (June 21 — July 21)
You may have to make a now-or-never decision about your love life this week, but whatever you decide — don't go back on it. Time to take a chance where a sudden opportunity is concerned — it'll pay off. Good news within the family circle makes everyone around you feel a lot brighter.

LEO (July 22 — Aug. 21)
A change of outlook which could be connected with your career may keep you busy fact-finding and writing letters this week. Keep your temper and refuse to be upset by someone who tries to make you look a fool in front of others — you'll show yourself in a new light if you assert yourself.

VIRGO (Aug. 22 — Sept. 21)
You may feel your friends aren't so friendly this week. Take their words with a pinch of salt, though, because they won't be saying what they really mean, and you'll have to wait to find out the real truth. Don't get too possessive with someone you haven't known long — you could frighten them off. You'll be feeling very calm and happy by the weekend.

LIBRA (Sept. 22 — Oct. 22)
You'll be busy with lots of light-hearted goings-on this week — shopping, sightseeing and writing letters. Make sure you don't ignore a friend who's in need of some practical advice.

SCORPIO (Oct. 23 — Nov. 21)
Travel plans are much in evidence this week, but things don't turn out quite the way you'd hoped! You could do a spot of matchmaking for a friend — but the boy in question isn't likely to be as pleased as you think. Wednesday could be especially lucky for you.

SAGITTARIUS (Nov. 22 — Dec. 21)
Watch out for another girl who could become your rival — she may try to take someone you fancy from right under your nose. It's not a week when anything really exciting happens. Watch out for an interesting letter on Thursday, though; and the weekend may turn out quite unexpectedly.

CAPRICORN (Dec. 22 — Jan. 19)
You could meet someone really interesting this week, but may later find that he's already booked! Don't give up, though — things may change very soon. You could suspect a secret regarding a close friend — but she doesn't want to talk about it yet, so curb your curiosity. Pink suits your mood and will be lucky for you.

AQUARIUS (Jan. 20 — Feb. 18)
You may feel that a family outing is standing in the way of a good time at the weekend, but go along with them and you could have a pleasant surprise! You could have the wrong idea about a guy you met recently, so save any decisions for the future.

PISCES (Feb. 19 — March 20)
Secrets abound this week — everyone seems to be whispering about something and it may get you annoyed. Hold onto your purse at the weekend — bargains aren't all they seem. A meeting with someone special towards the end of the week gives you a lot of pleasure.

ARIES (March 21 — April 20)
There could be some family upheavals this week — keep clear if you can! That boy you've fancied for so long — could be he'll finally notice you towards the end of the week. Fiery colours are lucky for you — wear some at the weekend.

TAURUS (April 21 — May 20)
You may have been made unhappy by friends lately, but this week sees an improvement in your relationships with them. This happier atmosphere extends to your love life, too — steadier relationships will seem much steadier, and those on their own could have some exciting meetings!

GEMINI (May 21 — June 20)
You could be all set for a financial crisis this week — there's something you desperately want and there just isn't cash around. Love is a whole lot happier though — someone is beginning to miss you when you aren't around. Good news by letter towards the end of the week.

HEAVENLY BODIES!

The latest in our series of cuddly zodiac characters, designed and created exclusively for you by Malcolm Bird and Alan Dart, is appealing Aquarius!

She's simple to make, and looks as though she'll create quite a splash in her stunning striped bathing costume and red hat! Make her to add to your own collection, or for that special Aquarian friend.

Watch out for the next in our series, Pisces, some time soon.

INSTRUCTIONS FOR MAKING YOUR ZODIAC CHARACTER

MATERIALS — 8½ in. squares of felt in white and flesh; a small amount of red felt; scraps of pink and brown felt; a skein of Anchor stranded cotton in black; white and flesh cottons; Kapok for stuffing; a tube of clear adhesive; red Dylon Color Fun fabric paint, or a red felt-tipped pen, or 60 cms of ½-in. wide red ribbon.

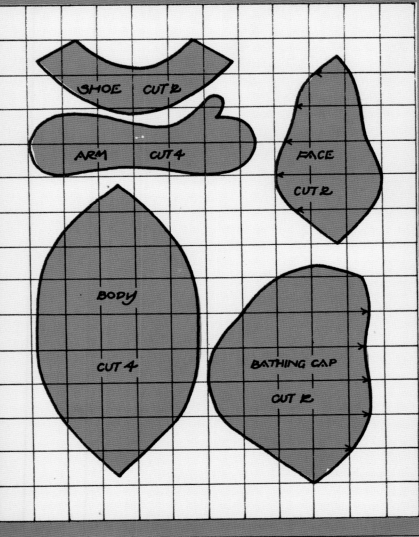

TO MAKE — Following diagram make pattern pieces in paper, each square representing 1 cm. Also cut a paper rectangle 3.5 cm x 4.5 cm for legs.

From flesh felt cut face, arms and legs. From white felt cut body. From red felt cut bathing cap. From brown felt cut shoes and two circles the size of one-pence pieces for shoe soles.

With black thread oversew face and bathing cap pieces, matching up arrowed edges, and leave a space open. Stuff firmly and oversew opening.

With white oversew body pieces together in pairs along one side. Either paint, use felt tip, or glue on ribbon for stripes.

With black oversew the two body halves together, leaving a space open. Stuff firmly and oversew opening.

Sew head to body.

With flesh cotton sew seams of arms, starting at thumb and finishing at shoulder.

Oversew top seam of arms in black, leaving a space open. Stuff firmly and oversew opening. Glue hand tips together, then position and glue arms to body.

With black thread oversew shoe tops to base of legs, fold in half lengthways and oversew leg seam, then sew soles to shoes. Stuff firmly. Position and sew legs to body, then glue shoes together.

Cut two pink circles for cheeks and a triangle for nose. Position and glue to face. Separate three strands from black thread and use to embroider eyes and mouth, and to oversew cheeks.

MADGE and BERYL

IT WILL BE SUNNY ALL DAY!

GOOD. I WON'T NEED AN UMBRELLA, BERYL

BUT, BUT..

HMPH!

I DID TRY TO TELL YOU THAT ALL THE BEST WEATHER FORECASTERS ARE ALWAYS WRONG!

MALCOLM BIRD

WEEKSPOT

Something nice or silly or both for you to do every day.

SUNDAY. Write all those Thank-You letters for your lovely Christmas presents now (even the Pink Carnation talc from your great-aunt!). Otherwise you may not get anything next year! Seriously though, people really do appreciate it.

MONDAY. Doodle. Then frame the best one and fool everyone into believing it's an early (very early) Picasso.

TUESDAY. If you've got short hair, make yourself some woollen plaits and swing 'em! (Lots of thin ones look great with long hair too!)

WEDNESDAY. Finish something you started last year. Like that scarf, that book, or that argument!

THURSDAY. Play some sitar music (Ravi Shankar is best) to your plant, and watch it move towards the music. Rumour has it that it will, honestly! Speak to it kindly and see how much better it grows.

FRIDAY. Pin some travel-agency posters of sunny Mediterranean seas or African skies on your bedroom wall, to warm yourself up through the coming cold months.

SATURDAY. Start being extra-specially nice to all those fellas you like. They may just get the hint in time for Valentine's Day.

Ed's Letter

I don't know how you feel about it, but to me, January is the greyest time of all. Of course, it's the weather—freezing cold and horrible. Somehow I always fool myself into thinking that as soon as we've turned the corner of the year it must start getting warmer and warmer. It's rather like going out to post a letter and expecting a reply to be waiting for you on your return—you know it can't possibly be true, but you can't help hoping all the same!

The only chills that are positively enjoyable at the moment are the ones we get reading Nicole Revin's specially-written serial "The Haunting Of Lucy Merrow". Sam read the whole story in broad daylight in the middle of the office and turned white as a sheet—so don't say you haven't been warned!

Actually there is one good thing about January—the sales. If they're still on in your area, and you're quite handy with a needle, then the place to go is the fabric department of any large store. This is the time when you really can pick up bargains.

It doesn't take an awful lot of material to make a blouse, for instance, so it might only cost a few pence to make one of the tops shown on this week's Fashion Page, "Getting Shirty". Can't sew? Then learn—you can't afford not to these days.

"How Do You Doodle" I wonder? I think the article on our revealing scribbles is absolutely fascinating—except for one thing: it doesn't explain mine. You see, I can only draw one thing, like this . . .

Those of you who did Botany at school may recognise it—it's a broad bean! Now don't ask me why I draw it—or what it means, because I don't know either!

Next week is a very special week for all Osmond fans—so mark the occasion of the Osmonds' visit, and to say 'Welcome back' from all of us here, we've got a super double-page pin-up of Donny and Marie, together for you. Plus a beauty feature all about the amazing things that yoga can do for you and the final part of our picture story serial, "A Time To Live, A Time To Die".

Have a nice week. *The Ed*

your A B C of Dating

GOING out with a boy can be lots of fun. In fact it's just as easy as ABC! And we've compiled an ABC of our own to help you on your way. So to start at the beginning . . .

ATTRACT: **You will, if you show you're interested in him.** If you shut up like a clam every time he comes near, he just won't know that deep down you're burning to get to know him. So take your courage in both hands and break the ice. If he's shy too, he'll really appreciate it!

BOYFRIEND: Never introduce him as this, boys hate it. Always use his name. Boys don't like to feel they're owned by anybody, even the girl they love. And don't presume that you're always going to do everything together, without bothering to wait for him to ask you. Always remember that he's not just an extension of you, he's an individual with his own likes and dislikes, his own hopes and dreams.

CATTY: Don't be. Boys may laugh when you make cracks about other girls, but are secretly afraid you may make fun of *them* on the quiet, too. Also boys usually find catty chit-chat pretty boring after a while, so make sure you keep his interest when you talk, that way you'll keep him, too!

DOUBLE DATE: Fun if you all four really enjoy going out together, but murder if you don't. Try not to get involved in blind dates; when your friend says "I just know you'll love . . ." you probably won't! But if it happens to you, make the best of it, you might even enjoy yourself!

END: When you feel it's almost over, be kind and tell him. Don't just drag on, being cool and hope he'll get the message. That's just a waste of time for both of you. Tell him that you'd like to stay friends, he might be a good one! If he ends it with you — give yourself time to cry and feel the sorrow; then like the song says all you can do is "Pick yourself up, dust yourself down, and start all over again!"

FLIRT: Why not — as long as you BOTH know it's just for fun. Otherwise it's heartless.

GIGGLES: Pointless, off-putting and a sign of nerves. Hide your shyness under a smile — it's much more attractive. Nothing makes a boy feel more uncomfortable than a girl who giggles uncontrollably whenever he says something. If you're confident that you look your best, are really interested in what he's saying and so feeling relaxed, you shouldn't be attacked by a fit of the giggles.

HANGER-ON: Don't be. Don't stick around your friend when she's with her boy friend, playing gooseberry. You'll feel happier on your own, and you'll have a much better chance of getting a boy yourself!

I-I-I: Have you listened to yourself lately? Do you sound like a record that's stuck on the I? If so, HE won't be for long (stuck on you that is!). Read the newspapers, take an interest in what's going on around you and you'll find that you won't talk about yourself so much.

JEALOUS: Say you never are and we'll say you can't really care! Everybody who loves somebody is jealous from time to time, it's part of life. The important thing is never to let it show, or make you do something you might regret later — like throwing a tantrum and pulling that blonde bombshell's hair! Boys don't like jealous, possessive girls who watch their every move. Remember — if you try to tie him up, he'll want to roam!

KISSING: If it embarrasses you — don't! If he's worth kissing anyway, he'll have the patience to wait!

LOVE: Show it in all kinds of ways. By putting him before you, being romantic, being a friend, always being loyal and letting him know you CARE.

MAKING UP: If you love him it doesn't matter who says sorry first. Don't let false pride prevent you from making the first move. That's the easiest way to break up a relationship. Remember love isn't a contest with points deducted if you're the one to break first !

NAG: You never do! Do you?

OLDER: He's older than you or you're older than him. So what's the difference if you get on together? As long as your parents are happy about him — go ahead. A few years' age difference is unimportant.

PARENTS: They all worry about you, even if they try not to show it. Do put their minds at rest and let them meet your boy. Get him to collect you from home sometimes. Once they realise he's not a teenage werewolf, or an old sugar daddy, they'll relax, which will make you relax too!

QUESTIONS: A good way to get a conversation going is by asking questions. Ask him what music he likes, where he goes at nights, whether he likes football or any other sports. But don't fire them at him machine gun style or he'll run for cover!

ROWS: Serious? Better look around for someone else. Trivial? Why are you wasting your time getting het up over nothing, can't you think of anything better to do when you're together? Seriously, everyone has rows from time to time, they clear the air and can do your relationship good. But don't make a habit of them, or he could start looking round for someone less aggressive.

SCENES: You'll never make it with him, if you make them!

TIME: Make a big effort not to be late for your dates, nothing annoys a boy more. Never keep him waiting for more than ten minutes if you can help it. And if your mum and dad have set a time limit to your dates, make sure you're home by the time they say. That way they'll think you're responsible and be ready to give you a bit more freedom.

US: The loveliest word in our alphabet guide. Never take your relationship for granted though, don't let it become boring and predictable. Once you know you've got him, don't stop bothering so much about the way you look. If you look a mess, it's just an insult to him and shows you don't care. Don't get into a routine, suggest new things to do, new places to go — and keep surprising him!

VAGUE: Don't be. Boys can't stand girls who can never make up their minds. Girls who never know where they want to go, what they want to do, who they want to do it with! You'll make a much bigger impact on him if you have a made-up mind.

WOLF: Don't fall for him, he can be a heart breaker if you take him seriously. He's not interested in a real relationship, he just wants to get you well and truly hooked before he moves on to the next girl, the next willing victim. Feel sorry for him, poor lad, he hasn't grown up yet.

X-X-X: Keep them private. There's nothing more sick-making than couples who are always indulging in heavy kissing sessions just where everybody can see them. Some girls think it proves how much their boy friend loves them. But most boys are embarrassed by this and don't like the way they feel about a girl being made public.

YOU: The most wonderful thing in his life. But don't let on for a moment that you agree with him!

ZAP: That's what you should bring to every date! It's the feeling that things are happening and he'd better stick around because it's going to be exciting. If you don't, he'll start to think that he could be bored by himself — and save money!

WHAT'S MISSING FROM YOUR LIFE?

BE warned — there's more to these pictures than meets the eye! There's something missing from each one, and your choice of what it is, will give away the clues to your personality!

So if you want to know what's missing in your life, just tell us what you think's missing from the pictures!

1. What should be in the centre of the fireplace?
(b) A magnificent gold statuette of a goddess, with surrounding cherubs, etc.
(a) A very pretty Dresden doll.
(d) A large Wedgewood plate with a peaceful pastoral scene.
(c) An intricately-patterned Chinese vase.

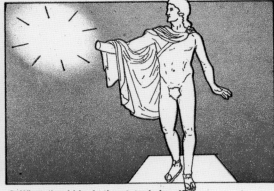

2. What should be in the statue's hand?
(d) A dove.
(b) A flaming torch.
(c) A sceptre.
(a) A wreath of flowers.

3. What should be in the centre of the island?
(b) A dense jungle.
(a) Lush countryside, with a huge lake in the middle.
(c) A weird landscape of rocks and volcanic mountain.
(d) Beautiful rolling hills, with an ancient, ruined monastery.

4. Which part of the castle is missing?
(a) A large, beautiful courtyard with miniature gardens and a summer house for lovers' meetings.
(c) Strange statues on large pillars, set around a chapel.
(d) The elegant castle lodge, complete with a huge lawn and fountain.
(b) Battlements and a look-out tower.

5. What kind of flowers should the boy be holding?
(b) Orchids.
(a) Roses.
(c) Sprigs of wild, meadow flowers.
(d) Snowdrops.

6. What does the missing door look like?
(a) A cottage door with planks across it, overgrown with creepers and pretty flowering plants.
(d) A plain, very heavy, dark wooden door.
(c) An arched doorway, heavily carved with designs in wood.
(b) A bright, panelled door with a gold lion's head door-knocker.

7. What stone is missing from her ring?
(d) A moonstone.
(b) An emerald.
(a) A sapphire.
(c) A ruby.

8. What should the figurehead on the ship be?
(a) A mermaid.
(c) A strange, African-type mask.
(d) A sea-gull.
(b) A warrior.

9. Who's the missing member of the group?
(b) An older brother, in magnificent soldier's uniform.
(c) An eccentric aunt in an Indian sari.
(a) An angelic little girl with flaxen ringlets.
(d) An older sister in a pretty white dress.

Now count your score — mainly (a) (b) (c) or (d), and read the conclusions.

CONCLUSIONS

Now you've ticked the missing alternatives, we'll tell you the meaning behind your choices. The idea is that the missing items which you've chosen symbolise the things you feel are missing from your own life — and there lies a clue to your personality.

So read on to find out what your subconscious has told you about yourself.

Mostly (a) — You're an emotional person, and at the moment you feel a lack of romance in your life. Your surroundings are too harsh for you — too lacking in sensitivity and feeling. You'd like to be able to trust and confide in people more, and most of all you'd like to communicate with them on a deeper level but you find it difficult to express your true feelings.

It's difficult to be an idealist, and find it difficult to accept harsh reality.

Don't let the missing elements in your life get you down, though. There is still plenty of romance around today, and if you haven't already found a very special person on your wavelength, don't give up. Many people feel as you do, and lots of boys, in their secret hearts, are really looking for a romantic, feminine girl like you!

Mostly (b) — You're the sort of person who thinks big, and won't accept anything commonplace or ordinary. Drama and excitement are the things you feel are missing in your life at the moment. Everything seems so dull and boring, and there doesn't seem to be any outlet for all the great dynamic ideas you have.

You really have to come to terms with the fact that everyone's life is largely made up of routine, day-to-day things — but that shouldn't stop you finding exciting, interesting life-style for yourself.

It's a horrible feeling being hemmed in and bored with drab surroundings, but you're basically a person with a lot of go. And if things seem deadly at the moment, your personality will inevitably lead you on to better things. Even if you have to fight for the sort of life you want!

Mostly (c) — A sense of wonder and creativity are the missing elements in your life. You're a dreamer and your mind's usually miles away, unable to gain satisfaction from the ordinary, day-to-day routine. You expect a lot from life and people, and so are often disappointed when things don't come up to your high expectations. Sometimes you retire to your ivory tower to be by yourself with your own thoughts.

Relaxation, as you've probably discovered, is one of the most difficult things to achieve in this age of hustle and bustle and unless you feel you just want to be by yourself. So do what you feel! Don't let other people influence you too much and try not to let them push you around. Go your own way and please yourself.

You're a truthful person with a great deal of sensitivity and if you learn to believe in yourself, you'll find things will be much easier for you.

Mostly (d) — Beauty and harmony are the things you feel are missing in your life at the moment — perhaps you need a bit of peace and quiet! Maybe you feel under pressure at home, school or work, or in your social life; or maybe you're not very happy at the moment.

This is why you tend to be attracted to anything strange and unusual and outside your own experience. You seem to be searching — for what you don't quite know! This can sometimes set you apart from others, but at the same time it makes you an interesting and unusual person!

You're a deep thinker, and will not accept life around you at face value. You feel the need to be constantly questioning yourself and your feelings.

David Cassidy

Jackie

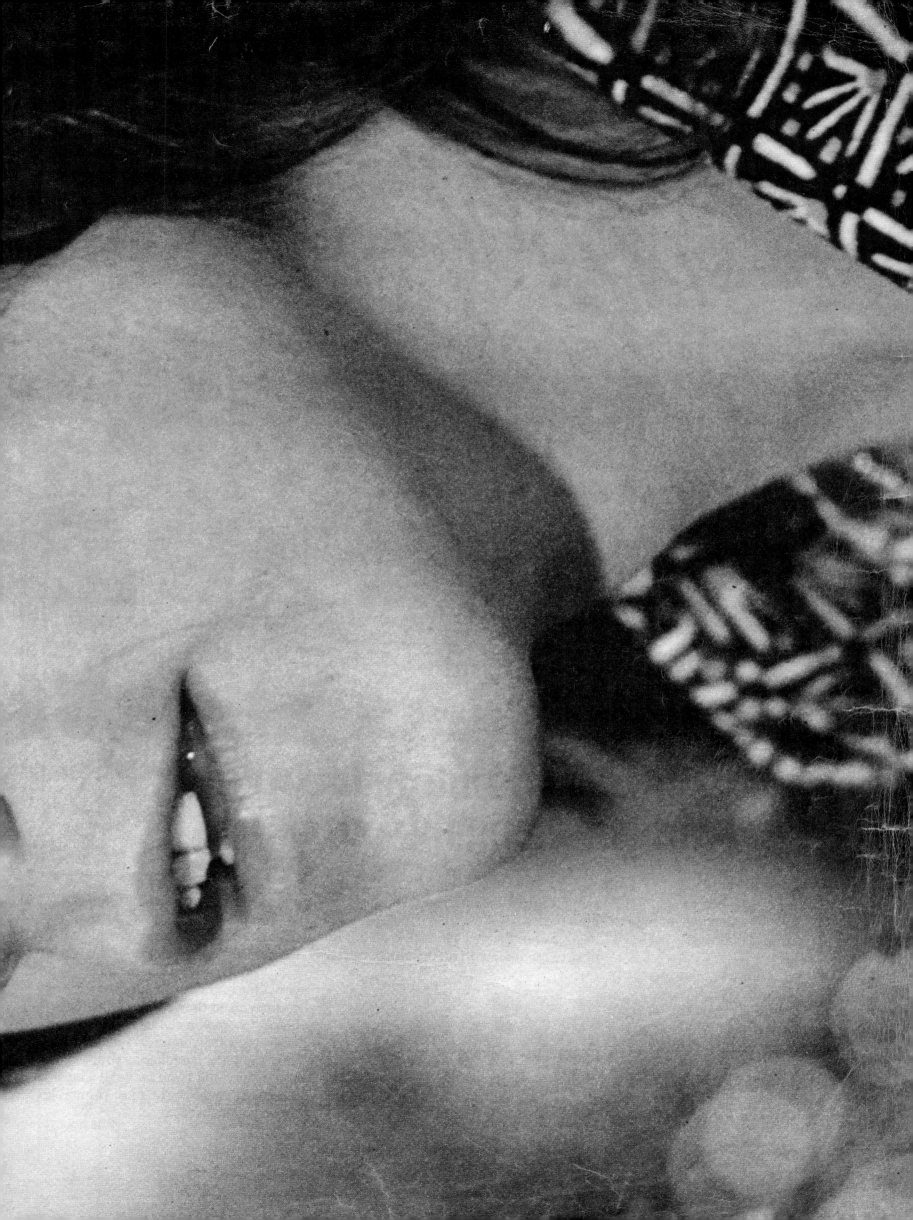

COVER STORIES

THE COVER STAR OF THE FIRST ISSUE OF *JACKIE*, way back in January 1964, was Cliff Richard. The artwork was a classic pose – hand up at his face and a wide grin baring such perfect, ultra-white teeth that he could easily have been starring in an ad for toothpaste.

The large masthead shouted out the name *Jackie* and the tagline made it clear who was the target audience. This brand new mag was "for go-ahead teens".

The wording promised to fulfil every young girl's desire, with full-colour pin-ups of Cliff, Elvis, Billy Fury and The Beatles, tips to make you more kissable, dreamy picture love stories, outfits to make you look pretty, even in the rain 'n' snow, plus way-out exclusives on all the "popsters". And let's not forget the FREE heart ring gift which was guaranteed to have you parting with your pocket money.

How could a teenage girl in the 60s possibly resist spending 6d (2½p) to get all this? You simply had to buy *Jackie* to be up on what was happening in the world of fashion, the juiciest pop star gossip and most importantly, get tips on how to find a fella. It was a real case of be there or be square!

So, what made *Jackie* stand out on the shelves? One contributing factor had to be its size. *Jackie* was far bigger than its competitors. Handbag-size would never have worked for the ever-popular pin-ups. Who would want a mini pic of David Cassidy when you could fill your entire bedroom wall with an enormous three-part poster?

The key to success for any magazine is engagement with its target audience through strong images and enticing wording. *Jackie* achieved this week after week, which is amazing when you consider the original lead time was a lengthy twelve weeks (the period between going to press and hitting the shops). The lead time gradually decreased over the years to a measly six weeks. But compare that to today's world and you realise what a challenge the magazine faced. Nowadays, as soon as a story breaks it's immediately out there all over the world via different forms of communication from mobiles to the Internet and multi-channel television.

Although every cover was put together with the same love and attention, some stood out for a variety of reasons!

The 15 January issue in 1971 featured a model dressed from top to toe in a crocheted outfit, complete with matching hat. It's just as well the fashion police weren't on duty! Throughout the Swinging Sixties the overall look was hippie and romantic. Several covers featured models wearing a dreamy expression and often sporting an enormous floppy hat. Others had loved-up couples, with the girls showing off their beautiful bodies in not too skimpy bikinis for summer issues.

Winning cover lines included, "What is a girl's greatest asset?" to the more daring, "The paper for young lovers" (11 October 1969).

Jackie sales were at their highest in the Seventies when David Cassidy and Donny Osmond were teen idols. Girls just couldn't get enough of them. David Essex and Marc Bolan were also big, but they were never in the same league as David and Donny. The best-selling issue of all time featured David Cassidy.

The cover wording continued to pull in sales with tempting lines such us, "How to kiss without touching!" (15 May 1971).

Hats of all shapes and sizes continued to grace the covers. Floaty dresses, dungarees and lots of flower power were the height of fashion. There was also a wide array of wonderful accessories including multi-coloured braces!

In the mid 1980s a change was made to the masthead and it was given a more italic look, but before the year was out it changed again. It returned to its roots, but this time with the addition of an outline for extra punch.

The final issue, which appeared on 3 July 1993, cost 50p and featured a model with a big wide smile wearing trendy specs with tinted lenses. The wording promised the readers all the info on Take That.

Throughout its life *Jackie* changed to reflect what was hip and happening, but it never wavered from its winning formula of eye-catching pictures, tantalising text and fabulous free gifts. And although times move on, when you look at today's top-selling titles you can see the same strategy is still being used!

Irene K Duncan

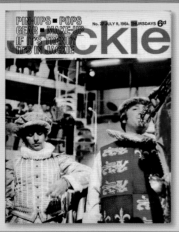
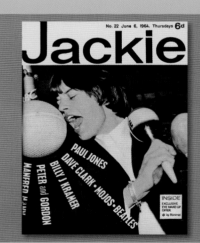
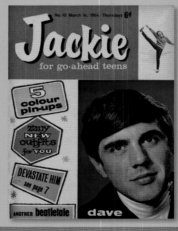
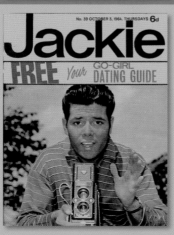

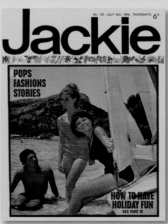

 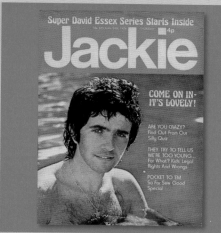  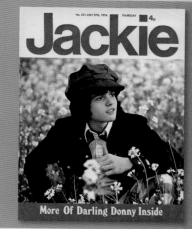

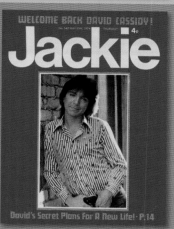   

THE LOVE MATCH

FIFTEEN ALL!

I CAN'T STAND IT ANY LONGER! NOTHING BUT TENNIS, TENNIS, TENNIS . . . MORNING, NOON AND NIGHT! WHY DOES EVERYBODY IN THE COUNTRY HAVE TO RAVE ABOUT A BUNCH OF IDIOTS HITTING A BALL ABOUT?

OH GOOD SHOT, BJORN! THAT'S A WINNER!

OH NO! HOW COULD I HAVE FORGOTTEN? IT'S WIMBLEDON TIME AGAIN!

Everybody except me, that is—I couldn't stand the game! But my flatmate had caught the bug, and it was driving me mad!

SSHHH, LUCY. DON'T MAKE SO MUCH NOISE. I'M TRYING TO WATCH THIS GAME.

OK, OK, DON'T MIND ME! I'M GETTING OUT OF HERE BEFORE I HIT A FOREHAND SMASH RIGHT THROUGH THE TELLY SCREEN!

I DON'T UNDERSTAND IT! OF ALL THE STUPID BORING GAMES IN THE WORLD, TENNIS MUST BE THE WORST! BUT FOR A WHOLE FORTNIGHT EVERY YEAR EVERYONE SITS GLUED TO THE TV. WHAT ON EARTH DO PEOPLE SEE IN IT?

As I turned away . . .

LOOK AT THEM ALL. I WONDER IF THEY KNOW HOW SILLY THEY LOOK, CHASING ABOUT AFTER A LITTLE BALL!

OH . . . !

OUCH!

I was all set to be sarcastic about people who didn't look where they were going, but . . .

I'M SORRY ABOUT THAT. ARE YOU OK?

YES . . . YES, I'M FINE . . . IT WAS MY FAULT ANYWAY. I WAS TOO BUSY WATCHING THEM . . .

WOW! WHERE DID HE COME FROM?

INTERESTED IN TENNIS, HUH? WELL, I CAN UNDERSTAND THAT. I'M THE SAME.

OH . . . UM—YES, YES, THAT'S RIGHT. I COULDN'T TAKE MY EYES OFF THEM . . .

OH BOY! I WOULDN'T MIND PLAYING GAMES WITH HIM!

THAT'S WHERE I'M GOING NOW—FOR A GAME. I'LL BE SEEING YOU!

OH—ER, YES! 'BYE!

LIKE I WAS SAYING . . . THERE'S A LOT TO BE SAID FOR TENNIS. IT'S A WONDERFUL GAME . . . AND YOU FIND THE NICEST PEOPLE PLAYING IT!

**A JACKIE MINI STORY
BY HILDA JAMES**

Shades
Of Blue

Blue is a happy, happy colour.
It's the colour of summer skies; of cornflowers and forget-me-nots and lovebirds. And Don's eyes. Laughing eyes that say, "I love you." Eyes that couldn't lie, because they're true, blue eyes.

And my eyes, too. Blue lagoons, Don said; deep enough to drown in. Blue as the sea on a soft summer's day. Like the dress I bought this morning. Lovely dress with a swirling kerchief skirt and huge puffy sleeves.

"Suits you," the salesgirl said, putting her head round the cubicle curtain.

The manageress came up. She was older, with a carefully painted face.

"It goes with your eyes, dear," she said in that condescending way they have.

I showed it to Mum and Dad when I got home.

"It's a bit cold, isn't it?" Mum said. "Blue's a cold colour."

"Oh, no!" I said. "Blue's warm and happy. Isn't it Dad?"

Dad smiled, slowly.

"It depends how you look at it," he said.

That's Dad! Always diplomatic. There are two sides to everything, he always says.

But how could anyone think blue is cold?

So I put on my blue dress this evening, because I was going to meet Don. And I put blue shadow round my eyes, and in the mirror they looked back at me, happy and blue, like two sparkling sapphires in a silver blue setting.

Usual time, usual place, Don had said. That meant at eight, under the big clock in the shopping precinct. It's only five weeks since I first met Don, but already eight o'clock in the precinct is our time and place.

"Don Howland! He has a new girl every week!" So friends told me, when they heard I was seeing him.

Well, I proved them wrong, because I was still his girl after five weeks, and his eyes still said "I love you." And I knew that Don and I had something really special going.

I was early. Well, I'm always early, because my bus gets in at seven-thirty. But I didn't mind. I ambled slowly through the precinct in a wispy cloud of expectation. Soon I'd be with Don.

We'd go to a film, perhaps, and sit in the hushed navy-blue warmth of the back row, holding hands. And soon Don's lips would find mine, and he'd whisper that he loved me.

He has a special way of saying it, that's like water lapping on the shores of a blue, blue lake on a warm blue summer's day.

I reached the clock. Its giant hands, smiling genially about at me, said one minute to eight.

I stood there, in the brightly lit centre of the precinct, my eyes focussed on the far corner where, any moment now, Don would appear.

He wouldn't be hurrying. Don never hurries. He'd be walking tall and straight, and wearing something trendy and immaculate, his hair gleaming silvery blond in the light, his eyes meeting mine across the square.

Perhaps, instead of going to a film, we'd have coffee somewhere. Meet some of Don's friends, and talk. And Don would chat up the other girls, and laugh with them, and I'd feel a tiny jealous hurt—until he turned his eyes to mine, and the secret smile in their blue depths would say: "Don't worry. There's only you. You're the only one."

Don was late. Well, he is sometimes. He'd look up at the clock in surprise, and say:

"Is that the time? I thought I was early. It's this watch of mine—it's always behind the times!"

And I'd tell him it didn't matter. Because it wouldn't. Not now he was there.

There were other people in the square—boys and girls, men and women. All waiting for someone.

I watched them meet, and smile, and walk away together. They looked happy. But not so happy as Don and I would look. When he came

Eight-thirty. He'd never been so late before. I shivered a little. I'd thought it was a warm evening when I started out, but now it seemed chilly. It was standing here waiting, that made me cold.

Why was he so late? Perhaps he was ill. 'Flu comes on suddenly sometimes. Or an accident. I imagined him, lying still and white in a hospital bed, and my throat tightened with fear.

The clock wasn't friendly any more. Its giant face mocked me as the long hands crawled relentlessly round.

Don wasn't coming. I knew that now. Something had prevented him. Something important, vital, disastrous. No point in waiting any longer.

I began to walk away, huddling into my coat.

Where should I go? Home? Mum and Dad were out, having dinner with friends. The house would be empty and uninviting. A coffee bar, then? Not without Don. The disco? Yes well, perhaps that.

I hurried through the precinct, out into the cold, night-blue street, lit by a regiment of steel-blue lamps.

The throb of music came from the hall where the disco was. As I went through the door the noise hit me. Laughter and voices; drums and guitars.

I was bathed in the rainbow glow from the revolving lights that threw psychedelic patterns on walls and ceiling. Green and mauve; red and orange and yellow, sliding and twisting over faces and arms; dresses and shirts. A moving, whirling sea of colour.

And one patch of brightest blue, picking out a boy and a girl, dancing together, laughing, touching. A tall boy, with blue-blond hair and a smiling face, in a shirt of vivid blue patterned with navy flowers. And I knew that his eyes, though I couldn't see them, were the deepest blue of all. Treacherous blue.

Don.

Somehow, I was in the street again, running on cold, grey-blue pavements. I stepped on a bus, and it jolted off into the dim blue-black night. Rain had started to fall, thin, steel blue pencils of rain slanting across the windows of the bus, and outside, the rooftops gleamed a dreary, wet, slate-blue.

I was home. My little room was cold and comfortless, the blue-patterned curtains drooping forlornly at the window. I dropped into the basket chair, with its dingy blue cushion and my mirrored face stared at me, the eyes tear-filled, like cornflowers in the rain. My blue dress looked sad, and tired.

I stood up and pulled it off, and it fell in a crumpled, drab, blue heap on the carpet. I sank on to the bed, burying my head in its softness. Tears spilled on to the coverlet, making a dark blue stain.

Blue. It's the colour of cold water and wintry landscapes. Of distant hills and sombre shadows and melancholy music.

Blue is a sad, sad colour.

Our specially designed Jackie Summer Set, which we're giving you over three weeks, consists of six parts — sarong and bra, beach-bag and sunglasses case, shawl and headband.

If you'd like to make all the the parts from the same material (like the clever girl on our cover did) then you'll need 5 1/6 yards of 36 in. wide fabric. Use crisp cotton or soft towelling.

Either way, have fun making it!

Here is the first part of your beach outfit — the sarong skirt and bra. You will need 3 yards of 36" fabric — use cotton or towelling. Cut the fabric as shown.

To make the sarong lay one 36" square on top of the other, and trim it to the measurements shown. Stitch one side, and run a gathering thread along the top edge. Join the waistband sections to form a long strip. Gather the skirt to fit your waist, and pin it onto the waistband.

Stitch the skirt to the band, then fold over the band and slip-stitch all round, turning in the edges of the tie pieces.

Hem the raw edges of the skirt and press.

The bra is made simply by joining the two bra sections and shaping the ends as shown here

Hem around the edge and just tie it on!

Around The Fan Clubs

Have Fun With Wings!

PAUL McCARTNEY has some of the most devoted fans in the pop world. When he and his wife Linda toured Britain with Wings last year, six American girls flew over to London from the States just to see him!

They flew to Heathrow Airport, hired a limousine for a month, and then drove around Britain, following Paul from city to city, staying at the best hotels, and managing to buy tickets to nearly twenty Wings concerts!

It was, after all, the first time that Paul had appeared in a concert tour since the break-up of the Beatles. And it was this that persuaded Sarah Nolte of Indiana, a Paul fan from way back, to organise the trip with five of her friends.

And all the girls were, of course, members of the Paul McCartney and Wings Fun club. (You couldn't expect Paul to have anything quite so ordinary as a *fan* club!)

The Fun Club has two secretaries — Sue who replies to all the American fan mail, and Nicky who looks after all the British fans.

It's not a vast club (like the Osmonds' for instance) and everything is organised on quite a modest scale, but the devotion is none the less extraordinary. In the States, the club has just over 1,000 members with another 170 in Canada; in Britain, there are nearly 2,500.

Sue and Nicky keep in touch with them all, sending out six newsletters a year, issuing membership cards, selling photographs that Linda has taken — plus calendars, music books, posters, T-shirts, badges, pens and so on.

It's all very cosy and friendly: the twelve-page newsletter is litho-printed down in Bristol, where Nicky lives, and tells the fans (or should they be funs?!) all about Paul and his work.

For instance, after the group came back from recording in Nigeria, the fun-club gave all the details in the next newsletter. For example information about "Helen Wheels" which was recorded out there in Lagos with Paul drumming. By the way, did you know that the single was named after the nickname of Paul's old Land Rover used on his Scottish farm? Just another gem!

More information included: "The band spent about six weeks in Lagos. They rented a couple of houses near the airport at Ikeja — an hour's drive from the recording studios . . . Heather spent hours catching lizards in a butterfly net . . . Paul wanted to swim, so they joined a country club. The manager said they could join if Paul signed a picture of the Beatles which was displayed on one of the walls."

Sue and Nicky can understand exactly how Wings' fans feel — they're fairly dedicated themselves.

For instance they went to Heathrow Airport to welcome Paul, Linda and the children back from Lagos — even though it meant waiting in the airport lounge until nearly 3.30 in the morning!

"I'd brought a bouquet of roses up from Glastonbury," said Nicky. "The plane was due to arrive soon after nine o'clock in the evening, but by the time they finally landed, the flowers had gone all soft and soggy! Still, they didn't mind at all! Some young girls stayed there through the night with us, and when Paul arrived he said 'hello' to all of us, signed autographs and chatted for ages before driving off in his Lamborghini, which had been left at the airport for him by his manager.

"That's one of the things that has always impressed me about Paul. Even if it's late at night like that, he will always stop and say 'hello' and he always remembers to say 'good night' to everyone before he leaves.

"He's very down to earth and a very nice person. Once I was in the office and Paul was doing a radio interview in the next room. He was due to go home afterwards and I knew he was in a bit of a hurry but he still popped in to say 'cheerio' before he left.

"He's a really super person. He doesn't ever behave like a great star, and when you see him face to face he's so much better-looking than he looks in photographs. And Linda is a much better musician than they all give her credit for, that's something I realised when I heard them rehearsing together."

Sue and Nicky are also given tickets for Wings' concerts and arrange for members of the club to be able to obtain seats — and even organise raffles for copies of Wings' albums.

But of course the main business is done through the mail.

"Sometimes we get letters with very personal questions, like does Paul put salt on his potatoes, or does he like cheese and onion crisps — the sort of questions you just couldn't answer however well you knew him. So these are a bit difficult.

"And then we get distressing letters. I had one from a girl who was on the brink of a nervous breakdown, but she felt she could turn to Paul as someone to talk to.

"And then there was a Japanese fan who wrote to say that' 'My Love' without Paul is like coffee without cream . . . ' and of course they always send loads of birthday and Christmas cards and fluffy toys, things like that.

"When Paul used that photo on the back of the 'Red Rose Speedway' album sleeve of a bouquet lying on stage, a girl wrote from France to say that she was the person who threw the bouquet, and how flattered she was that Paul had used the photograph.

"And then we have Justin, our only honorary member — he is six years old and lives in Boston in the States. By the time he was five, Justin had learned the lyrics to every Beatles song that had ever been written — so we made him an honorary member of the Fun Club."

If you would also like to join, write to:
Nicky,
Secretary,
Paul McCartney and
Wings Fun Club,
P.O. Box 4UP, London W1A 4UP

SUMMER SET (2)

The beach bag and sunglass case – the second part of your beach outfit are made from 1 yard of fabric. Use the same as you used for last week's sarong skirt and bra. Cut the fabric as shown here. Stitch the two bag sections together round three sides leaving a shorter end open. With the bag still inside out, turn over the top 4", and stitch as shown, the first row of stitching 2" down from the fold – the second 3" down.

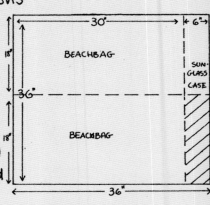

Now turn the bag the right side out, and open up just that section of seam between the two rows of stitching, at either side of the bag.

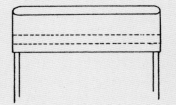

Oversew firmly either end of the gap to stop it opening up further. Now thread a 1½ yard length of cord through the top of the bag and fasten it securely. Just draw up the cord to close the bag. The sunglass case is made exactly the same way, using the piece of fabric 18"x6", folded in half lengthways, the top turned over 2" and stitched then threaded with fine cord or ribbon.

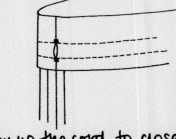

SUMMER SET (3)

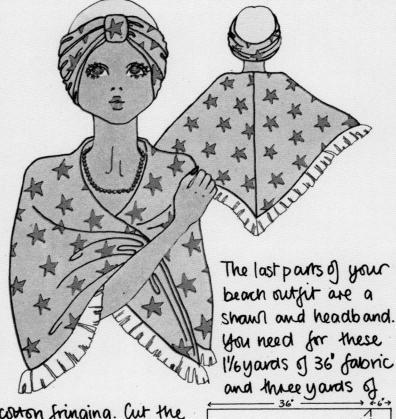

The last parts of your beach outfit are a shawl and headband. You need for these 1⅙ yards of 36" fabric and three yards of cotton fringing. Cut the fabric as shown here. Re-arrange the two triangles of fabric to form a larger triangle – you'll see when you do it how it shapes.

Stitch the centre seam, neaten the seam edges and hem all the other edges. Stitch the cotton fringing onto the two shorter sides of the shawl.

To make the headband join the ends of the 24" x 6" strip to form a tube. Hem the edges. Fold the 4" x 6" piece of fabric neatly around the head-band, over the seam and stitch it firmly into place.

QUICK AND EASY RECIPES

ICED LOLLIES

Drawings by Jenny Williams   Recipe by Marguerite Patten

Needed : for 4-6 iced lollies

½ pint canned orange juice (2 teacups)
½ pint water (2 teacups)
1 tablespoon sugar

can opener
teacup
jug
tablespoon
lolly moulds and sticks

1 Open the can of orange juice by making 2 holes with the can opener.

2 Measure out ½ pint or 2 teacups of juice.

3 Pour into the jug.

4 Add the water and sugar.

5 Stir together.

6 Fix the sticks into the lolly moulds.

7 Pour in the orange mixture and freeze.

8 When frozen pull out of the moulds.

For a change : Use all orange juice and no water. Use blackcurrant or other juice mixed with water.

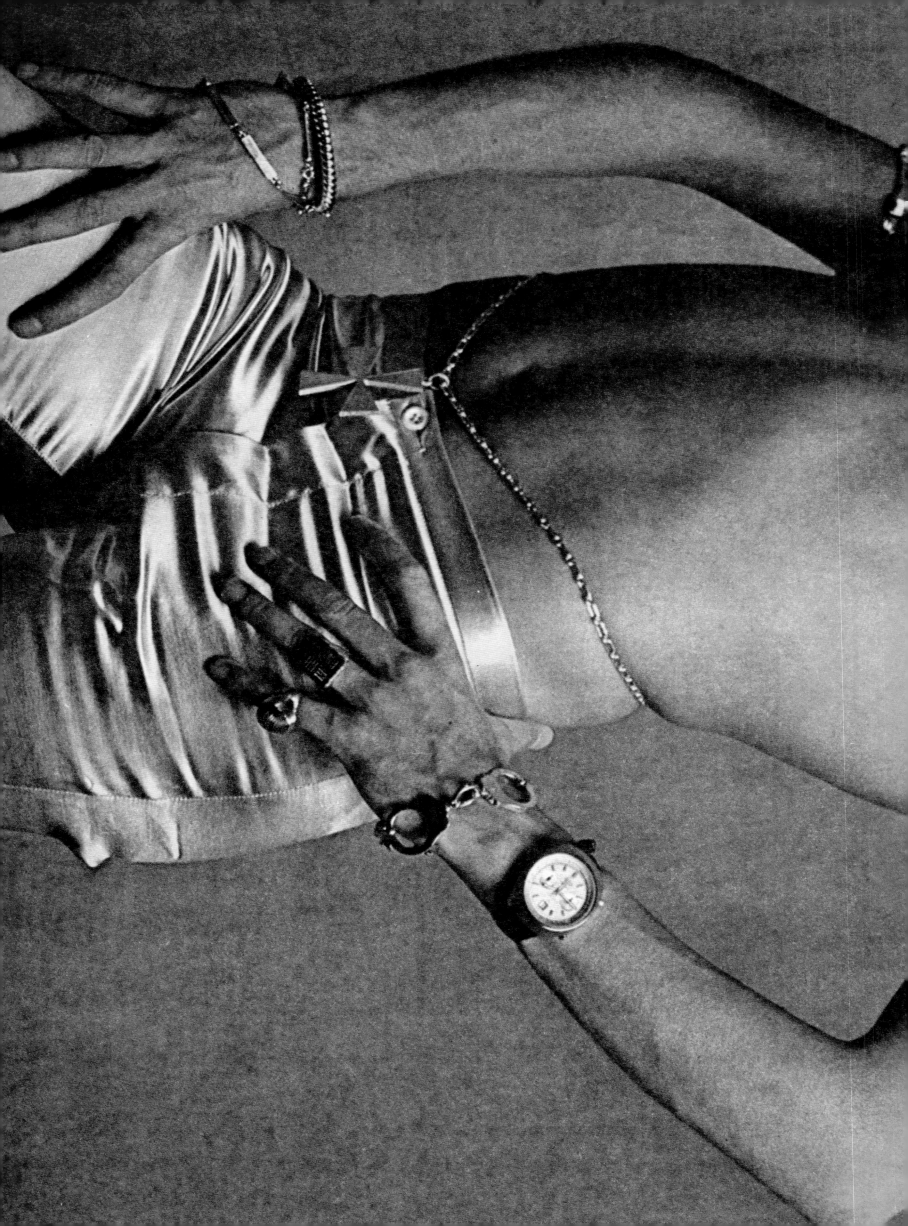

jackie
Rod Stewart

1 *Red print dress with tie collar and ties at the back, comes from Dorothy Perkins. Style No.: 2219. Price: £11.99. Fabric: Rayon. Colours: Assorted prints. Sizes: 10 to 14. Available from main branches of Dorothy Perkins.*
Red/white stripe square comes from a selection at Peter Robinson. No Style No. Prices range from 95p to £1.95. Fabric: Cotton. Colours: Assorted. Available from Peter Robinson, Oxford Circus, London W.1. and branches of Peter Robinson throughout the country.
Red ribbon-front string espadrille with long laces, has woven side and back, and comes from Saxone and Lilley & Skinner. Style No.: Salon. Price: £2.49. Fabric: Cotton tapes and string soles. Colours: Blue, red. Sizes: 3 to 8. By post from Lilley & Skinner, 360 Oxford Street, London W.1., plus 48p postage and packing.

2 *Brown/orange paisley print waistcoat with ties comes from the range Concept by Samuel Sherman. Style No.: 6668. Price: £6.95. Fabric: Cotton/polyester. Colours: As shown. Sizes: 10/12, 12/14. Enquiries for stockists to Samuel Sherman, 10c Hanover Square, London W.1.*
Cream cheesecloth shirt with button-down pockets on front, comes from Etam. No Style No. Price: £2.99. Fabric: Cotton. Colours: Cream only. Sizes: 10 to 16. Available from all branches of Etam.
Orange/white print skirt with frill round hem comes from Laura Ashley. Style No.: LSK 110. Price: £5.50. Fabric: Cotton. Colours: Assorted prints. Sizes: 10 to 14. Available from all branches of Laura Ashley.
Cream/white cross strap sandal with woven strap and wedge comes from Russell & Bromley. Style: Dude. Price: £12.99. Fabric: Kid/rope. Colours: Cream/white. Sizes: 4 to 7. Available from Russell & Bromley, 24 New Bond Street, London W.1., and branches throughout the country.

3 *White peasant top with embroidered front and drawstring neck comes from British Home Stores. Style No.: 5460. Price: £3.50. Fabric: Polyester/cotton. Colours: White with multi-coloured embroidery. Sizes: 10 to 16. Available from all branches of British Home Stores.*
Navy/blue/red print skirt with frill around the hem comes from the Co-Op. Style No.: BU 427. Price: £4.99. Fabric: Cotton. Colours: Navy/blue/red, navy/blue/brown, navy/blue/lime. Sizes: 12 to 18. Available at most Co-Op branches.
Navy canvas wedge with open toe comes from Russell & Bromley. Style: Bouncy. Price: £10.99. Fabric: Canvas. Colours: Navy, red, black, cream, green. Sizes: 4 to 8. Available from Russell & Bromley, 24 New Bond Street, London W.1., and all branches.

GIPSY

We're gazing into the future this week, predicting gorgeous gipsy dresses with matching shawls, cool cotton skirts with embroidered cotton tops and espadrilles to lace up your legs. Add crisp, cotton scarves, knotted over your hair and a pair of hooped earrings for the total gipsy look . . . you'll love it!

4 *Cheesecloth top with elasticated bodice and frill top comes from C & A. No Style No. Price: £3.25. Fabric: Cotton. Colours: Natural or white. Sizes: Small, medium, large. Available from all branches of C & A.*
Purple/green/yellow tiered skirt comes from Coopers. Style No.: CG 219. Price: £10.75. Fabric: Cotton. Colours: Red/white/blue, purple/green/yellow. Sizes: 8 to 14. Available from Quorum, 52 Radnor Walk, London S.W.3; Top Shop, Peter Robinson, Oxford Circus, London W.1.; Annie's at Barkers, Kensington High Street, London W.8; and all Quorum shops.
Chinese-look yellow sandal with woven wedge comes from Russell & Bromley. Style: Jap. Price: £9.99. Fabric: Kid. Colours: Yellow, red, navy, white, green, brown. Sizes: 4 to 7. Available from all main branches of Russell & Bromley.

FASHION!

jackie fashion

5 Scoop neck dress in black with pink floral print has full length three tier skirt and a matching shawl with fringes. Dress and shawl come from Dorothy Perkins. Style No.: 2184. Price: £9.99. Fabric: Cotton. Colours: Assorted prints. Sizes: 10 to 14. Available from all branches of Dorothy Perkins.

Slim-heeled, pink canvas sandal with slim rope weave platform comes from Russell & Bromley. Style: Carina. Price: £12.99. Fabric: Canvas. Colours: Pink, navy, grey, red, green, lilac, khaki. Sizes: 4 to 7. Available from all branches of Russell & Bromley.

6 Red dress with shoe-string straps and embroidered bodice and frill, comes from Woolworth. No Style No. Price: £8.99. Fabric: Cotton. Colours: Red, yellow, black, green. Sizes: 12 to 16. Available from most Woolworth fashion stores.

Red shawl with long fringes comes from Woolworth. No Style No. Price: £1.29. Fabric: Viscose. Colours: White, black, ecru, red, green, black. Available from most Woolworth fashion stores.

Low blue wedge espadrille has blue/white string front and leg laces, comes from Saxone and Lilley & Skinner. Style No.: A52/6704/37. Ketch. Price: £5.99. Fabric: Cotton. Colours: Blue/white. Sizes: 3 to 8. Available from main branches of Saxone and Lilley & Skinner. By post from Lilley & Skinner, 360 Oxford Street. London W.1., plus 48p postage and packing.

7 Small green crochet scarf with fringes comes from Bombacha at Peter Robinson. No Style No. Price: £1.95. Fabric: Synthetic. Colours: From a selection. Available at Peter Robinson, Oxford Circus, London W.1. and branches of Peter Robinson throughout the country.

Green suede shoe with woven edge and ankle strap comes from Russell & Bromley. Style: Ghobi. Price: £9.99. Fabric: White kid; grey, green, navy suede. Sizes: 4 to 7. Available from all branches of Russell & Bromley. Enquiries for stockists to Russell & Bromley, 24 New Bond Street, London W.1.

8 Green/white print smock top comes from Pixie. No Style No. Price: £5.50. Fabric: Cotton. Colours: Green/white, blue/white, brown/white, red/white. Sizes: 10 to 16. Available from Pixie, 32a Fulham Road, London S.W.10., mail order 50p extra.

Green/white print two-tiered skirt (to match smock top) comes from Pixie. No Style No. Price: £6.00. Fabric: Cotton. Colours: Green/white, blue/white, brown/white, red/white. Sizes: 10 to 16. Stockist as for the smock. Cream cheesecloth shirt as for Fig. 2.

9 Red dress with frilled hem, lace-up front and cap sleeves, comes from Earlybird. Style No.: 510. Price: £12.95. Fabric: Cotton. Colours: Red, black, navy, green, blue, white. Sizes: 10 to 14. Available from Earlybird, 20 Park Walk, London S.W.10., mail order 30p extra; Topaz, 2 Brighton Square, Brighton; Park Walk, Meeting House Lane, Brighton and North Street, Guildford.

Red turban with plaits comes from C & A. No Style No. Price: £2.75. Fabric: Polyester. Colours: Assorted. Available from all main branches of C & A.

10 Wooden wedge espadrille with beige front and leg laces, comes from Dolcis. Style No.: A15/15303 Rome. Price: £3.99. Fabric: Synthetic. Colours: Tan, white. Sizes: 4 to 7. Available from main branches of Dolcis. By post from Dolcis, 350 Oxford Street, London W.1., plus 48p postage and packing.

HEAVENS ABOVE!

Have you ever thought how much the sky influences the way we feel? How much happier we all look for example, when the sky is a bright, sunshiny blue and how our spirits droop when we wake up in the morning and see the sky is dull and grey. In the same way, we all look at the sky through the filter of our own emotions and so the way we see it can tell us a lot about ourselves and the way we look at the world.

Interested? Then try our special quiz. All you have to do is look at each picture of the sky carefully and choose the description which you think suits the mood of the sky best. After that turn this page upside down for your own special reading of the writing in the sky!

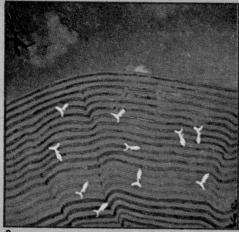

1.
(a) Astronauts
(b) Lovers
(c) The mysterious inhabitants of another planet.

2.
(a) The colour of the sea is only a reflection of the sky
(b) The beginning of the world
(c) The unfathomable depths of sea and sky.

3.
(a) My smallness
(b) Eternity
(c) The vastness of the galaxy.

4.
(a) There's nobody else alive in the world
(b) The cold hardship of winter
(c) The purity of the world without people.

5.
(a) Wet country fields
(b) Pity the people without shelter
(c) The sky's moods reflect human nature.

6.
(a) How great to be alive on a day like this
(b) The perfect order of nature
(c) Unpolluted air.

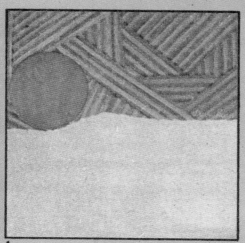

7.
(a) What incredible shapes you can see in clouds
(b) Some people say that clouds are omens of good and bad luck
(c) There's probably a storm coming.

8.
(a) The yearly migration of birds
(b) The eternal search for faraway places
(c) The birds are flying away to make new nests with their mates.

9.
(a) I wish I could fly away behind the clouds
(b) Now we can live high in the sky like birds
(c) The city stamps out nature.

SCORE
No. 1: give yourself 5 points for A; 3 for B; 1 for C.
2: 5A; 1B; 3C.
3: 3A; 1B; 5C.
4: 3A; 5B; 1C.
5: 5A; 3B; 1C.
6: 3A; 1B; 5C.
7: 1A; 3B; 5C.
8: 5A; 1B; 3C.
9: 3A; 1B; 5C.

CONCLUSIONS

IF YOU SCORED LESS THAN 21 POINTS: You have a free flowing imagination and tend to live in your own dream world. In fact you often prefer your imaginative world to the real one you find around you. Not that you don't like ordinary life, but you have many friends and are a lively, active girl; but you know how to take advantage of every occasion to escape, and you deeply enjoy what nature offers you.

IF YOU SCORED FROM 21 TO 34 POINTS: You are a gentle soul, delicate and sensitive in your feelings. You need tenderness and understanding and are deeply emotional and romantic. You like to feel in contact with nature although you are frightened by lightning and thunderstorms. Your idea is to walk barefoot in a soft summer meadow and feel at peace with everything around you.

IF YOU SCORED FROM 35 to 45 POINTS: You have a clear headed, common sense approach to life. You're not given to flights of fantasy and your friends rely on you for sensible, unemotional advice. For you the sky is an element of nature which you hardly notice, and when you do think about it — it's usually only to wonder what the weather will be like!

WHO'S THE GIRL
with
THE KISSIN' LIPS?

Let loose on the lipstick lark and you can make things really whizz! Buzz on the brown bea[...]—way out in front for '64. We're gone like ten, guess you will be, too. Colours range from dee[...] coffee, bronze, ginger, russet . . . . to a burnished sandalwood colour, peach and tangerine, jus[...] made for honey blondes.

Chalky palesters take a downbeat! Catching on fast, the light, bright pinks. Some have a hin[...] of lilac or apricot for extra zing!

Liplure Lowdown! Start with lips clean and softened with lipsalve if necessary. Smooth tinte[...] foundation followed by a pat of powder over lips, smiling slightly as you go. Gives a supe[...] surface for your lipstick! And almost blots out natural lip shape, so that, if you like, you ca[...] re-design it.

Model-girls always, always use a lipbrush for that smoothie, sleek outline. With a bit of practice it's easy to use, result is more attractive and it's more economical, too.

A magnifying mirror is super for a close-up view, but otherwise use an ordinary one set in a good light. Load lip-brush by sweeping round the sides of the lipstick . . . then, resting the little finger on your chin to steady your hand, draw in outline on top lip. Follow your natural shape, working from the centre of your "cupid's bow" outwards, in long, smooth strokes. End just a fraction away from the corner each side.

Do same as for bottom lip, but take colour right into the corners this time. See why? Gives a wowee smiling effect!

Now for the fill-in. Straight from the stick if you like (just skimming the outline as you go), or you can carry on using your brush. Blot with a tissue, lipstick again, and blot carefully.

Lip-shape Pretty-up! Using your lip-brush you can outline a prettier, zippier lip-shape over your natural one! Looks super so long as you use tinted foundation and powder as a blot-out basis first of all. Here're the how-to's, along with some diagrams:

THE LIPLINE LARK

Cupid's Bow too pointed? Outline with a slightly oval shape, just skimming the tips of the bow and tapering down towards the corners.

Lips too thick? Take outline very slightly inside your natural shape, gradually following through to outer corners.

Often lip shapes are rather crooked, but you can easily change this by outlining the odd side of your mouth slightly outside or inside your natural shape to match the other prettier side.

Lips too thin? Take outline slightly outside your natural lip shape, but follow the natural line as you work into the corners.

Oooh . . . that kiss! But left him with any tell-tale lipstick marks? If you paint over lipstick with transparent sealer, colour just can't come off. Try Lipcote.

So your lipstick's super, but how about nail varnish? Mod bods go for match-ups. Loads of manufacturing smarties make go-together lipstick 'n' varnish shades . . . like Gala, Max Factor, Miners, Outdoor Girl, Cutex . . . .

Lips feel tingly or slightly sore after applying lipstick? This means your lips are extra sensitive to the dyes used in ordinary lipsticks. So it's Innoxa to the rescue. They have a range designed just for you, in all their usual sizzling shades, called Innoxa No. 22.

Cracked, dry lips, which feel (and look) grimsville? Smarties smooth a very fine film of lip salve or Vaseline over their lips every night before tumbling into bed. Try it—works wonders!

To find out true colour of new lipstick before you buy, stroke a tiny line from sample stick across the inside of your wrist. This will give you the best idea of what it will look like on your lips.

Here's something to try—looks very swish. Outline your lips in a shade darker than the colour you're using to fill in the centre. Gives a much clearer, neater look. Put one colour on top of another, too. Discover zingy new shades this way!

For fun-type dates, try Gala's latest frostie lipstick. They have the faintest whisper of silver or gold through them.

SOULD OUT!

As well as being widely accepted as the most brilliant and successful singer in soul music today, Stevie Wonder also has the distinction of being one of its longest serving members. When he first rose to fame at the age of twelve, he was known as "Little Stevie Wonder", but since he grew over the years to more than six feet tall, the 'Little' had to be dropped.

In those early days, Stevie made very simple, catchy records, but now he's become much more sophisticated, and albums like "Innervision" and "Talking Book" have been praised by critics all over the world.

And Stevie is totally involved in music. He says himself that it's the greatest love of his life.

"I've always loved music," he said. "Even when I was tiny I was always listening to the radio.

"My first memory of actually playing is during a family picnic in the country. There was a lot of singing and playing going on, and I kept saying that I wanted to play the drums. I was only six, so I wasn't big enough to reach the drums on my own — I had to sit on the drummer's knee to play!

"But I remember I really enjoyed it. I seemed to have a natural rhythm for it right from the start. I loved music then, and it still makes me happy today!"

It seems only natural that someone as brilliant as Stevie Wonder should have musically talented people around him — and that's definitely true in the case of his ex-wife Syreeta.

Although Syreeta and Stevie are no longer married, they're still good friends, and they have great respect for each other as musicians. In fact, Syreeta describes Stevie as a "musical genius". And, as her hit records "Spinnin' And Spinnin'" and "Your Kiss Is Sweet" have proved, she's pretty special too!

IN the music world, things are changing all the time. There are always new people coming along with bright new ideas — that's why it's so exciting!

And recently, as you've probably noticed, there have been even more new names than usual appearing in the charts. This time a year ago, hardly anyone had heard of George McCrae, The Three Degrees or Sweet Sensation — but now every record they make goes straight up the charts. So what's the secret of their success? That's easy — they've all got soul!

Soul, of course, isn't a new sound. But right now, it seems that more people are listening to it and enjoying it than ever before. And, in fact, it's become so popular with everyone that we've decided to take a closer look at it.

There are lots of reasons behind the sudden new success of soul music. It's great music to dance to, and when you're in the mood, it's equally good just to sit down and listen to! But for lots of girls, such as 16 year-old Chris Simpson from North London, the best thing about it is that it's romantic!

Chris is still at school, but she works in her dad's sweet shop at weekends, and saves up the money she earns to buy the latest records by her favourite — Barry White.

"When I first heard Barry, I got shivers up and down my back," she told us. "His voice really did something to me. It was so sexy! But it was more than that — it was romantic, too. I pictured him as a really handsome man, and I must admit I was a bit disappointed when I first saw his picture in a magazine, and discovered he weighed about twenty stone!

"Still, it hasn't changed my mind about his music — it's fantastic.

"Whenever I'm feeling a bit fed up I go into my bedroom and just shut the door and listen to his records for hours on end. My favourite album is 'Can't Get Enough'. It seems to build up a dreamy atmosphere every time I play it. As far as I'm concerned, it's the greatest thing around."

Angela Lucas, a schoolfriend of Chris, agrees that she finds soul music soothing and romantic. And in her case, soul actually helped her to get over a broken romance.

"Last year, I was going out with a boy called Vince," she said. "I was mad about him, but one evening he didn't turn up for a date and I discovered he'd gone out with another girl. I was really shattered. I was left feeling really alone — I don't think I've ever been so miserable. For ages I didn't go out. Instead I just sat in my room and listened to doomy music.

"When that record, 'What Becomes Of The Broken Hearted' by Jimmy Ruffin came out, I bought it and played it non-stop, because that was exactly how I felt. At first it made me even more depressed, but after a while it made me realise I wasn't the only person who'd ever felt that way, and it helped me get over it. I'm not saying it was a wonder cure or anything, but it did help."

But soul isn't just music for sad people — and it doesn't only appeal to girls!

It's popular with everyone! And 14 year-old Alex Ford from Sussex has very definite ideas about why he likes it.

"I think soul acts are best at entertaining their audiences," Alex explained. "They wear really great costumes, and they're always so polished and professional. A lot of ordinary groups just stand around, trying to look good. They might wear bright clothes and make-up and things, but they don't have any idea how to put their songs across.

"Black singers are really good at that — they seem to enjoy themselves so much when they're onstage that you can't help getting in the spirit of things as well!

"I saw the Three Degrees playing live recently, and I thought they were out of this world. I was knocked out by them. They're lovely girls, and their stage act is just terrific!"

So, soul is good to listen to, and good to watch. But there's one other very important thing about it — it's great to dance to as well!

And lots of soul records become hits without ever having been played on the radio or appeared on "Top of the Pops". Instead they become popular with people who go to discos regularly and choose their favourites from the music they hear there.

Pauline Wright, a 17 year-old secretary, says she spends at least three nights a week dancing — and she only goes to discos that play soul.

"Pop music's okay to listen to in the car or something," Pauline told me, "but I don't find people like Mud, David Essex, Bay City Rollers and the others very good to dance to. They've got a long way to go before they match somebody like Stevie Wonder. My favourite dance record of all is Stevie's 'Superstition'. When that's playing I can really let myself go!"

So there you are — lots of reasons why soul has suddenly become so popular. Of course, everyone has his or her own idea on the subject. But one thing's certain — whatever it is that causes the magic of soul music, the spell's certainly working!

The biggest sound in soul music today is the Philly Sound, which originates from Philadelphia. And right at the head of this movement are the Tymes, a five man group from North Philadelphia who first stepped back into the spotlights last year with a single called "You Little Trustmaker". That was followed by "Ms Grace", a lovely record which was an even bigger hit.

The Tymes aren't a new group — in fact they've been making successful records since the early sixties. Since then, their musical style has changed quite a bit, but their basic outlook hasn't.

"We still believe in the same things we always have," the group's lead singer, George Williams, told me. "We believe in peace and love, and the best way we can spread that message is through our music."

The Three Degrees are without a doubt the top girl group in soul today. They have lots of style, and a very sexy sound! As well as having a sensational live act, the girls — Fayette Pinkney, Sheila Ferguson and Valerie Holiday — have made some beautiful records. The best known of these is probably "When Will I See You Again" which was one of the biggest disco hits of 1974.

"The three of us are all great friends," Fayette said. "I used to be very nervous onstage, but when I have Sheila and Valerie beside me, nerves don't bother me at all. It's nice having them there with me.

"We've had lots of good moments in our career so far, but one of the biggest thrills was when we first heard that 'When Will I See You Again' had gone to number one in Britain. That was tremendous!"

One thing that makes Sweet Sensation different from every other soul group is the fact that they come from Manchester. That really is something new in the soul world, because up till now, all the world's top soul sounds have come from America.

Sweet Sensation are an eight-piece group who've been together for four years now. Their first big break came last year when they made an appearance on TV's "New Faces". Soon after that, they had their first single hit with "Sad Sweet Dreamer" and then at the beginning of this year, they had another big hit with "Purely By Coincidence".

There are four lead singers in the group, but the best known one is 17 year-old Marcel King.

"We started the group because we wanted to show that a British soul band could be just as good as all the American acts," Marcel explained. "I have to admit it wasn't exactly easy when we first started. We had very little money and it was difficult to find work. Some nights we ended up sleeping in the back of our van, because we couldn't afford to stay anywhere else!

"Still, the success we're having now makes up for all that!"

Barry White is a big man — with a talent to match. He knows how to produce those beautiful, smooth, soulful records that can conjure up a very romantic atmosphere!

Barry was born in Texas on September 12, 1944. When he was just a baby, his family moved to Los Angeles where he started his musical career — singing in the church choir! Then, when he was only ten, he became the church organist, and at 16 he joined a soul group called "The Upfronts", and he also began to write hits for other people.

Today, he writes and sings his own hits, such as "Never, Never, Gonna Give You Up" and "Can't Get Enough Of Your Love, Babe". And he's also made very successful albums like "Can't Get Enough" which has been in the British LP charts for a while now.

And Barry's also the man behind Love Unlimited, who've produced beautiful singles like "Walking In The Rain" and their latest, "It May Be Winter Outside".

And Barry hasn't stopped there, either! He's now writing film scores, and in future he may well be starting a new career altogether — as a film actor!

It seems there's just no stopping him!

SATURDAY
Sun rises at 5.35 a.m. today. Will you?

SUNDAY
Build sandcastles on the beach — or mud pies in the garden.

MONDAY
Find out how easy it is not to talk to anyone at all . . . or is it?

TUESDAY
Search for tea leaves floating on top of your tea — letters are coming, if there are.

WEDNESDAY
See how many reflections you can see in two facing mirrors . . .

THURSDAY
Bury something for posterity — who knows, your old bottle of nail varnish may be somebody's grand find in a few hundred years !

FRIDAY
Help old ladies across roads (but first make sure they want to go!).

·ED'S LETTER·

So what's new? You don't know? Well, actually, to tell you the truth, we weren't too sure either—until we read Jenny's carefully researched feature on page 34.

We all wondered why Jenny had been lounging about behind pot plants, dressed in a kimono and plastic sandals, reading a comic and sucking a Kojak lolly while talking non-stop about horse-riding and Princess Caroline or Monaco. Of course, you don't have to go THAT far, one plastic sandal and a comic would do!

It's one way to be noticed, anyway. And you'll find another 20 ways to be noticed on page 25. The one I like best is riding a tandem by yourself. I've often wondered about that . . . do the little pedals on the back part go round as well? And, if you were riding a tandem WITH someone, could you tell if the one at the back wasn't quite doing her fair share? Maybe somebody, somewhere can tell me . . .?

If you can, though, don't put your hand up until you've read our beauty page on hands! After I'd seen it, I felt so ashamed of my hands, I went around wearing gloves for a week. Have you ever tried to get eight pence out of your purse on a crowded bus in the middle of summer while wearing furry mitts? It's not easy. I know.

I know, too, that you're going to enjoy the last part of our super serial, Jilly By Herself. It's quite—well—sniffy, but sort of sad and nice at the same time. Read it for yourself and you'll see what we mean.

BAY CITY ROLLERS COMPETITION Huge apologies! In our July 26th Pop Gossip, Pete told you that you could win two weeks with the Rollers in Bermuda.

In fact, first prize is a week's holiday—still a fantastic prize. Good luck with your entry.

The Ed

MY LIFE WAS SO EMPTY...

A READER'S TRUE EXPERIENCE

YOU know, there's a certain stage in life when nothing seems to matter any more. Every day seems to be the same — empty, grey and deadly boring. The slightest little task seems to be too much to handle. You want to burst into tears with the emptiness and frustration of your dull, drab life.

Parents of course, just don't understand that sort of feeling. To them, if you're young, then the world is at your feet. You should be bursting with happiness and enthusiasm . . . or at least, grateful for what you've got. And if you're not, then you're just in a silly, self-indulgent "mood." *Snap out of it, can't you? Grow up, etc., etc.*

But they don't understand what it's like to feel empty and alone . . . without Grant . . .

We'd met quite by accident, Grant and I. In the supermarket, of all the ridiculous places. I ran my trolley straight over his foot.

"Oh! Oh, I'm sorry," I'd stammered, embarrassed. But he just laughed and took command of the situation right away. He was like that — strong and self-assured.

I went out with him that night. He took me to the cinema where we saw an old James Bond film. I don't remember a single bit of it. All I could think of was Grant.

Grant. Even the name makes tears come to my eyes.

We'd been going out together for six weeks, and I thought it would last forever, when the blow fell. He'd met another girl, and wouldn't be seeing me any more. He was sorry.

Just like that.

It felt as if someone had cut me in two. I'd just never suspected anything. I thought he loved me — just like I loved him. One moment we saw each other four, maybe five nights a week and the next, nothing. For a while I even prayed Grant would change his mind.

But he didn't. Pretty soon he even stopped bothering to say hello, when he passed me in the street. I'd see him in the distance and my heart would lurch, my mouth would go dry. I'd will him to stop . . . just for a moment. But he never did.

He'd just dropped me out of his life completely, like I'd never existed.

Then I really accepted it was all over, and my life became nothing.

I've never been one of those girls who are fanatic about clothes and their appearance. As long as I looked presentable, it was all right by me. Sure, I was interested in fashion, but it didn't bother me if I couldn't afford to rush out and buy the latest stuff.

After the split with Grant, though, I hardly bothered at all. I slopped around in any old clothes that came to hand when I opened the wardrobe. Usually it was a pair of tatty old cords plus a T-shirt.

I stopped wearing make-up too, never even bothering to put on mascara. After all, there was no one worth putting on a front for; there was only one single boy I'd ever been interested in, and now I'd lost him. For good. I let my hair go all straggly and tatty and when it got a bit dirty I just tied it back off my face, and that was that.

ICOULDN'T have cared less about what I looked like, or what people thought of me — or anything, come to that. I suppose I thought: well, this is me, take me or leave me — I don't mind.

It was no fun now going to the disco without Grant so I simply didn't bother. If I could work up enough energy to go into town I'd buy a box of chocolates and a few magazines. Then I'd lock myself in my bedroom most evenings with my store of goodies. I knew Mum was worried because she kept trying to get me interested in things. She'd come up to my room and talk, but I never listened. My mind wasn't taking in any of her chat.

I couldn't even make the effort to meet my friends for the usual Friday gossip. We'd always met up together, Friday lunchtime for a coffee in the Wimpy, even when we had steady boyfriends. It was a sort of ritual, and I'd always looked forward to it. We'd get all our problems out in the open, and always ended up having a really good laugh about things.

I couldn't face it any more, though.

No one said anything about my absence the first couple of weeks. I began to think they hadn't even missed me — after all, nobody really cared about me, did they? But on the third week Gayle met me in the street, grabbed my arm and stopped me dead in my tracks.

"What's happened to you then, Chrissie?"

I looked at her quite blankly, wondering what she meant. These days it was a job for me to think about anything except getting through the day.

Gayle's been my friend for as long as I can remember; she's one of those lucky people with natural corn-coloured hair and amazingly slanty green eyes. She could wear an old sack and still look great.

Added to that she's one of the nicest people you could hope to meet.

"You look terrible," she went on. (She's also very, very honest.) "A real boot. I never thought you'd let yourself go like this. You're absolutely bursting out of those old jeans and that hairstyle makes your face look like a full moon! Why on earth are you slouching around like that? Honestly, if I didn't know it was you inside that outfit, I'd begin to think you'd been taken over by some alien power or something!"

I stared at her, feeling just the stirrings of real murder in my heart. Who was she to talk? She wasn't the one who had just lost

the only love in her life. She didn't know what it was like. She'd never been crazy about a boy; it was always the other way round for her.

A stunned silence — I couldn't remotely think of an answer to a slagging like that!

"I know just what you're thinking," she said. "Well, forget it. It's just self-pity. Have some respect for yourself, for goodness sake. Have a bit of pride. And then have a think about coming to the disco with me tomorrow night, eh?"

And before I could draw breath to answer, she rushed off to catch her bus.

I was near to tears by this time, but what Gayle had said really did start me thinking, after the resentment had worn off. She was right. I walked home very slowly, head down, kicking at stones.

When I got in, I went straight to the mirror and took a good long look at myself; I rested my chin on my hands and examined every single inch of my face. It was definitely dull — empty expression, lifeless hair, and there wasn't even a sparkle in my eyes

BUT I wasn't really plain — I knew that. It was just that the way I'd been feeling for weeks, since Grant dropped me, had reflected in my face. I could do something about the way I looked, and I would, too. Gayle's strong words had given me the inspiration.

So I shouted to Mum to give me a hand. She washed my hair, cut and set it, flicked it back off my face, gently. Not scraped back as it had been before! Then she gave me a pair of gold, stud earrings. They were beautiful — I knew they were her favourites, but they set off my hair perfectly.

Knowing that I was looking better already, I set about doing my face. I hadn't experimented with make-up for months — but now I really felt excited about it. And when I'd finished, I looked completely transformed. It wasn't just the make-up and the new hairstyle — it was the real me, underneath it all, that was completely different. I was cheerful again, at long last — and it really did show in the way I looked.

When I dressed that evening, I knew I looked all right. All right? — I hardly recognised myself! Gayle was waiting down the street for me, along with some of the others. She slipped an arm through mine. I was going to tell her how stunning she looked in her black velvet suit, but she didn't give me a chance. Gayle's like that.

"You look smashing, Chrissie," she said straight away. "We're going to have a great time tonight. It'll be just like it was before."

And it was. I hadn't enjoyed myself so much for ages. Everyone seemed so pleased to see me, I was quite surprised and a bit flattered. It was almost as if I'd been ill for a long time and had just got back into circulation again. Everyone seemed so eager to see that I enjoyed myself. I never realised before how many really good friends I had. All in all, that evening made me feel I was pretty lucky after all — boyfriend or no boyfriend.

I'd like to be able to say that I won Grant back, after I got back on the scene again, but of course I didn't. He's had three more girlfriends since me but — he never seems to stick to any of them for very long. It's all over between us now; I'm well aware of that. But there's plenty more fish in the sea, as my mum says and that's what I keep telling myself now.

I've got my self-respect back, that's what's important. And it's the one thing that I'm determined not to lose ever again . . .

WHAT ARE YOU FRIGHTENED OF?

IT'S amazing how many little things can make you scared. I know from talking to you and reading your letters that many of you are afraid of quite little things.

Older people often tend to dismiss your fears saying that young people can't possibly have phobias, but believe me these are genuine and you need help in coming to terms with them. Worrying won't help, but learning to understand why you feel this way will.

It's funny how many things there are to fear. Quite little things, which commonsense tells us we ought not to mind, are called phobias. But common sense doesn't always help much! It doesn't come to the rescue of girls who are perhaps afraid of going into lifts, of walking along certain streets, or of tiny creatures like spiders and mice.

Most phobias are triggered off by much earlier experiences. Some unpleasant little incident, long forgotten, keeps on nagging away at us, in disguise.

If we were afraid of absolutely nothing, we wouldn't last very long in this world. Some degree of fear is essential as a kind of safety mechanism. We have to learn, for instance, the dangers of fire and traffic, and of savage dogs. So it's quite natural to worry about falling off tall buildings!

Phobias start when we worry about dangers that don't exist. It's an awful nuisance if you can't go into a lift without fearing that it will stick and you'll be trapped. And there's another peculiar but fortunate thing about phobias. People who dread doing such awful things practically never do them! And so the girl who's scared to hold her sister's baby in case she drops it, would never let it fall.

FRIGHTENED OF DYING

A lot of fears and phobias disappear as mysteriously as they come. It's quite common for young people to be afraid of dying, but you don't meet many old people with similar fears.

I know a girl who was frightened of going to sleep at night in case she never woke up. Eventually she had to have her appendix out. She was terrified at the thought of having an anaesthetic, but it cured her for good. It proved to her that she would wake up!

The trouble is, that it's so easy to get a fixed idea about something. Sandra used to love going to the swimming baths, splashing around in the shallow end. Then, one day, she became a little more daring and went a little deeper.

Suddenly she found her feet wouldn't touch the bottom. She panicked when this happened, with the result that she swallowed gallons of water, and really believed she was going to drown.

And now, the very thought of swimming brings back that choking

sensation. She can't go near the pool, and, worse still, she can't bear to be left in the bath at home without her mother or sister in the bathroom. It's going to be a very gradual process to build up Sandra's confidence again, but she will regain it through time.

FEAR OF THE DARK

Another young patient of mine has a completely different fear, but an equally disturbing one for her. Liz is afraid of the dark. Not an

uncommon fear in the least. It's a nuisance more than anything else.

Her fears began when she had a nightmare one night and woke up in the dark screaming her head off. What made things worse for her was that she was alone in her bedroom.

Now her sister shares her room and, in addition, she keeps a small bedside light on all night. Again it will be a long time before Liz regains the confidence and trust to go to sleep with the light out but it will come eventually—time, as in

all illnesses, is the all-important factor.

Of course, some people are more likely to become anxious and afraid than others. Liz and Sandra are probably more "highly strung" or just plain nervous than a lot of people. Point to note—anxious mothers can produce nervous daughters!

Some phobias are a part of growing up. So it can happen that a young girl or boy develops a very real fear of going to school. Yet they are perfectly happy once they get in to the playground. It's just the thought of going which gives them "butterflies in the tummy" every morning.

What they are really afraid of, in fact, is being separated from their mothers. Perhaps they dread something awful happening to her whilst they are away at school. A similar fear of going off to work can develop.

INSECTS AND MICE

On the other hand, it's harder to shake off a fear of insects, spiders, or mice. The main thing to remember is that lots of people have these phobias, so it's certainly nothing to be ashamed or embarrassed about. We simply have to learn to live with our fears, avoiding the dreaded thing where possible.

The one phobia which really does interfere with normal life is the fear of going out. It's rather difficult to say how this one starts, but it's enough to say it can be quite crippling. There are less severe forms, such as being afraid of wide open spaces. The opposite, fear of being shut in, often called claustrophobia, is very common too.

It's not necessary to go to your doctor if your fear is unimportant and easily avoided, like mice. But no one's life should be made a misery. Your doctor will certainly not dismiss fears and phobias as being too trivial to bother with.

He or she can help by explaining what the fear is all about. Sometimes he will prescribe a medicine or mild tablet to calm the nerves. Or if he feels your phobia requires special treatment, he will make arrangements for this too.

Treatment for a more serious phobia will take the form of learning to relax and getting used to the dreaded thing gradually, by degrees. This therapy is simple, but effective.

And don't worry if you don't have any fears. Just as it's perfectly normal to be afraid of something, it's equally normal not to be! It depends entirely on your temperament.

I am simply bringing to your attention little fears and not so little fears which may trouble you at some time. And I hope that by helping you to understand such fears, far from making you neurotic and likely to start imagining things, you won't be entirely ignorant of the possibilities of developing such phobias.

SPOTLIGHT ON
Toyah

We've all admir
actress/sing
TOYAH WILLCOX
screen and stage,
now's your chan
to see her in a diff
ent light — as
model for o
fashion page
Toyah picked out
the clothes hers
using her own
dividual style to p
them all togeth
Which, for Toyah
just doing wh
comes naturally!

BEING SMALL, I ALWAYS LOOK FOR CLOTHES WHICH MAKE ME LOOK A BIT TALLER," TOYAH TOLD US.

"FOR INSTANCE, I'D NEVER CHOOSE ANYTHING WITH HORIZONTAL STRIPES WHICH WOULD MAKE ME LOOK FATTER THAN I AM!

"Smaller people do have a problem when it comes to buying clothes and I have to be very careful to make sure that I go for darker colours, which tend to be more flattering."

Toyah likes to shop for her clothes in unusual, back-street shops.

"I prefer the not so well-known shops because I don't want to go somewhere and find someone else in exactly the same outfit," she told us.

Toyah is very interested in fashion and feels that it's very, very important.

"What you wear should reflect your own personal taste. I don't always believe in being told what to wear!

"Clothes are a very big part of your individuality. You should feel good in what you wear. Above all, though, your clothes should be comfortable."

Toyah spends a lot of money on clothes now, particularly on her stage clothes, but she wasn't always in this position.

"When I was a drama student I couldn't afford many new clothes, but I still really cared about what I dressed in.

"I got all my clothes from places like jumble sales and the wardrobe department of the theatre!

"If you don't have much money to spend on clothes, I think it's important to buy outfit that you really like, and wear it al time — rather than buying lots of access and things.

"When I was a drama student I used around in this long black coat and a pa heavy black platform shoes — I loved the and wore it all the time!"

TOYAH FEELS THAT HER CLOT ARE A VERY IMPORTANT PAR HER IMAGE. SHE'S WELL KN FOR APPEARING IN S STUNNING STAGE OUTFITS, WOULD HATE TO BE PRE ABLE, WHICH IS WHY SHE LIKES U YOUNG, NEW DESIGNERS.

Whereas before, she didn't feel that ac sories were important if you haven't got a money to spend on clothes, Toyah feels tha jewellery she wears on stage is an esse part of her look.

"On stage, the accessories are jus important as the outfit."

Judging by the selection that Toyah br along to our photographic session, her accessories are as individual and drama the girl herself!

Finally, we asked her if there was an she admired for their clothes sense.

"James Dean and David Bowie. B always looks so fantastic. Whereas so ma his generation have let their style sl become dated, he's managed to stay up th

"Grace Jones is amazing — her style's individual and unique.

"Marilyn Monroe is someone who I always looked good in clothes, too — alth in her case, her fantastic figure made clothes look good."

Which is something Toyah feels is tant — but looking at the shots here, it just to show that personality counts for quite too!

PLAN the basics for your winter wardrobe . . . start with a jacket and build up from there, adding warm skirts, trousers and soft stripy knitwear. We find the best value jackets and show you what to put with them for the latest looks in fashion.

Jackie Fashion

TAKE

1 Zipped-up brushed cotton jacket with two slit pockets at the front, by Johnathan Miller. Style No.: 6033P. Price: £6.95. Fabric: Brushed cotton. Colours: Assorted. Sizes: Small, medium, large. From Dickins and Jones, Regent Street, London W.1.: Renton of Oban: Binns of Manchester and branches. Enquiries to Johnathan Miller International Ltd., 34-36 Margaret Street, London W.1. for other stockists.

Knee-length skirt with its own belt comes from Dorothy Perkins. Style No.: 4707.

Price: £4.99. Fabric: Polyester/viscose. Colours: Moss, brown, mulberry, airforce, chestnut. Sizes: 10 to 16. From all branches of Dorothy Perkins.

Brogue front shoe with detailed platform and heel from Freeman Hardy Willis. Style No.: A4210. Price: £6.99. Fabric: Synthetic. Colours: Black, brown. Sizes: 3 to 8. From main branches of Freeman Hardy Willis. By post from Freeman Hardy Willis, Oxford Street, London W.1. plus 40p for postage and packing.

2 Denim patchwork-look jacket with two patch pockets from Brutus. No Style No. Price: Approx. £8.95. Fabric: Cotton denim. Colour: Blue only. Sizes: 1, 2, 3. From all branches of Milletts.

Denim patchwork jeans to match with one patch in the back, also from Brutus. No Style No. Price: Approx. £7.95. Fabric: Cotton denim. Colours: Blue only. Sizes: 26 to 32 waist. From all branches of Milletts.

Black lace-up shoe with brown wood-look

wedge, from Dolcis. Style No.: A01/00992. Price: £7.99. Fabric: Leather. Colours: Black, tan. Sizes: 3 to 8. From main Dolcis branches or by post from Dolcis, 350 Oxford Street, London W.1. plus 40p for postage.

3 Warm tan jacket with hood and two patch pockets comes from Marks & Spencer. No Style No. Price:£18.00. Fabric: All wool. Colours: Green, red, tan, camel. Sizes: 10 to 18. From most branches of Marks & Spencer.

Floral print cord skirt from British Home Stores. Style No.: 6413. Price: £6.99. Fabric:

COVER!

Jackie
Bryan Ferry

MY FRIEND CAROL...

I'VE got a problem. No, it's not buck teeth or baldness, it's emotional. A heart condition, if you like. Okay, so you've got enough problems of your own without having to plough your way through mine. So, I'll start somewhere else . . . with Carol . . .

My friend Carol is twenty one. That's around the waist. She's pretty trim and pretty pretty, if you know what I mean.

Like when we walk down the street together, all the boys look at her.

"I'm exercising the dog," she tells them, and they pat me on the head. That shows how closely I capture their attention when she's around. I mean, I might not be England's answer to Raquel Welch, but then I don't bark, either. For all that, though, I like her and we get along fine.

"Carol," I say, "I've got this problem . . ."

Funny — when you've got one on your mind you keep coming back to it. But Carol's a good friend. Thoughtful and sympathetic. She leans her head to one side and looks me up and down.

"Julie," she says. "You've got several . . ."

I ignore that and proceed to tell her about David. She listens attentively while chomping her way through an enormous Brunchburger, two jam doughnuts and a chocolate eclair. These slim, dainty girls can get away with it. The rest of us eat one stale peanut and put on half a stone. I like Carol, but that doesn't mean I don't hate her.

"Whelmph Joolmnie," she begins, and pauses to swallow. "It happens to all of us at some time or another — it's what they call the sweet orchestration of love."

Yep, she actually said that! I'm forever telling her to lay off the magazines and stay with the telly, but she's a dedicated reader, Carol. With a bit of luck she'll need glasses before long.

"There's no sweet music in being packed up by someone you've been going out with for three months," I tell her. "It hurts!"

"Sure, sure, sure," she says. "But it hasn't come to that yet . . . pass the menu, would you?"

I pass the menu and sit strumming while she thinks about it. You have to be patient with Carol, but she gets there in the end.

It was Carol, in fact, who helped me catch David in the first place. That was at the beginning of the summer. We went swimming nearly every day, and I would sit and look at him. He started off white and after three weeks he was a gorgeous brown — like he went to sleep every night in a huge can of Golden Syrup.

And the sun bleached his hair blond, and the darker his face became the more his teeth would shine. And his eyes were the palest cornflower blue . . . and he didn't take the slightest bit of notice of me.

Of course, there was no reason why he should. I hid every time he came near in case he said anything and I made a fool of myself trying to reply. I'm not kidding, I'm so shy I have to make an appointment before I can look at myself in the mirror.

Carol put a stop to all that, though. She waited 'til he was glancing in our direction then pushed me in the deep end. He noticed me then, alright. So did everyone else. My gurgling screams were heard on the other side of town.

David pulled me out and insisted on giving me the kiss of life even though I was standing up and adjusting the strap of my swimsuit at the time.

"You might have checked that I could swim, first," I complained to Carol afterwards.

"Why, can't you?" she asked, all airily innocent.

But that's Carol. She solves other people's problems like other people solve crossword puzzles. Clever, she is. And hungry. I watch her tucking the food away and decide she needs prompting.

"It hurts," I remind her.

"Waffle!" she says.

"Is that your considered opinion?"

"No, it's a sort of pancake. I think I'll have one."

I wither her with a look, but Carol isn't the wilting type and I don't have the right kind of face. She just laughs.

"Okay, Julie," she says. "Carry on, I'm all ears!"

SO I start again. I tell her how the wonderful romance has developed into a series of squabbles and rows. How every date seems to end up with one of us stomping off in a huff.

I tell her how he's been glancing at Tracy Simmons a bit too much, and how I suspect the end is near.

"In a sense," I say, "I wouldn't mind it ending. We don't really seem to enjoy ourselves as much as we did, though I'm sure I still love him. It's . . . well it's pride. I mean, if he packs me up, I not only lose someone I love, but I lose all my self-confidence, too! And how can I go and find somebody else when I'm all weighed down with an inferiority complex?"

She ponders that one, nibbling sugar lumps as an aid to concentration.

"Julie," she says at last, "there's a sweet side to your nature that I like. So I'll tell you what to do. Phone him up."

"What . . .? Why . . .?"

"Tell him you're going to Blackpool for a holiday."

"But I've been on holiday already! He knows that."

"Tell him it's a second holiday."

I try to guess what's in her mind, but it's beyond me. I can't even do crossword puzzles.

"And what will that do?" I ask.

She shrugs.

"Who knows? But boys are funny creatures. They get jealous and uppity when you don't include them in things. This provokes a sort of possessiveness, they start laying down the law, and then . . ."

And then I see what she's driving at!

"It might work!" I say. "By jolly jingo it might work!"

She gives me a disdainful look. "You know, you really should lay off the telly and start reading magazines . . ."

So we're crammed into this phone-box and contorted round the earpiece. I've already told David about the holiday, and now I'm waiting for his reaction. There's a lot of heavy breathing and little else, then:

"Why haven't you mentioned this before?"

"Slipped my mind," I tell him sadly.

"Well you're not going."

I pause for effect, then try my little-girlie-whining-whisper: "But please David, I must . . ."

"Out of the question!"

"But . . ."

"Look, if you love me, you won't want to leave me, right?"

"But . . ."

"So it's a straight choice between me and your holiday, right?"

"But, David, I can't get out of it now . . ."

"So that's your choice?"

"David, I have no choice . . ."

"Well that's it, then, isn't it?"

"That's what? David, I . . ."

"You've made your decision."

"But David, listen . . ."

There's a definite click at the other end of the line and I realise he's gone. Knowing David as I do, I realise also that this time he means it. It's all over. We leave the phone box.

"Did you hear that, Carol?" I ask.

"I did," she replies smugly. "Easy, wasn't it! Now his pride is spared, he has no complex to worry him, and all he's lost is you. Next problem, please!"

"But Carol, you dummy — it wasn't this pride I was worried about. It was mine."

"So? Your pride is spared too — it was your decision, after all." I frown at her a little doubtfully. "So what do I do for a boyfriend?"

She smiles and puts her hand on my shoulder. "Ah, well, I was just coming to that. There's this really dreamy fella — name of Bob — he's just dying to meet you. Asked me to fix something up as a matter of fact."

It all figures. "So you planned this, eh, Carol?"

"I'm admitting nothing," she replies evasively.

I heave a big sigh of resignation. That's the thing about my friend Carol — sometimes she's just too clever . . .

FOOD Glorious FOOD!

CHRISTMAS is coming . . . and so is all the scrumptious food that goes with it. But, before you tuck in, stop and think about what it could do to you . . . like making you fat (or fatter!) or making you spotty, for instance. We take a look at the problems of Christmas eating and tell you how to cope!

Christmas eating's becoming a bit of a joke these days. Everyone giggles nervously as they tuck into the chocs saying, "Oh, well, it's Christmas," and by New Year we're all wondering why we're feeling so pudgy and spotty and lazy.

If you're too thin, of course, you'd think that all that extra food would help you to put on weight, but that's not always the case . . . you might put on a few pounds but you'll also collect a few spots on the way!

THE SPOTTIES' CHRISTMAS

If your skin is liable to erupt in a thousand spots at the sight of a chocolate, Christmas could be a very unhappy time for you! Tables groan with orange and lemon slices, sticky dates, mint creams, etc., etc.

Even if you can steer clear of those, you've still got to face the Christmas Pudding, the cake and everything else your mum has lovingly cooked for you and you know you can't refuse!

WHAT YOU CAN DO . . .

Avoid chocolates and sweets like the plague and try not to nibble crisps and biscuits.

If you've got a weight problem you can eat nuts and, of course, as much fruit as you want Those tiny oranges, tangerines, mandarins, satsumas etc. are usually very plentiful at Christmas so reach for one of those instead of the chocolate box when you get the urge for a nibble!

If you're sitting around during the day and in the evening in hot stuffy rooms, you'll probably get quite thirsty and drink gallons of coffee, tea and sweet drinks. These aren't good for your skin, either, so try not to drink too much of them, drink lots of water, instead, and for really clear skin drink hot water . . . marvellous!

Try to get plenty of fresh air, too. Go for brisk morning walks or late afternoon ones when the sun's just setting . . . try to persuade someone else to go with you; to make it worthwhile.

Keep up your cleansing routine, too. Don't be lazy just because it's Christmas. Use a cleansing lotion such as Boots Medicated Skin Wash, Clearasil Cleansing Lotion, Helena Rubinstein Bio-Clear Medicated Wash or Innoxa Skin Shampoo 41 to make sure your skin is really clean and to discourage spots and blackheads.

Tone the skin with a good toner such as Lemon Delph Skin Freshener, Boots 17 Herbal Toner or, if your skin is very oily, try Innoxa's Solution 41 which may be dabbed directly on to spots to help clear them up and may also be used to tone and brace the skin.

Remember, too, that oily skins need to be moisturised with a light moisturiser. Try Pond's Lemon Cream, Boots 17 Herbal Moisturiser, Coty's Equatone Moisturiser, Cyclax Moistura Moisturiser for normal/oily skin or Weleda Rose Velvet moisturising lotion (from Health Shops, about 60p).

THE FATTIES' CHRISTMAS

Fatties have the same problems as spotties at Christmas. Faced with mountains of goodies it's really hard to lay off for the sake of a few pounds!

Once Christmas is over, though, you'll be horrified at all that extra weight, so make sure you behave yourself and avoid all that post-Christmas depression!

CHRISTMAS CALORIE COUNTER

Dates 1 oz. 85
Cake 1 slice 210
Chocolate 1 oz. 150
Almonds 1 oz. 90
Peanuts 2 oz. 335
Walnuts 1 oz. 185
Cream double 1 fl. oz. 130
Christmas Pudding 2 oz. 160
Crisps, small bag 160
Fruit Jellies, each 30

Those are just some of the things you can and should avoid over Christmas! We're not saying you should give up your Christmas Dinner entirely, but do try to avoid the trimmings. Drinks can be a problem too. Choose Schweppes Low Calorie drinks, Weight Watchers own Jaffa Orange or Jaffa Lemon drinks which need to be diluted or Boots own Low Calorie drinks.

Try not to sit around with nothing to do, that way you'll get bored and you'll have to eat to compensate. Help your mum in the kitchen and around the house. (Mums usually have a dreadful time at Christmas because they have so much to do and no-one helps very much!), exhaust the dog by taking it for long expeditions or annoy all your friends by walking to visit them all in turn! That way you won't have much time to think about food. Reach for a 40 calorie orange when you feel really peckish. That'll keep you quiet for a while, especially if it's a big one you have to spend ages peeling first!

THE SKINNIES' CHRISTMAS

If you're trying to put on weight, Christmas is a great time for you. Skinnies are often that way because they burn up the calories very fast, so the answer is to eat more foods with higher calorific values!

Surprisingly, they aren't always the obvious ones, some nuts have more calories than sweets for example, as you'll see from our calorie chart.

HIGH CALORIE COUNTER

Bread 1 slice 70
Chipped potatoes 4 oz. 270
Fruit cake 1 slice 210
Almonds 1 oz. 90
Peanuts 2 oz. 335
Walnuts 1 oz. 185
Honey 1 oz. 80
Christmas Pudding 2 oz. 160
Roast lamb 4 oz. 230
Pork sausages 4 oz. 145
Tongue 4 oz. 290
Baked beans 4 oz. 100
Milk 1 pint 370
Milk, Channel Island 1 pint 490
Cream double 1 fl. oz. 130

Those are just some of the things with relatively high calorific values, that will help you to keep your weight up and even to put some more on! You'll notice that we haven't included sweets, chocolates and crisps and things, because we don't think that large amounts of them are good for anybody.

Legs are often a problem with skinnies, and that's usually where you need the extra pounds. There's no guarantee that they will actually go to your legs, though, so don't go too mad with all that food and get a fat middle instead. Legs have a habit of fattening up suddenly, sometime between the ages of about 14/15 to 17/18. The calves lose their stick-like appearance and you find you can wear shoes with low fronts instead of all those straps you'll have been forced to wear!

Remember, though, whatever shape you are, your diet should be balanced if you're to stay healthy. Eating too little is just as bad as eating too much . . . your body needs fuel to keep it going and any great change can upset it for weeks. So, even though it is Christmas, try not to go too mad. You might enjoy all the extra goodies but your body won't appreciate them quite as much!

HANDS UP!

BEAUTY BOX

HANDS up everyone whose hands are problem free, with neat nails and soft, smooth, skin.

Thought so — not a hand to be seen! Shame on you, hands are just as much on show as face and hair — so isn't it time you gave yourself a helping hand?

TO START WITH...

ALWAYS make sure that you wash your hands regularly. It's so easy for dirt to become ingrained, and once that happens, it's really a full time job to get hands clean again.

If you *do* happen to get stains on your hands (from ink, typewriter ribbon or what have you), you'll know that it takes a few days of scrubbing and washing to remove the marks, and at the end of it all, your hands are left red and rather sore into the bargain.

A much more pleasant way to get rid of stains, then, is to soak your hands in freshly squeezed lemon juice, which whitens the skin as it soaks. Just squeeze the juice into a bowl and let your hands rest in it for a while. Follow this treatment once a week and those stubborn marks will soon fade, leaving your hands much softer and beautifully white, too!

Of course, it isn't always easy to keep your hands soft and white, unless you wear gloves all day long! No matter what you're doing, from deskwork to housework, hands are bound to suffer somewhere along the line.

But there *are* precautions you can take — like wearing rubber gloves if you know that your mum is likely to have you washing dishes or cleaning floors.

Rubber gloves really do protect hands from abrasive cleansers — though getting into the habit of wearing them can be difficult at first! So make sure they're always in the kitchen where you won't forget to put them on. It helps as well to put a bottle of hand lotion alongside the kitchen sink, in the office drawer and on your dressing table, because it's important that you moisturise your hands with a soothing lotion as soon as they've been in water. If you don't do this, they're bound to dry up and that's when the skin becomes hard and flaky.

A good tip to remember when you've neglected your hands, is to save them with a simple dose of glycerine. It's an old, old, method but it works! Just rub a little of the glycerine on to your hands and leave it overnight. After a few doses, you'll notice that your hands have lost their roughness.

Glycerine, as well as an enormous

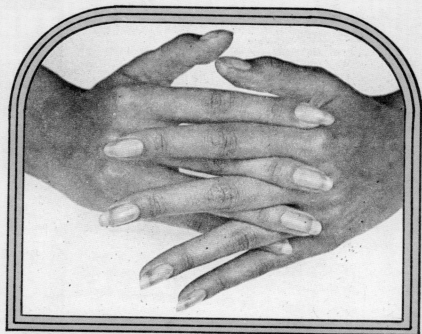

selection of good hand lotions, is available from any chemists. By the way don't spend the earth on a perfumed hand lotion, unless it's for a special occasion. Daily usage means you'll get through a lot, and cheaper brands are just as good.

Try Nulon, Boots 365, Baby Lotion, Nivea Creme, Atrixo or Cuticura.

HAVING nice hands means having nails which aren't bitten, brittle, and which don't flake. But it isn't always so easy when nails are really troublesome.

One of the most common troubles is that, once nails reach a certain length, they just seem to snap and you're back to square one. The basic problem here is that the nails are weak, and although they'll grow to a certain extent, they really need added strength to promote further growth. Don't despair, though! There are

several steps you can take to strengthen nails. Firstly, step up your intake of calcium (this is found in dairy foods like milk and cheese) and you'll find that in time there will be a noticeable difference.

The second thing is to use one of the many nail strengtheners available just now. You could use a cream like Sally Hansen's nail strengthening cream, Eylure Nail Cream or Proteinail, which should be massaged onto the nail daily. Carnate Paste works in the same way and also adds a shine. However, if you'd rather paint on strengthener, then you could choose Cutex Nail Hardener or Sally Hansen's Hard as Nails. Both brands come in a wide selection of colours.

Of course, strengthener alone won't keep your nails looking good, because when it comes to nails, nothing is as important as a manicure

— something you should give yourself once a week, at least.

Before you begin to file your nails, make sure all the old polish has been removed with polish remover. If it's difficult to get at the odd particles of polish that tend to stick to the sides of your nails, you'll find that a cotton wool bud dipped in remover will get into those awkward corners!

Once your nails are clean, use cuticle remover to get rid of that stubborn and often hard skin around the nail edge. Go gently around the cuticle with the remover, then dip your fingertips in soapy water for a few moments. Once you've done this, gently scrub nails with a soft nailbrush and dry your hands on a soft towel. Now very carefully push back the extremely soft skin with an orange stick.

After you've filed nails into a simple neat shape (working from side to side — never straight across!), don't forget to smooth away any rough edges with the reverse side of your emery board. As well as making them look better, this ensures that nails won't split or accidentally tear your tights. At last you can start to put on nail polish — though that doesn't just mean a quick brush, hoping for the best. Hurriedly applied nail polish can easily look messy if it isn't applied properly.

Remember to use long, even strokes, and make sure you never put on a second coat before the first one has dried. if you want, you can put on a third coat — not only will it deepen colour but it can help to strengthen nails too!

I hate to say this, but even after all your work, nail polish *does* chip — and when this happens, don't ignore it. Strip the nail of its polish and start again. There's no point in covering up chips — it results in an uneven, lumpy looking finish. So remember that when it comes to wearing this season's super new shades.

Look out for Boots 17 soft Autumn shades with names like Harvest Moon and Country Green. Or for a more glamorous look there's the Movie Queen look from Miners with colours like Roxy and Rialto. Not to mention loads of other fun colours you really can't afford to miss if you want a show of hands!

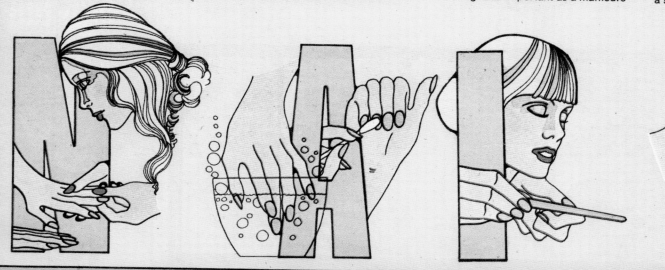

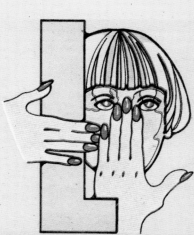

Anyone Can Make A Mistake...

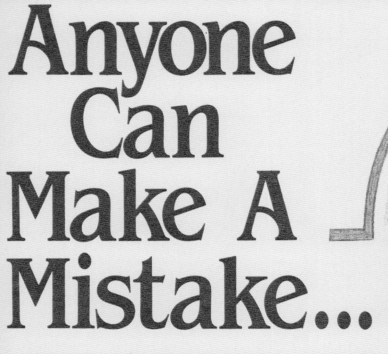

Marti was usually able to tell whether someone was asking her for a dance or not. Where Gary Morgan was concerned, she found it difficult to tell about anything . . .

EXCUSE me," he said. I looked up hopefully. He was wearing a blue sweatshirt with the words 'Are you ready for love?' written on it in white, and he definitely wasn't the worst-looking boy I'd ever seen.

A Jackie Short Story by Mary Hooper.

"Yes?" I said intelligently and smiled encouragingly. It was the first time that anyone so good-looking had come within a mile of me, let alone spoken.

"Would you mind?" he said, making a funny movement with his hand. He looked a bit embarrassed, as if he hadn't had too much experience of asking girls to dance.

"Of course not!" I said. I leapt up and took his hand. They were playing a fairly fast record but I was prepared to do a slowie if he wanted. Well, it would give us more chance to talk and get to know each other a bit . . .

"No!" he said sharply. He pulled his hand away from mine at the speed of light. I stopped dead in my tracks.

"I beg your pardon?"

"I was just asking if I could take the chair next to you," he said. "My mate wants it. He hasn't got a seat."

I stared at him, horrified. Then I turned a pretty unappealing shade of pink.

"Er . . . did you think I wanted to dance with you . . .?" he asked, his voice tailing away to nothing.

"No," I said loudly, "of *course* I didn't! I was just getting up to pass you the chair."

"Oh," he said looking relieved. "That's all right then."

He took the chair and I counted ten, then rushed into the cloakroom and burst into tears.

IT was all so humiliating — I couldn't bear it! The only decent boy *ever* to ask me for a dance and he'd actually been asking for a chair. The shame of it all.

Sandra came in just as I was gathering my breath for another howl.

"What's up with you?" she said cheerfully. "You look terrible."

"Well, I've just had the most terrible experience," I said, sniffing loudly but trying to look dignified. "I thought a boy was asking me for a dance and he was actually asking me for a chair."

She creased herself laughing. "I saw you rushing across here," she said, wiping a tear from her eye. "I thought you looked a bit funny."

"I feel so *stupid*," I wailed. "There I was, thinking he'd asked me for a dance and . . ."

"Yes, you already said," she interrupted, briskly. "He was asking you for a chair. Who was he, anyway?"

"I've seen him here a couple of times,"
I said mournfully. "He's good-looking, tall and dark — and he's wearing a blue sweatshirt with 'Are you ready for love?' on it."

"Well, *you* certainly were!" she choked, and dissolved into helpless giggles again.

I gave her what I thought was a withering look. It had no effect.

"Well?" I inquired, with great dignity. "I suppose *you* know him?"

"Gary Morgan," she said promptly. "Only Gary Morgan! Fancy you thinking he was asking *you* to dance!"

"Who's Gary Morgan? And why shouldn't he ask me to dance?" Sandra was beginning to annoy me just a little.

"The boy that simply everyone in the place is mad about, that's who," she said. "Be realistic, Marti — he's not liable to fancy you!"

I took a swipe at her with my make-up bag. "You're supposed to be my friend," I said, through clenched teeth. She grinned at me.

"I am!" she said. "I'm just trying to stop you getting hurt, that's all!"

I FELT too niggled to reply, so I just walked straight out of the cloakroom — and straight into a blue sweatshirt with 'Are you ready for love?' written on it.

"Hello," he said. "Want to dance?"

"Oh, very funny! Wit is obviously your strong point! I suppose you've been laughing with your mates over my perfectly natural mistake?"

"No, I . . ."

"I'm afraid I haven't time to talk to you, so if you'll excuse me, I have a prior appointment," I said, pushing the sweatshirt to one side.

It didn't move and its occupant looked at me even more intently. "Have you been
crying? Don't tell me you've been crying about what happened!"

"I most certainly have *not!* How dare you suggest . . . think . . . that I've been crying over *you!*"

"But your eyes look all funny. And your nose is red."

"Thank you very much," I said bitterly, hanging on to the remains of my temper. "I realise that I may not come up to your exacting standards of female excellence, so if you've quite finished criticising me, move aside and I'll leave. Then you won't have to look at me any more."

He was persistent, I'll say that for him. "If you really haven't been crying," he said, "I suggest you change your eyeshadow. Pink does nothing for you!"

"Well!" I gasped, practically speechless for a moment. I stared at him, open-mouthed. "You certainly have a way with you," I said, knowing that it wouldn't do me a bit of good to burst into tears all over again. "Which charm school did you go to?"

As I said this, I shoved hard at the sweatshirt just where it said 'Ready' and he stepped backwards. It was enough to let me pass by him, so I rushed up the stairs and outside as fast as I could.

I paused at the top for a breather. Never, never again, I vowed. No more discos, no more letting myself be humiliated by boys who thought they were wonderful. From now on, I'd stay at home and read books, do embroidery, learn to knit — really *enjoy* myself for a change. I would listen to everyone else's tales of their boyfriends and smile wisely. I'd be a wonderful
daughter, always in and helping to wash up and I'd learn all those little homemaking skills that Mum had given up trying to drum into me.

There was a clattering on the stairs behind me.

"Where is he then, your prior engagement?" Gary Morgan said.

I stared into the distance and pretended not to have heard.

"I do hope you're not going to be stood up," he said helpfully, leaning forward to look right into my face.

I COULDN'T decide whether to stand still and scream loudly, or run down the road shouting for help. In the end, I did neither.

"I wish you'd go away," I hissed. "My boyfriend will be here in a minute and he's very jealous. He won't like you talking to me."

"Do I know him?" he said. "Is he one of the regulars down here?"

I hated Gary Morgan more every minute. "No," I said, "*He's* nice!" and started to walk briskly down the road.

"You'll miss him if you go now," he shouted after me. "Can I give him a message?"

I forced back a sob and started to run but before I'd taken more than two strides, he'd caught up with me.

He took hold of my hands. "Sorry," he said, "I'm really sorry. I didn't know you were that upset."

I hung my head and swallowed hard.

"I felt terrible afterwards — about the chair," he said. "I looked for you so I could apologise, but you'd disappeared. I really did want to dance with you just now, too — I wasn't being funny."

"Really?" I said. I couldn't bring myself to look him in the eye.

"Yes, really. You got it all wrong."

He peered at what he could see of my face. "Friends?" he said.

I took my courage in both hands and looked up into his eyes but then remembered that mine were red and maybe even puffy, so I looked down again in a hurry.

"Hey," he said. "Look at me! I didn't mean all that about your eyes. They're lovely. Really."

"Don't be silly," I muttered, feeling all hot and bothered.

"I'm not! And, well, if I tease you sometimes, you know what people say . . ."

"What?" I wasn't sure I really wanted to know, but somehow I just had to ask.

"You only tease people you really like!"

I heaved a big sigh, and he laughed.

"Shall we start again? Will you come back in with me?"

I nodded and couldn't help thinking of Sandra's face when she saw us. She'd die of envy. Not that it mattered what she thought.

Gary put his arm round me and we walked back down the stairs. I remembered the slogan on his sweatshirt and grinned to myself. "Yes," I thought, "I think I am . . ."

ARE YOU READY TO ROCK?

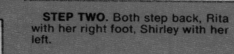

Rock has a strong western influence — so these boots should be great if you're jiving with a clumsy rocker. Best in tan, Mexican boots like these should be worn with straight jeans. (Available from Westerner shops.)

Look out for black or brown leather cowboys belts like this one with white stitching and ornate silver buckles. (Westerner shops, Great Western Trading Company.)

IT all started in 1955 when Bill Haley belted out "Rock Around The Clock." At that moment, Rock was born, and it's refused to lie down ever since. So if you want to join the boppers and bobbysoxers to find out just what you've been missing, here's how — Rock ON!

"PUT ON YOUR ROCK 'N ROLL SHOES . . . (AND DANCE AWAY YOUR BLUES!)"

The jive is of course the ultimate dance and everybody should know how to do it. So grab a friend and follow our basic jive steps with Rita and Shirley! Try them to "Rock Around the Clock" and add your own variations. Look closely at old Elvis Presley films on TV for new ideas!

STEP ONE. Feet together, facing each other. Rita's right hand holds Shirley's left hand, her left hand is on Shirley's shoulder, Shirley's right hand is on Rita's waist.

"EVERY SHA-LA-LA-LA, EVERY WOE, WOE WOE . . ." THE MUSIC.

Try dancing and listening to these Rock single classics;
"Long Tall Sally" — Little Richard
"Great Balls of Fire" — Jerry Lee Lewis
"Be-Bop-A-Lu-La" — Gene Vincent
"Roll-Over Beethoven" — Chuck Berry
And if you really get into it . . .
"Elvis's Golden Discs Vol I" (including "Hound Dog" and "All Shook Up").
"Chuck Berry's Golden Discs Vol 1" (including "Johnny-B-Goode").
"The Very Best Of Eddie Cochran" (including "Summertime Blues", "C'mon Everybody.").

Like the song says, you've just got to have a pony tail! Wear it with a heavy fringe, very black mascaraed eyes, very light foundation and white or pale pink lips!

"SATURDAY NIGHT AT THE MOVIES . . ."

Rock films to try and catch —
"That'll Be The Day"
"American Graffiti"
"Jailhouse Rock"
"Let the Good Times Roll"

STEP TWO. Both step back, Rita with her right foot, Shirley with her left.

STEP THREE. Rita steps forward onto right foot. Shirley steps forward on her left, both leaning to Rita's right.

Repeat steps two and three a few times in time to the music. Then,

STEP FOUR. Rita's right hand holds Shirley's left, and she does a complete clockwise turn on her right foot, under Shirley's arm. Then back to STEP ONE and start all over again!

"CHANTILLY LACE AND A PRETTY FACE AND A PONY TAIL HANGIN' DOWN . . ." THE LOOK.

Rita wears: A shiny, circular, shocking pink skirt and stretchy belt from a selection at Biba. Blue off the shoulder top from main branches of Tesco. White ankle socks from Lillywhites; pink satin pumps from Anello and Davide (or any ballet shop).

Shirley wears: Straight-leg denims, by Levi, skimpy white T-shirt from a selection at Biba, white plimsolls from Woolworths.

Other Rocker touches which you can adapt are turn-ups on narrow black jeans, Levi shirts and spotted neckerchiefs. Full net petticoats to billow under circular skirts (your mum might still have one!), seamed tights (Biba), silky pleated skirts (Guys and Dolls, Oxford Street) and plastic, poppet beads to swing round your neck (Woolworths).

And that's it! All you need to rock back (and around) the clock!

COUNTDOWN TO CHRISTMAS!

WANT to look your best for all those Christmas parties, dances and discos? Then follow our special countdown to see how it's done!

What's the first thing you do when you want to look nice? Wash your hair, of course, to make it shine!

Make sure you choose a shampoo for your particular hair-type, preferably one with a built-in conditioner, like the shampoos in the Alberto Balsam or Bristow ranges.

Give yourself plenty of time, too, so you can wash your hair properly! Dampen it first, then apply shampoo sparingly in little dots all over your head. Work into your hair as directed on the bottle and leave for the amount of time stated. Rinse well, then repeat and wrap your hair up in a towel, or put in rollers if you use them, while you have your bath or shower.

Colouring your hair just before a big night out isn't a good idea at all, unless you use a colourant regularly and are sure of the results! You can add colour to your hair by spraying on Nestle's Streaks 'n' Tips which spray on and brush out again, so you can experiment and brush out if you don't like the results!

Having a long hot bath is an inviting idea, but is likely to make you feel tired and more like going to bed than going out to enjoy yourself!

If you're lucky enough to have a shower, use that. It'll make you feel really fresh and ready for anything. If you haven't got a shower, have a quick bath, but make sure it isn't too hot!

Whichever you do, pamper yourself with something nice like the new Aquasoft range from Boots. There's Aquasoft Bathing Foam, 49p, which is a pearly blue, contains a deodorant and helps to moisturise your skin. For shower users there's the Aquasoft Body Shampoo, 49p, which you use instead of soap, and is best applied with a sponge or flannel. It contains lanolin to help soften your skin.

Don't be tempted to use a face pack just before you go out. The chances are your face will go quite pink and not settle down for a few hours. Facepacks are best used when you've got the whole evening to yourself . . . always remembering to follow the instructions very carefully of course!

Now, leap out of your bath or shower and dry yourself thoroughly.

It's a good idea to clean your teeth now while you're in the bathroom. You won't want to clean them after you've applied your make-up, it'll ruin your lipstick!

Use your anti-perspirant, following the instructions on the bottle or can and allowing it to dry before you apply a fine dusting of talcum powder. Baby powder such as Johnson's is very soft and isn't perfumed, which is useful, or you can try Boots Aquasoft talc, 45p, which is very soft and contains a light sparkle dust to make your skin gleam. Use your favourite cologne now, too, all over for a delicious but *light* smell!

Dry your hair next. Blow-drying is best and if you want a really smooth look use a circular styling brush such as the Kent Curly or the Harold Leighton styling brush.

If you aren't blow-drying you must use a comb with widely spaced teeth if your hair is wet, not a brush as this will damage your hair and cause split ends.

Experimenting with different styles isn't a good idea just before you go out. Stick to the style you know suits you best and you know you can manage. Billowing curls won't feel or look right if your hair is normally straight!

The same goes for ribbons and bows and things. If you're going to be fiddling with them all night, don't bother. Slides look nice and tend to stay in place quite well, so try them if you want to look a bit different. Buy them from Woolworth or Boots in all sorts of shapes, colours and sizes!

Nails next. Give them a good manicure pushing back cuticles gently with an orange stick and cotton wool and shaping with an emery board.

Always file in one direction only, from the outside of the nail to the middle, then from the other side to the middle. Softly rounded nails are the thing to have now, really long pointed ones are out of fashion, so no need to worry if yours aren't all that long!

Nail polish should be applied carefully, using three strokes for each nail, one down the middle and one down each side. Make sure there's enough polish on the brush, but not so much that it will smudge.

Allow the first coat to dry thoroughly and then apply a second coat. Use a lighter, pearlier colour to give a muted effect. Make sure your nails are completely dry before you dash off to do anything else, though, otherwise you'll undo all the good work you've just done!

Now slip into your underwear, tights etc. . . . everything but your dress or whatever you're going to wear on top. (Hopefully, that's hanging up somewhere, neatly pressed with hems neat and buttons sewn on properly!)

Now you're ready to start your make-up. Pop a little toner on to a piece of cotton wool and apply to face and neck, then moisturise with your usual moisturiser. Allow this to settle down before you apply foundation evenly over face and neck. Use your fingers to put little dots of foundation all over and then blend into face and neck with your fingertips.

If you tend to get all hot and bothered and flushed when you're out somewhere, try Boots No. 8 Colour-Corrective Moisturiser. This is a green cream which goes on underneath your usual foundation to counteract redness.

Cream blusher goes on underneath face powder, powder blusher on top, so that's the next step. Powder blushers are usually best for girls with greasy skins, cream blushers for drier skins, so choose yours accordingly.

Apply your blusher in a triangle shape starting with the round bit of your cheek-bones out to the temples. Large red dots in the middle of your cheeks won't look nice at all!

Next comes face powder. The loose kind is lovely for evenings, especially if it sparkles like Max Factor's Swedish Formula face powder with added glitter! If you're using powder from a compact, make sure the puff is clean and don't grind the powder into your face, apply it gently! Translucent powder is probably the best because it doesn't have a colour of its own, but allows the colour of your foundation to show through.

Eyes come next with carefully applied colours to make them look really big and sparkling!

Brows should be tidy, but not too thin. Just follow the natural line, whipping out the stragglers. Choose eye colours that tone with the clothes you'll be wearing, not to match your eyes.

The number of different colours you use is up to you. If you feel you can manage two or three then use them by all means, but if you aren't too good at putting on your eye colours just stick to one or two at the most.

Crayons are very useful. Use one in a muted colour such as grey or brown to draw a line in the crease between lid and brow-bone (socket line), and also below lower lashes. Use a pale pearly colour such as 17's Starry Eyes shadows on lids and a sparkly shadow on brow-bones to highlight them.

Apply two coats of mascara, one at a time, allowing the first one to dry before going on to the next. It's a nice idea to use a colour that tones with your eyeshadow. Try the 17 range of liquid mascara which comes in all sorts of lovely colours including maroon, bottle, aubergine and charcoal.

Lips are very important for parties, so take care with your lipstick. It isn't easy to change the basic shape of your lips but you can disguise certain shapes if it's absolutely necessary.

A very full bottom lip, for instance, can be made to look thinner by outlining with a dark shade and filling in the middle with a lighter colour and using the light colour on the top lip, too. Don't try to paint over the edges of your lips, it will be very noticeable and won't look nice at all!

If you put on your lipstick with a brush you'll find that it stays on longer, because you paint into all those little cracks in your lips. Finish off with a slick of lip gloss such as Max Factor's Lip Potions which come in different flavours like Spiced Apple and Strawberry.

Now for your clothes, being very careful not to smudge your make-up while you're dressing.

If you've got perfume to match the cologne you sprayed yourself with earlier, put the tiniest touch on pulse areas, wrists and behind ears. Not too much, though, especially if it's a "heavy" perfume such as Musk!

Now for the final check in a full-length mirror to make sure you look as wonderful as you think you do. Check your bag, too, making sure you've got comb, make-up, hanky, etc., plus 2p for a phone call and money for bus or train fares in case you get stuck! Have fun!

THE CHRISTMAS THEY'LL NEVER FORGET

RINGO —

DON'T have to stop and think: it was Christmas, 1962. I hadn't long joined the Beatles. We were in Hamburg. We had had a bit of a hit with our first disc. We were feeling good. We raved it up every single minute possible—eating, drinking, playing. (I believe John played the same guitar solo in every number!)

During Christmas and the days that followed, the one thing we got little of was sleep. I don't know how we ever managed to drag ourselves on to the plane which took us to a New Year's Day date in Britain.

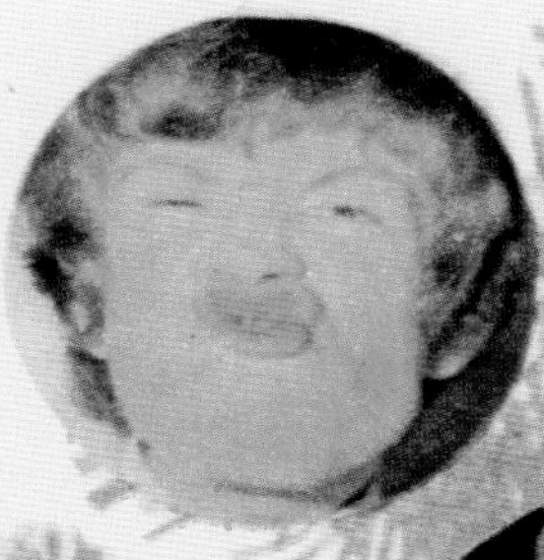

HERMAN —

CHRISTMAS, 1955. I was eight years old. My folks bought me one of those big toy horses that move forward when you mount. I thought this was fabulous. So did my mates when they heard about it. They started queuing up for rides till I finally called a halt. Sure: I've still got the horse. Maybe I'll have a bit of a canter along the passage this Christmas!

MILLIE —

A PARTY in the sun—that's what I threw a couple of Christmases ago back home in Jamaica. My discs had been doing pretty well out there— I felt like celebrating—so I did! We sat outdoors in lovely hot weather: my folks, my seven brothers, my four sisters, lots of other relatives—and me! We had curried goat meat and rice—which tastes smashing. We drank coconut milk and Cokes. I think I gave the longest singing performance of my life that day!

DAVIES (KINKS) —

AST Christmas—because we were at last getting some -paid dates after having it tough for a long time. 's face it, it's not a very rry Christmas if you have ney problems on your mind!

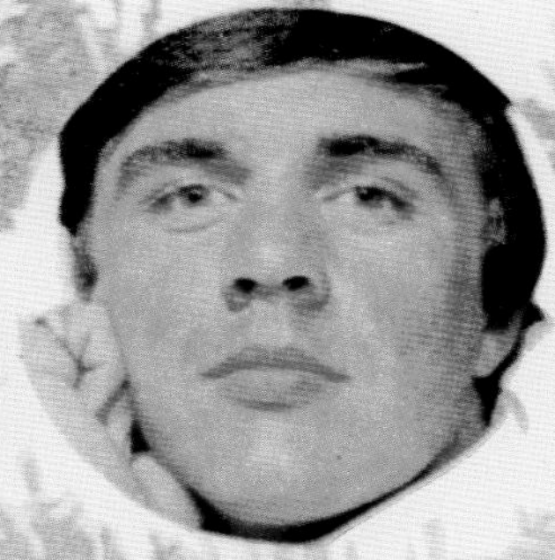

EDEN KANE —

WHEN I was 16 my mother gave me a gold watch at Christmas — wonderfully made and the most beautiful present I have ever had. I always wear it.

I never forget what Mum told me when she gave it me, "One thing more precious than gold is time: never waste a minute of it." That has been one of my rules of living ever since: to realise that you have but one life—and to live it to the full.

LULU —

I WAS nine years old. I had taken up skating. About ten days before Christmas, I broke the old pair of second-hand skates I had been using. Mum said it didn't look as if they could be mended. I felt so blue—thinking I might have to give up the hobby I was so crazy about.

Christmas morning—about five-thirty!—I opened the parcels on the end of the bed. The one from Mum and Dad contained a pair of brand-new skates!

DAVE CLARK —

CHRISTMAS, 1960 . . . For the first time, my Boxer dog Spike was part of the family gathering. I had bought him on the Christmas Eve at some kennels in Essex—after first phoning to make sure they would be open.

I went with the idea of buying a white Alsatian. But when I saw Spike, I couldn't resist him. Nor could my folks when I brought him home—even though they had always said, "You can't possibly keep a dog in this flat!"

GERRY —

I SUPPOSE I was about seven when I was first in a Christmas play at school. I was one of the three kings. Mum, Dad, and practically all the neighbours were out front— and I was dead scared in case my flipping crown fell off.

With about a minute to go I felt a whacking great sneeze coming on. I held it back as best I could—being dead scared of looking a fool in front of everyone. I just made it.

DOWN came the curtain—OUT came the sneeze—and OFF came the crown!

CILLA —

LAST Christmas tops the lot for me. Being in a show with the Beatles—that alone would have been excitement enough for any girl. But on top of that I had two plane trips.

One was to Liverpool on Christmas Eve—after rehearsals in London. The other was back to London on Boxing Day for the opening of the show. In between flights I had a slap-up Christmas at home. I won't forget it if I live to be a hundred.

LESLEY GORE —

THREE years ago—when my white poodle Buffee came on the scene. We let him have fun with all the wrappings as we took them off the presents. He had a whale of a time— ending up festooned with all kinds of coloured ribbons. This has since become a regular part of our Christmas routine.

CLIFF RICHARD —

THIS takes me back to the age of eight, when I was still living in India. There in the living-room on Christmas morning was something I had wanted for ages but hardly dared hope to get: a new bike! I remember how I was out of doors in a flash with it. I must have done a round trip of close on twenty miles by lunchtime!

SIMON SCOTT —

THE Christmas of 1962—for I had just come to Britain and saw snow for the first time! Before then I had been in Pakistan—where the Christmas temperature is normally around eighty.

Anyway, I thought the snow was so fantastic, I just stood in it and let it fall on me for about an hour. For the rest of the day I had snowball fights with more or less anyone who was willing to oblige!

NEWS AND TELEVISION PRESENTER FIONA BRUCE and actress Leslie Ash share something pretty unusual. They both featured in *Jackie* magazine long before their careers took off big style.

In Fiona's case, she was still at school when her mum nagged her to get a Saturday job. She headed off to her local newsagent where she spotted an ad in the window that immediately grabbed her attention. A photographer was looking for models to star in *Jackie*'s photo love stories. What was even more exciting was the payment of £3 an hour, which was mega-bucks back in the 1980s. The prospect of starring in *Jackie* and getting paid a fortune was too good to miss. Fiona couldn't wait to get started!

She recalls her mum insisting on going to meet the photographer to ensure that there was nothing dodgy about the work. All was well, the photographer was totally genuine and Fiona went on to star in a number of photo stories that usually involved meeting boys and kissing!

Fiona joined the BBC in 1989 and has gone on to present many flagship programmes including the BBC's *News at Six*, *News at Ten* and the *Antiques Roadshow* – a bit more serious than the world of photo stories.

Leslie Ash is probably best known for starring as Debs, the girlfriend of Tony (Neil Morrissey) in the 1990s sitcom *Men Behaving Badly*. But, *Jackie* magazine wasn't Leslie's first time in the limelight. At the tender age of four she starred in a television advertisement for Fairy Liquid and asked the legendary question, "Mummy, why are your hands so soft?"

In her *Jackie* days, Leslie starred on the front covers. She was the ideal model with her wide smile, big eyes and blonde flowing locks. Dressed in the very latest fashion, she was what every teenage girl wanted to be. Leslie went on to star in several successful television series including *Holby City*, *Judge John Deed* and *Where The Heart Is*.

Her sister, Debbie, also started on the road to fame with *Jackie*. Three years older than little sister Leslie she, too, was a cover girl. Her friendly, smiling face on the 3 February issue in 1979 encouraged readers to buy this special issue which had a fantastic free gift – a choice of button badges! Debbie went on to have several claims to fame. She was part of the "Hot Gossip" dance group in the early Eighties and could be seen on the small screen in *Angels*, *Red Dwarf* and *The Bill*. She also starred in Freddie Mercury's "I was born to love you" video.

Other well-known faces who appeared in *Jackie* include the gardening expert Rachel de Thame, who had a former career as a model.

Well-known broadcaster and journalist Nina Myskow began her career on *Jackie*. Back in the early Seventies, editors were always male, but after working on the teen title for several years, Nina broke the mould and in 1974 became the first female to occupy the editor's chair.

During her time on *Jackie*, Nina was the "Queen of Pop"

and interviewed all the top teen idols including David Cassidy, the Osmonds and Elton John.

For many years, she has been a regular on the box and the radio, with appearances on *This Morning*, the *Alan Titchmarsh Show* and *Big Brother's Bit on the Side*, plus Talk Radio's *Breakfast* and BBC's *Woman's Hour*.

Another well-known and respected broadcaster who cut her teeth on *Jackie* is Jackie Bird. Working on *Jackie* was her first job, and Jackie spent her time "running about after pop bands". Today, she's one of the best-known faces on television and is the anchor of BBC Scotland's flagship news programme *Reporting Scotland*. Every year she plays a leading role in the New Year programme *Hogmanay Live* and *Children in Need*.

Many more top journalists and writers kicked off their careers on *Jackie*. Fiona Gibson, journalist and author of six successful novels, including *Pedigree Mum* joined *Jackie* at the tender age of 17 and then moved to the bright lights of London to work on rival teen title *Just 17*. Top-selling children's authors Dame Jacqueline Wilson, Cathy Cassidy and Karen McCombie also worked on *Jackie*.

But it wasn't just the girls who went on to make it big. Mike Soutar, one-time pop editor on *Jackie* revolutionised the magazine world with the launch of "freemium" titles *Stylist* and *Shortlist*. After *Jackie* he went on to become the editor of *Smash Hits* aged just 23 and was also involved in the launch of lads mag *Nuts*. And then there are the celebs who didn't star in the magazine, but who were *Jackie* fans. Michelle Collins, Trisha Goddard and Anthea Turner are among the millions of fans who couldn't wait to get their hands on the latest issue to keep up to date with everything from fashion trends to pop gossip.

Jackie was a special magazine and can take the credit for making many celebrities "special", too.

Irene K Duncan

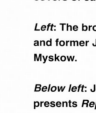

Above: Debbie Ash (left) and her sister Leslie (right) on the front covers of *Jackie*.

Left: The broadcaster, journalist and former Jackie editor, Nina Myskow.

Below left: Jackie Bird, who presents *Reporting Scotland*.

Opposite far left and above left: Rachel de Thame had a successful career as a model before training in horticulture and now helps to present coverage of events such as the RHS Chelsea Flower Show.

Opposite middle and below left: Fiona Bruce featured in various photographically illustrated stories in *Jackie*.

SECRET LOVE

ROSIE AND PHIL HAD BEEN MATES FOR YEARS . . .

DID YOU GET THAT FRENCH HOMEWORK DONE LAST NIGHT? IT TOOK ME AGES. IN THE END I GOT DAD TO HELP ME, AND HIS FRENCH IS WORSE THAN MINE!

YEAH . . .

THERE'S DEFINITELY SOMETHING WRONG WITH PHIL. HE'S BEEN ACTING REALLY WEIRD FOR THE LAST FEW WEEKS. I WONDER WHAT'S GOING ON?

SO, ARE YOU COMING TO DRAMA CLUB AFTER SCHOOL TONIGHT?

WHAT? OH, I DUNNO . . . I'LL SEE HOW I FEEL.

OH . . .

THIS JUST ISN'T LIKE PHIL AT ALL. HE'S USUALLY SO KEEN ON COMING TO DRAMA CLUB. MAYBE I SHOULD TRY AND GET HIM TO TELL ME WHAT'S WRONG.

PHIL, ARE YOU OK?

WHAT — WHAT DO YOU MEAN? I'M FINE —

COME OFF IT! YOU'VE BEEN ACTING REALLY STRANGELY FOR AGES NOW! WHAT'S GOING ON? ARE YOU IN LOVE OR SOMETHING?

WHAT? DON'T BE STUPID! LOOK, I'VE GOT TO GO — I'LL SEE YOU LATER.

PHIL! WAIT A MINUTE —

I JUST DON'T UNDERSTAND — I WAS ONLY JOKING, FOR GOODNESS' SAKE!

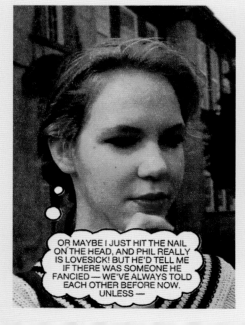

OR MAYBE I JUST HIT THE NAIL ON THE HEAD, AND PHIL REALLY IS LOVESICK! BUT HE'D TELL ME IF THERE WAS SOMEONE HE FANCIED — WE'VE ALWAYS TOLD EACH OTHER BEFORE NOW. UNLESS —

HI, ROSIE! DID YOU GET THAT FRENCH HOMEWORK DONE LAST NIGHT? IT WAS A REAL KILLER, WASN'T IT?

ER — HI, BECKY . . .

IT MUST BE ME! PHIL FANCIES ME! OH NO, THIS IS TERRIBLE . . .

ROSIE, ARE YOU OK?

ER — YEAH, I'M FINE . . .

WHAT DO I DO NOW? IF PHIL REALLY DOES FANCY ME — THE QUESTION IS, DO I FANCY HIM?

LATER THAT DAY . . .

I HAVEN'T BEEN ABLE TO GET PHIL OFF MY MIND ALL MORNING. MAYBE I'M JUST JUMPING TO CONCLUSIONS, BUT IT ALL SEEMS SO OBVIOUS. PHIL'S BEEN ON EDGE BECAUSE HE'S REALISED HE FANCIES ME, AND HE DOESN'T KNOW WHAT TO DO ABOUT IT . . .

ROSIE? ARE YOU SURE YOU'RE OK?

I WISH YOU'D STOP ASKING ME THAT! I'M FINE —

COME OFF IT — YOU'VE BEEN IN A DREAM ALL MORNING! AND I BET I KNOW WHY — YOU'RE DAYDREAMING ABOUT ANDY JACKSON ASKING YOU FOR A DATE!

HUH! AND PIGS MIGHT FLY!

I LIKE PHIL . . . I SUPPOSE IN A WAY I EVEN LOVE HIM. BUT HE DOESN'T MAKE ME GO ALL WEAK AT THE KNEES LIKE ANDY JACKSON DOES!

BUT THEN I'VE FANCIED ANDY FOR MONTHS NOW, AND HE DOESN'T SEEM TO HAVE NOTICED. IF PHIL DOES FANCY ME, MAYBE I SHOULD GIVE IT A GO.

OI — WAKE UP! YOU'RE DOING IT AGAIN!

ER — HI . . .

HELLO, PHIL . . .

PHIL LOOKS TOTALLY EMBARRASSED. OH, THIS IS AWFUL! IF HIM FANCYING ME IS GOING TO RUIN OUR FRIENDSHIP, I'D RATHER HE WENT OFF AND FOUND SOMEBODY ELSE.

I WAS WONDERING . . . D'YOU FANCY GOING DOWN THE CHIPPY?

NO, I'VE GOT TO GO TO THE LIBRARY AND FINISH MY ENGLISH PROJECT.

I NEED SOME TIME AWAY FROM PHIL TO THINK THIS OUT . . .

I'LL BRING YOU A CHEESE ROLL OR SOMETHING FROM THE CAFE, OK? OTHERWISE YOU WON'T GET ANY LUNCH.

THAT'S PHIL ALL OVER — KIND, DEPENDABLE, NICE. I JUST DON'T FANCY HIM! OR MAYBE I DO, SECRETLY . . . I JUST WISH I KNEW.

YOU COMING TO THE LIBRARY, BECKY?

NO, I'M GONNA SHOOT OFF AND GET MYSELF SOMETHING TO EAT. I'LL NEVER LAST THROUGH DOUBLE MATHS THIS AFTERNOON IF I DON'T!

A LITTLE LATER . . . .

IT'S NO GOOD, I JUST CAN'T CONCENTRATE. ALL I CAN THINK ABOUT IS PHIL AND ME . . . I KNOW I LIKE HIM, BUT I JUST CAN'T SEE HIM AS MY BOYFRIEND, THAT'S ALL. MAYBE IT'S BECAUSE WE'VE KNOWN EACH OTHER FOR SO LONG . . .

ANYONE SITTING HERE, ROSIE?

OH! N-NO, THAT SEAT'S FREE. HELP YOURSELF.

NOW IF ONLY PHIL MADE MY HEART TURN SOMERSAULTS LIKE ANDY JACKSON DOES! THEN I WOULDN'T BE ABLE TO SAY YES FAST ENOUGH WHEN HE ASKED ME OUT!

ER — MIND IF I BORROW YOUR MATHS TEXTBOOK? IF YOU'VE GOT IT ON YOU. I'VE LEFT MINE IN CLASS.

THE END

ARE YOU IN LOVE?

A Cathy And Claire Special On That Special Feeling.

YOU'RE always thinking about him, you grab any opportunity to talk about him, you cover endless scraps of paper with his name — but are you in love?

You have a great time together, you like the way he looks, you think he's got a smashing personality, you know you're fond of him — but still you wonder are you in love?

Believe us, it's not always easy to tell. Just because you go weak at the knees when he's around, blush when he looks at you and feel as if you're melting away when he speaks to you, doesn't mean you're in love with the guy. It could very well be a crush, which, once you've known him for a while, will leave you wondering what you ever saw in him!

Some couples, of course, are hit right from the beginning with that fantastic, "This is it!" feeling. They **never** have any doubts that they're in love!

For others, though, love grows quietly and slowly, and this growing, developing relationship between a boy and a girl often has three stages.

At first you're attracted to him, you fancy him and want to get to know him better. Once you start going out with him you move into the second

> ❛ Protesting that you're not in love, is often a pretty sure sign that you ARE! ❜

stage; you like being with him, you start to lose interest in other guys, you'd even go so far as to say you love him, but at the same time if he did walk out of your life, you don't think that your whole world would collapse, because you don't feel totally committed to him.

This gives way to the third stage; you find him just as attractive and knee weakening as you did when you first fell for him, but now you've really

got to know him, you find that your personalities go together so well that you wonder how on earth you ever got by before you knew him!

The three phases of love blend so subtly into each other, that it's very difficult when you're involved, to know which stage in the development of your relationship you've arrived at! And sometimes of course you don't go right through the love process. Perhaps the first attraction doesn't lead to anything; either he doesn't feel the same about you or you have a few disastrous dates. Or very often the relationship ends in the second phase when one of you gets bored after going out for a while and starts looking around for somebody new.

But assuming you've been going out with the same guy for a while, and you know you feel more for him than any other boy, how do you tell whether you're really in love? We're afraid there's no surefire answer. There are no rules to love, there's no checklist you can tick off, saying, I feel this and this so I must be in love.

Your feelings will follow their own pattern because we're all individuals and so we all fall in love in different ways. But there **are** some telltale signs you should be on the look out for until the day dawns when you don't have to ask if you're in love any more — you know it! And you know that . . .

WHEN YOU'RE IN LOVE . . . You can't wait to be with him, you're full of things to tell him which only HE can really understand.

The hours and days when you're apart crawl by and just don't have any sparkle. You wait impatiently for

> ❛ You feel so much happier, life seems rosier, all your friends say how well you look and you smile knowing the reason why — you're in love. ❜

every letter, every phone call, but when you're together, the time whizzes by and everything is dazzling again. The time you spend with each other never seems long enough and sometimes you think you'll never get the chance to tell him all the important things you want to; about how you feel and just what he means to you.

WHEN YOU'RE IN LOVE . . . You know all his faults and love him in spite of them, and sometimes even because of them — they can be very endearing!

Nobody's perfect and if you're sure he is, the chances are you've got a crush! Being in love means totally accepting your boy for what he is, loving him because he IS him and not trying to change him into somebody different. If you think, I would love him, if only . . . then you wouldn't! If his faults make you unhappy or miserable you should think seriously about your relationship. Do you really love him enough to put up with them? Love is a two way street, and if he truly cares for you he should treat you with kindness and real concern.

WHEN YOU'RE IN LOVE . . . No other boy seems half so interesting or exciting or lovely to be with, as your guy.

Suddenly the pop stars you fancied

like mad don't seem half so desirable. Why should you bother about Les McKeown or Steve Harley, when you've the boy you love right next to you!

Of course just because you're in love doesn't mean that you never notice other guys or don't feel flattered when they look at you. Of course you'll probably wonder what it would be like to go out with somebody else. But deep down you'll know that there's nobody else for you. If your boyfriend is in love with you the same will go for him. He'll find you far more attractive and interesting than other girls, and will prefer to be with you to anybody else. OK he's only human. He'll probably still look admiringly at other girls in the street or at parties, but if he's in love he won't be interested enough to do anything about them!

WHEN YOU'RE IN LOVE . . . You feel totally relaxed with your boy. You can both sit quietly saying nothing and still be having a marvellous time.

You don't feel you HAVE to keep up a conversation all the time. You no longer feel you have to impress him with your wit and brilliance. There's no need to put on any act, and you know you can tell him silly little personal things without him laughing at you. And that's because he's in love with you, not with an image you put on for his benefit. He loves you for what you are and that's the greatest compliment you can have!

Some girls try to change their real personality to fit in with a boy and make him think they're different to the way they really are, but pretence can never lead to a true, deep, love relationship. So if you really care about your boy, stop acting. You might find that he really loves YOU.

WHEN YOU'RE IN LOVE . . . You want to be with him in the bad times as well as the good.

When things aren't going too well for him, you don't immediately start looking for somebody else; you encourage him and let him know he's still the tops as far as you're concerned.

Boys are always expected to do the he-man bit and stand by girls when they have problems at school, at work or with their families, but boys have their problems too! So you let him know you'll always be sympathetic and helpful and that he can always come to you with his troubles, and he'll know you love him when he's weak as well as when he's strong.

WHEN YOU'RE IN LOVE . . . You laugh together and feel sad together.

If you both share the same sense of humour and can always smile at things, your love will be that much stronger. When you're in love, you're lucky, because you know what it's like to love and be loved, to give and receive loyalty, kindness, care and trust. Put all these together and add that magic which draws people together, makes them never tire of each other, and you don't need us any more . . . because you're in love!

SPANDAU BALLET

A JACKIE MEDICAL FEATURE
An insight into spot problems — by the doctor.

DON'T LET SPOTS MAKE YOUR LIFE A MISERY

Almost half of all the queries you write to me about concern spots. And so I think it would be a good idea to go into the whole unfortunate spot business in more detail, discussing the different problems which trouble you.

WHY?

First of all, there is a tendency for acne to be inherited — by acne I mean spots, blackheads, open pores, the lot. Even if your boyfriend has bad spots, you are unlikely to become an acne sufferer yourself unless you have inherited this tendency from your family. You could, however, be infected by the odd spot from him and so if this applies to your boy, encourage him to have his spots treated!

WHEN?

Skin problems are particularly troublesome in adolescence because the *adrenal* or sex glands which are responsible for your physical development at puberty, stimulate the grease glands in the skin at the same time. Lots of you will be prone to the odd spot at period time when these glands are at their most active. People who have inherited a tendency to acne usually find two things: —

1) Their skin is particularly greasy (this is because the grease glands are very sensitive to the sex hormones circulating in their bodies).

2) The opening of these grease or sebaceous glands in the skin are very small and block easily.

HOW DO THE SPOTS DEVELOP?

As I have already said, at puberty, extra grease or sebum is produced and this blocks the opening of the gland on the surface of the skin. This little plug is discoloured by the air and a blackhead is formed. This, in turn, can become infected and a spot is the result.

The face, neck, shoulders and back have more grease glands than anywhere else and, consequently, these are the areas most prone to spots.

If your back is not too troublesome and you just want to keep the spots at bay or avoid any forming — use a back-brush or loofah (your own of course — tell the rest of the family, hands off!) and Simple Soap. Rinse with warm water and finally splash with cold to close the pores.

Lots of you spend so much money on lotions and potions without much success in banishing the dreaded spots.

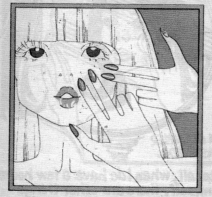

Don't squeeze spots – this spreads infection.

What can you do to get rid of open pores, blackheads and spots if not for ever, to at least keep them under control? We'll deal with them one by one.

OPEN PORES

Some people are troubled not so much with spots, but with the large open pores which can collect a lot of dirt and look unattractive. Unfortunately, we can't cure this type of skin, but a lot can be done to help. A regular routine of cleansing, toning and nourishing the skin is essential.

First step, using cotton wool, wash open pore area thoroughly with warm water and Sebbix Soap to remove all traces of dirt and make-up. Close pores with a toner. Follow with a light film of moisturiser to nourish your skin. Follow this routine morning and night and through the day if you're applying make-up and you will begin to see an improvement.

BLACKHEADS

Treatment is aimed at preventing blackheads being formed and getting rid of those which have developed, before they become infected.

Washing the face frequently with warm water and an unperfumed soap such as Simple Soap helps. (Never use a face flannel — in case of germs.) The warm water opens the pores and the soap washes away the grease. After cleansing it is necessary to pat on toner to close the pores again. Elizabeth Arden's Velva Smooth lotion is very good.

This type of skin also benefits from the application of a lotion which causes peeling (2 per cent. solution of sulphur in Calamine is one such lotion). Applied morning and night after washing, it causes peeling of the skin — thus opening up the blocked pores.

Recent research in America and Germany has shown, encouragingly, that applying Vitamin A (Retinoic

Avoid gooey cakes.

Acid, or Retin A for short) to the skin results in the disappearance of blackheads and whiteheads. It is thought that the Vitamin A produces a change in the outer layer of skin. This is a real break-through for acne sufferers because early treatment with this could prevent the next stage — spots. Your doctor will prescribe this for you.

You often ask my opinion about blackhead extractors. It is quite safe to use one for the odd particular large blackhead. They are available from most chemists. The blackhead extractor is a small tube, the edge of which is pressed round the blackhead so that it is squeezed into the tube. There will be a pressure mark left behind but this will soon disappear. Again, the open pore which is left should be

Let sunshine help your complexion.

dabbed with toner to close it up again. But the real answer, of course, is to reduce the number of blackheads in the first place.

SPOTS

The blackheads or blocked pores are liable to become infected by germs on the skin — and develop into spots or boils. It is always wise to go early and get treatment for these before the skin becomes permanently blemished and scarred.

A small daily dose of *tetracycline* helps a great deal to reduce the infection in the skin. Your own doctor will be able

to prescribe this lotion too. The treatment may have to go on for a few months but, along with the peeling lotions already mentioned, this drug can really help.

HELP YOURSELF BY REMEMBERING THE FOLLOWING RULES:

1. Don't squeeze the spots or blackheads or touch your face at all. Your fingers can spread germs on to your skin.

2. Cut down on sweets, chocolate, fries and pastries.

3. Get out in the sun whenever possible — real sunlight is more benificial than a course of ultra-violet light, although this is a good substitute when there's not much sun around.

4. Cleansing, toning and moisturising the skin is all that's advisable as far as make-up is concerned. Avoid thick make-up which is apt to clog the pores.

5. The red areas left after a spot has gone usually clear up very quickly because there's a very good blood supply to the skin. Elizabeth Arden's Soothing Cream can often speed up the healing process. Scars can be hidden quite effectively by applying a smear of Max Factor's Erace Plus.

That takes care of the physical side of the great spot problem, but there's the emotional angle to consider too. It does seem most unfair that at the same time as you are experiencing so many physical and mental changes simply by growing up, you have to suffer from spots as well.

Cleanse, tone and moisturise your skin regularly.

It's not much consolation to say it will improve as you grow older — you want help now! Obviously spots on the face cause most distress because they are visible all the time. It is very important, therefore, to have the skin treated at an early stage.

Don't hide yourself away in your misery — follow the routines I have suggested, and if your spots are particularly bad, seek help from your own doctor, who will sympathise with your problem and you'll be able to face the world with a lot more confidence.

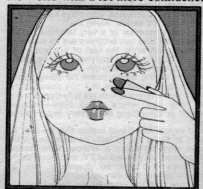

Disguise spots effectively with a smear of Max Factor's Erace Plus.

YOU'VE GOT TO SPEC-ULATE TO ACCUMULATE!

TO accumulate boy friends, we mean! A pair of smoothie-style specs can have the males buzzing around like a bee on a spree.

Why? It's mod in mood!

So, get wise to the go-hep specs line!

Large eyes: Flip for frames with heavy, upswept tops and sides, at pastel or rimless bottom curves.

Small eyes: The biggest, boldest pair you can find, slightly squarish with upswept tops.

Round, close-set eyes: Choose frames with stunning side interest, such as tiny marcasite jewels on the top "wings" or heavy, old side curves. Keep the bridge of these frames light and smallish.

Oval, wide-set eyes: A heavy, top-curved frame, narrowing towards the outer part will balance this, plus a fairly heavy bridge.

Big, slightly heavy-looking eyes: These need pretty yet bold frames with upswept tops which follow the curve of your brow-line, give an illusion of swish-looking specs instead of heavy eyes.

Slanting eyes: Lucky you! For frames in a gorgeous upswept, slightly oblong or oval style would suit you!

Specs can be a boon to girls with facial faults, as, if you choose a flattering frame style, they can be disguised to make a prettier you!

For instance, if you've a rather large, long nose, dark, upswept frames will disguise the length of your nose and give balance to enhance your other features.

High brow? A heavy, slightly "winged" at the top style, with very light lower curves to the frame, would be fine.

Low brow? Go for light pastel-coloured frames which dip low-at the bridge and sweep upwards, following the curve of your eyebrow.

Heavy jaw-line? Pear-shaped faces look most appealing in specs with wide-set side interest and heavyish top curve to give width.

Round, chubby face? Choose a style with darkish frames in an upswept, oval shape with high-hinged sides.

Long, narrow face? Deep, roundish frames with a gentle upward tint will give a striking contrast.

The shade you choose for your specs is important, too! Try to team up with your hair colour as a basic: honey or tortoiseshell for blondes; black, navy or deep green for dark brown or black hair; reddish brown for chestnut hair.

There are some zippy, slightly more expensive styles with interchangeable tops—so you could have a range of super coloured ones which you can change in a flash to match all your fashion-buys!

DEAS ON MAKE-UP

Any girl can have lovely eyes! But behind your specs you've got to have slightly more definite (not heavy, though!) make-up to bring out your eyes' true vivacity.

Brows get the Very Important Part tag.

Using a pointed pencil, draw in your natural brow line, working upwards in short, light flicks, so that the colour goes on the hairs of the brow and not the skin. Use two different shades for a more natural effect.

Now for liner and shadow: Two-toned colour hits the headlines this year, so choose shades in go-together colours which also match in with your specs. Try out offbeat shadow shades, too, like navy, turquoise, mauve-blue and bottle green.

Apply, following the line of the glasses instead of your natural eye shape. For example, if your specs are upswept, apply one shadow from inner corner outwards, triangular-wise, pointing up towards your brow. Oval frames? Smooth in shadow from inner corner, then fanned up over the lid to dip slightly towards the outer edge. Squarish frames? Try the newest fad from Italy, lots of shadow applied in a box-like shape, and a heavy "comma" drawn just above the natural line of the lashes.

Finally, apply lots of mascara. Powder lashes, apply one thin coat, allow to dry, then brush on a heavier layer, sweeping lashes outwards. Allow to dry, then brush briskly with dry brush to separate lashes.

Brows coming above the top curve of spec frames and skilful eye make-up makes small eyes look larger.

Gentlemen prefer blondes who wear bold tortoise-shell specs. Sleek hair style shows them off perfectly.

If you have large eyes, specs with upswept tops and rimless or pastel coloured bottom curves take a trick.

THE HEIGHT OF FASHION

WHEN *JACKIE* FIRST STARTED IN 1964, the era of the Swinging Sixties was in full force, with much more focus on fashion as part of popular culture and a more relaxed mode of dressing than the rather formal wear of the Fifties with its suburban housewife style largely borrowed from America.

Girls were becoming more independent as well, and were able to buy clothes from the money they earned themselves, rather being beholden to either their families or husbands.

The problem was that the latest fashion tended to revolve around London and the iconic Carnaby Street. Other larger cities had their own burgeoning fashion scene, too, but in terms of showing new fashions to their readers, *Jackie* had to rely on samples being sent to them by the Public Relations (PR) companies who worked for the larger fashion retailers.

The clothes were sometimes sent directly to artists who worked for DC Thomson, or sent to the offices in Dundee. The illustrated fashion style was very similar to the photo stories, with gorgeous long-legged, long-haired girls wearing the clothes.

The occasional fashion spread was photographed, and in fact, the very first fashion spread in January 1964, was entitled, "Love me in the sunshine, Love me in the rain" and featured a model wearing rain clothes, but taken in a studio. Later shoots would be much more adventurous, and done on location in parks, or in the houses of pop stars and celebrities. It was only from the late Eighties and into the final issues in the Nineties, that photographed fashion became the norm. Sometimes the clothes

sent to up to Dundee and we went out on location with local models – usually staff! – wearing the clothes.

But the most cost effective way to get several fashion spreads done at once was to send the fashion editor down to London to spend a week there, doing enough fashion spreads for the next season. We worked three months ahead so spring fashion had to be photographed in the depths of winter! It was hard work, involving many many players. First, we had to choose the models, from the books which model agencies sent us. Then we had to ask the fashion PRs if we could borrow the clothes – which they were usually very happy to do, because of *Jackie's* huge circulation.

We would often focus on a theme – like a particular colour, or if there was a sudden fashion trend which looked like it was going to be huge – such as dungarees (yes, really!) we would feature that. Then, of course, we always had high days and holidays like Easter, Christmas, holiday wear, office wear, disco clothes, etc that we could use as themes.

The fashion editor would then go down to London on the overnight sleeper train (no flights out of Dundee to London in those days!), check into a hotel and set off in a taxi to do the rounds of the PRs. Often, they would let you choose whatever you wanted from the racks and racks of garments in their store cupboards. Sometimes, however, a fashion PR had ideas above their station. One such, who shall remain nameless, but who is know very well known, kept me waiting for two hours before deigning to see me.

beautiful · denim

A FASHION AND BEAUTY SPECIAL

GET YOUR SKATES ON!

INSIDE or out, skating's all the rage at the moment. So choose the nicest, cheapest gear you can find, add a warm hat — and you're off!

Slit the outside of the sleeves of a t-shirt to the shoulder, hem the edges and put eyelets all the way down, evenly spaced. (Eyelet machines and eyelets are available very cheaply from craft shops and department stores) Now lace up loosely with cord or fine ribbon. Once you've got the machine you can put eyelets on lots of things — hats and bags and belts!

I wanted to borrow watches for a particular spread, and she wasn't sure *Jackie* was quite the market they were aiming for. However, when I told her we were selling a million copies a week, she changed her mind and gave us the watches!

Fashion shoots went on all day, with make-up artists, hairdressers and stylists all employed to make the models and clothes look their best. Frequently, when the models first came in to the studio, I would worry whether I had chosen the right ones; they didn't look anything like they did in their photographs. But with the help of the various experts, after a couple of hours they would be transformed into the gorgeous beauties we needed to show off the clothes.

At the end of a long week in the studios in London, all of the clothes had to go back to the PRs, so the taxi journey took place in reverse.

I think the concierges at the hotel I always stayed in thought I was rich. I was always coming in with bags and bags of clothes and they would help me to take them up in the lift — I am sure they were disappointed when I didn't give them a big tip! It was always a rush to drop off all the clothes, with the correct belts and other accessories, to the correct PRs and make it onto the train back to Dundee late on a Friday afternoon, but it was good to have another twelve weeks of fashion all sorted!

Anne Rendall

LOVE IS IN THE AIR

— so dress up to match the atmosphere. There's no saying what might happen . . .

1. Gloves by Dents, £4.95. From Selfridges, Owen & Owen and Dingles. Straw Boater from a selection at The Hat Shop, 58 Neal St., Covent Garden, London WC2. Dress, £24.95. From Top Shop. Shoes by Faith, £14.99.

2. Straw Boater as for 1. Two-piece outfit by Flowers, £32.95. From Islander, Covent Garden, London; Next-to-Nothing, Oxford; Catch, Reading. Gloves as for 1.

3. Straw Hat as for 1. Dress by Adini, £25.95. From branches of Peter Robinson; Fenwicks of Bond St.; and Caprisco of Lewis, Sussex. Gloves as for 1.

4. Pink Straw Hat as for 1. Dress by Adini, £31.95. Stockists as for 1. Gloves as for 1. Also available in black.

5. Straw Hat as for 1. Dress, £17.99. From Top Shop. Gloves as for 1.

FASHION'S gone beautifully bitty with warm woolly jackets, tweedy skirts, thick twinsets, super trousers and loads of warm scarves and mufflers. Mix the autumn browns, rusts, camels and greens with tans, creams and pale blues for the newest looks, add warm toning tights and you're all set!

1. Sling-back shoe with platform, from Curtess. Style No.: A5297. Price: £4.99. Fabric: Synthetic. Colours: Black, bronze. Sizes: 3 to 8. From all Curtess branches.

Chunky, wraparound cardigan with two pockets and tie-belt, from Dorothy Perkins. Style No.: 3153. Price: £5.99. Fabric: Acrylic. Colours: Brown, paprika, bottle, black, camel. Sizes: Medium. From all branches of Dorothy Perkins.

Check skirt with pleat in the front and flapped pockets, from Marks & Spencer. Style No.: 5200. Price: £5.40. Fabric: Acrylic. Colours: Black/white, brown/white, camel/white, navy/white. Sizes: 12 to 18, standard and long lengths. From major branches of Marks & Spencer.

2. Cosy, cream cardigan jacket with zip front and tan fake fur collar, from Marks & Spencer. Style No.: 9876. Price: £4.90. Fabric: Orlon with fake fur. Colours: Cream, black, bottle. Sizes: 12 to 16. From major branches of Marks & Spencer.

Button-through, corduroy skirt with two pockets, from Dorothy Perkins. Style No.: 4530. Price: £6.99. Fabric: Cotton. Colours: Camel, black. Sizes: 10 to 14. From major branches of Dorothy Perkins.

Tan shoe with tongue front and wedgy sole, from Saxone. Style No.: A55/4824/60. Isla. Price: £6.99. Fabric: Synthetic. Colours: Tan, black. Sizes: 3 to 8. From all branches of Saxone and Lilley & Skinner.

3. Stripy, wrapover cardigan with pockets, by Brutus. Style No.: CL/20. Price: £7.95. Fabric: Acrylic. Colours: Brown, navy, black. Sizes: 1 and 2.

Matching polo-neck jumper, Price: £4.95. Buy them from all branches of Army & Navy Stores; Debenhams branches; Owen Owen and branches.

Knee-length skirt with four front pleats, from British Home Stores. Style No.: 6723/4. Price: £3.92. Fabric: Polyester/rayon. Colours: Black, brown, navy, green, prune. Sizes: 12 to 18. From most branches of British Home Stores.

Two-tone shoe with strap, from Dolcis. Style No.: A11/50501. Strand. Price: £7.99. Fabric: Leather, Colours: Beige, black, amber with

WARMING UP!

cream. Sizes: 3 to 8. From all branches of Dolcis.

4. Checked jacket with tie-belt and side pockets, from British Home Stores, Style No.: 9400. Price: £14.99. Fabric: Wool/acrylic mixture. Colours: Brown/gold, black/red. Sizes: 12 to 18. From major branches of British Home Stores.

Brown trousers with button-down flaps for a belt, from British Home Stores. Style No.: 7438. Price: £4.99. Fabric: Polyester/rayon. Colours: Airforce blue, navy, brown, black. Sizes: 10 to 18. From major branches.

Leather shoe with medium heel, chunky sole and buckle trim, from Russell & Bromley. Style No.: Spartacus. Price: £10.99. Fabric:

Leather. Colour: Tan. Sizes: 4 to 8. From all branches of Russell & Bromley.

Brown wedgy shoe with 3 buckle fastening, from Freeman, Hardy Willis. Style No.: A32/77. Price: £7.99. Fabric: Leather. Colours: Black, brown. Sizes: 3 to 8. From selected branches of Freeman Hardy Willis.

5. Edge to edge cardi with tie belt and ribbing at the wrists, from Bellmans. Style No.: 5214/04. Price: £5.99. Fabric: Acrylic. Colours: Chocolate, red, natural. Sizes: 14 to 16. From all branches of Bellmans.

Blue trousers with button-front, from Bellmans. Style No.: 7955/03. Price: £5.99. Fabric: Polyester/viscose. Colours: Black, grotto blue. Sizes: 12 to 16. From all

Bellman's branches.

6. Flecked cardigan with five button front, tie-belt and two pockets, from Richard Shops. Style No.: 2354. Price: £8.95. Colours: Brown, green, wine. Sizes: Medium and large. From most branches of Richard Shops.

Long-sleeved shirt with pockets and acorn print, by Brutus. Price £3.95. Fabric: Polyester/crepe de chine. Colours: Assorted. Sizes: 10 to 16. Stockists: details from Brutus, 167 Hermitage Road, London N.4.

Brown trousers with flower embroidery detail at the waist, from Dorothy Perkins. Style No.: 4604. Price: £8.50. Fabric: Polyester/viscose. Colours: Brown, bottle, airforce blue. Sizes: 10 to 14. From major branches of Dorothy Perkins.

7. Blue cord jacket with three buttons and patch pockets, from Marks & Spencer. Price: £9.80. Fabric: Cotton corduroy. Colours: Navy, rust, black, brown, beige. Sizes: 10 to 16. From major branches of Marks & Spencer.

Zig-zag print skirt with snake-look belt at the waist, from Dorothy Perkins. Style No.: 4540. Price: £7.99. Fabric: Rayon and cotton. Colours: Brown on blue. Sizes: 10 to 14. From major branches of Dorothy Perkins.

High-heeled shoe with snake-look front, from Saxone. Style No.: A55/7341/63. Price: £7.99. Fabric: Leather. Colours: Red, tan/brown. Sizes: 3 to 8. From all branches of Saxone, Lilley & Skinner.

ALL PRICES APPROXIMATE.

ARE YOU A CHRISTMAS CRACKER?

·ED'S LETTER·

With Christmas only a week away, everyone in the office is in a panic about who they've forgotten to send cards to and how many last minute presents they have to buy. Even Alison, who's usually well organised, keeps on remembering people she should have bought a present for and sits racking her brains until she thinks of something to get for them. For Pete, the most disorganised person in the office, this is the time he starts writing apology letters to send to the people he completely forgot.

Still, despite the Christmas rush, we've still managed to find great things for this week's packed issue. The emphasis is on parties and Cathy and Claire have a fascinating guide to getting the most out of the party season. There's a beauty guide to help you look your best at any gathering and some exciting new party outfits to add the finishing touches. On top of all that we've still found room for the second part of our super new serial, "A New Life For Kathy" and an exclusive interview with Chris Spedding.

Oh no! I've just remembered another Christmas present I haven't bought—I'll have to go, see you next week.

Love,

The Ed!

IT'S Christmas, the season of goodwill to all boys, and suddenly every girl you know is having a party!

So are you quietly confident that you'll be the centre of attraction, monopolised under the mistletoe, the sparkly fairy at the top of the Christmas tree? (In which case you don't need us!)

Or does party-time find you dragging your feet, hoping things'll be called off due to an outbreak of frostbite and wishing you had a handy pair of cruel stepsisters to make you stay at home? (In which case you do!)

You see, parties are there to be enjoyed (believe it or not) and while we may not be fairy godmothers, we think we *can* help you to have a fantastic time!

So starting right at the beginning, you'll want to be sure you're looking your very best. Well, all you have to do is consult our Jackie Christmas beauty and fashion pages for super sparkly ideas, then actually *put them into practice.*

Give yourself the whole afternoon before the party, to go through the whole routine, and you'll be sure to leave your house feeling relaxed and rather gorgeous!

But however gorgeous you look, now comes the testing time, as you leave the safety of your own home to venture on to the wilder shores of the Christmas party. Suddenly you start feeling like Cinderella again as music thumps out, hundreds of happy revellers rush past you in the hall and everybody seems to be having a great time but you.

This is *not* the time to go and lock yourself in the loo, hide behind the curtains, or pretend you've only come to wash the glasses. Instead, take your courage in both hands and ask the guy nearest you if he knows where the girl holding the party is.

If he says, "No, haven't a clue!" — move on, he isn't interested. But, if he says, "Who *is* holding the party?" you've got a ready made opening for conversation. And if he says, "I don't know but I'll help you look," then you're made!

IF you can't quite pluck up the courage to approach a boy directly, though, the first place to make for at any party is the kitchen, where you'll probably find some dishy hunk doling out the punch.

Don't take this — it's too easy. Instead, choose a bottle with a nasty looking screw-cap and pretend you're having trouble opening it.

Look all fragile and feminine and as if all you need is a big strong man to open your bottle for you. This gives a guy a perfect chance to chat you up — but if nobody bothers, stick to the punch.

Otherwise, you *could* pretend to be poisoned by your cheese whackies or choke on your celery stalk so somebody (preferably male) will have to pat you on the back.

If you don't want to be *quite* so dramatic, though, pick up a plate of food and, as the saying goes, circulate. First of all head for the guy you fancy most and then work your way down!

But remember, don't be put off just because the most fanciable boy in the room doesn't keel back in ecstasy when you ask him if he'd like a sausage roll. Instead, be prepared to carry on and talk to the ordinary, more average guys, too.

For one thing, it's good practice and for another, you might even find you like one !

So now you've cornered the boy, what do you say to him? Well, try to avoid, "Cold weather for the time of year, isn't it?" Or, "Did you come here by bus then?"

Try instead to say something mysterious, enigmatic, feminine or just plain flattering. Like, "You're the first boy I've seen here tonight with really perfect blue/green/brown eyes." Or "I've got the feeling you're a Sagittarian, for some reason I was inexplicably (practise saying it) drawn to you." Or "Can I read your palm? I just know it will be interesting."

As a very last resort you could say, "Do you mind if I talk to you? I don't know a soul and I feel really lost." This is a bit dangerous because he could say, "Yes I do mind. Push off."

But in fact it's surprising how often boys respond to an appeal like this and come over all protective with the 'lay your little head on my shoulder' kind of approach. Or they may even admit that they were feeling a bit lost too, but that's more unlikely.

Anyway, whatever you decide to use for an opening line, say it with a smile! Nothing knocks a boy out more than a dazzling, sincere smile, and apart from anything else it will light up your face and make you look ten times more attractive. So even if he hates astrology and thinks palm reading's a load of rot, he can't help but think you look friendly and nice to know!

NOW usually at parties there's one room set aside for dancing, and this can be a trap for the potential wallflower. It's very tempting to stand along an empty wall with a group of fellow lone girls and make catty comments about everybody else there. But this should be avoided at all costs.

If you're really brave and a firm believer in Women's Lib, you'll have no qualms about asking a boy to dance. But unfortunately most of us find that just too hard. So move away from the herd and next to a boy you like the look of, then get that smile out again and say, "I really like dancing, but I'm not much good . . ."

This leaves it open, so that if he just doesn't like dancing he can say, "No, neither do I — let's go and have something to eat instead." Or "Who cares? Will you dance with me?" Of course his reply might be something *totally* different — but nothing ventured, nothing gained!

Another good rule is to dance with everybody who asks you (unless they're totally repulsive) because boys will be put off if they see you refusing other guys and won't dare ask you. Also dancing is a good way of being seen by the guys you do fancy and the more they see you dancing with different boys, the more popular they'll think you are and popular girls always interest boys!

You see it's only human nature to want what someone else has got. So don't be too choosy. Be prepared to be friendly to every boy at a party and you'll find it works like a chain reaction. Once other boys see you're approachable and ready to enjoy yourself they'll come to you too . . .

So throw yourself into whatever's going on at the party. Don't sit back and expect everybody to come to you. At Christmas time especially, people often play a lot of silly fun games like getting two teams to compete over who can get an orange up the line quickest, using only their chins!

If you want to be a wallflower, you'll say you feel far too embarrassed and shy and sit gloomily watching while everyone else has all the fun. If you don't, you'll say, "It doesn't hurt to make a fool of yourself once in a while and if everybody else doesn't mind, why should I?"

In other words, spread yourself around. Just because you haven't perhaps managed to get the guy you first fancied, don't sit trying to look as if you're far too good for this place anyway and it's awful to be beautiful but bored. This won't mysteriously draw the most interesting boy in the room over to you because he'll be with the most interesting girl!

So if you haven't managed to get yourself into a cosy twosome by the first hour and a half, put our next plan into action and create a crowd instead. Look for another girl who seems a bit lost and start chatting to her. It's amazing how two girls have much more confidence than one.

So pick out a lonely looking boy and start talking to him. Then the three of you can start chatting to someone else, pretty soon other people will come up to your lively looking group and before you know what's happening you'll be in the centre of a crowd!

So there you are. We've given you a guide to getting on (or off) at a party. Now all *YOU* have to do is put it into practice. And remember — if you really want the party to be a success, concentrate more on other people than yourself.

Try to help the lonely guy in the corner, or the girl pretending to be totally absorbed in the LP covers, to fit in and lose their shyness, then we bet you'll lose your shyness too! That's what being a party-smarty's all about — try it and you'll see!

THE CATHY & CLAIRE PAGE

We can't promise the perfect solution, but we'll do our best. If you're stuck with a problem and you can't see the way out, write to us at this address: Cathy & Claire, Jackie, 185 Fleet Street, London EC4A 2HS. Please remember to enclose an S.A.E.

DEAR CATHY & CLAIRE — My friends laugh at me because I'm so interested in sport. I spend nearly all my spare time taking part in sporting activities and I have a great time. There are lots of boys at the club I go to and I don't think I'm missing out on anything but all my school friends won't stop teasing me.

How can I make them understand that I'm having a great time and really enjoying my life?

Well, if they insist on teasing you just because you enjoy yourself in a different way from them, they probably won't ever understand or believe that you *are* having a good time.

These school "friends" of yours sound a bit narrow-minded to us. It's our guess that they think people can only possibly have a good time at a disco or party. They don't realise you can meet lots of boys and have a great if not better social life, just by being a member of a club or interested in a certain activity.

So try to ignore these girls' remarks and keep on enjoying yourself! And if they really knew how *much* you enjoyed yourself, they'd probably all be green with jealousy!

DEAR CATHY & CLAIRE — I went out with Neil for three months before I met his brother, Danny. Danny's 25 and he's married but I really fancy him. He's always really nice to me and puts his arm round me and things when we go and visit him and his wife.

Neil knows this but he only laughs and teases me about it. I don't think he knows I'm serious about Danny.

I keep hoping that Danny will ask me out. Do you think he will?

Well, we're sorry if this sounds cruel, but we very much doubt that Danny will ask you out. We think you've mistaken Danny's friendliness for something else. He obviously just feels affectionate towards you because he's fond of you — not because he fancies you.

You're his brother's girlfriend and he likes you, but you'd be very wrong to try and make more of this. Remember that Danny is *married*. He's not free to go out with you, even if he wanted to.

Neil laughs about this because he knows Danny isn't serious. He'd probably think you were very stupid if he thought *you* were serious.

So don't let your imagination run away with you. Enjoy your relationship with Neil . . . and your friendship with Danny.

DEAR CATHY & CLAIRE — I know it's stupid but I fancy my friend Kathy's boyfriend. He's the best person I've ever met. I used to get on great with him but then I realised I fancied him so I kept out of their way.

Well, now they both keep phoning me and asking me why I don't go down to see them anymore. You see I used to go down about twice a week to her house to see them and play records. It used to be a good laugh, but now I can't bear to see them together.

I can't tell her my real reason for not going down so I make up stupid excuses and I know she doesn't believe me. When Simon, her boyfriend, phones me up I find it impossible to talk to him.

I think I've really offended them now and I don't know what to do. Do you think I should just go and see them anyway and try and hide my feelings?

Well, that really depends on how good you are at hiding your feelings. If you're going to go down and be really miserable, we don't think there's much point in you going.

But, if you feel you could go and try and learn to accept this situation we think it would be much better.

Try to accept the fact that he's your friend's boyfriend and try to keep your relationship friendly.

It would help, too, if you found yourself some new friends to go out with at weekends. Go to discos and parties and we're sure you'll soon find a real boyfriend of your own . . . and you'll still have Kathy and Simon as friends.

DEAR CATHY & CLAIRE — Our mother died just over a year ago and although we still miss her very much, my sister and I have gradually accepted the situation. The problem is our father. His attitude towards us has really changed. He never allows us to go out with friends — never mind boys — and we seem to spend all our time doing housework or watching T.V.

Neither of us have been out with a boy yet, although we have been asked out by quite a few. We just can't seem to talk to our father at all. Do you think there is anything we can do to change this situation without causing a row? I'm 15 and my sister is 14.

You really should try to talk to your father — we bet he's very sad about this communication barrier between you two and him, and we're sure he'd welcome a serious talk with you both.

Explain to him that you'd like to go out with your friends and if he still isn't keen, ask him if it's okay for you to bring a crowd of your friends, both boys and girls, home, so he can meet them. When he sees what a reliable bunch you are, we're sure he'll relent.

Your dad is probably worried that he won't be able to bring you up well enough alone, so do your best to show him you won't let him down. And be nice to him. He's lost his wife — your mother — and he must still be feeling that loss. So let him know you understand — and try to be patient with him. OK?

DEAR CATHY & CLAIRE— A couple of months ago, my friend and I met these two boys at our local youth club. They were really friendly and my friend and I fancied them a lot. The third week we had been there, one of the lads came up to me and told me that he liked my friend. I told him that she liked him too and he was really pleased. So he asked her out.

A few days later the other lad phoned me up asking me out too and now we go out in a foursome. The trouble is, I can't help thinking he just asked me out for convenience — just for the sake of the foursome. This is making me really unhappy. Can you help?

We think you're making a mountain out of a molehill! We honestly don't believe this boy would have asked you out if he didn't *want* to go out with you. So just try to enjoy yourself with him — and don't take things too seriously. We're sure you'll find out in the near future how much he likes you — and meantime — have a great time! And don't worry!

DEAR CATHY & CLAIRE — I used to be really keen on my boyfriend but now I'm afraid I've gone off him. The trouble is, though, that it's my birthday in a week and I know he's bought me a solid gold locket I admired recently.

I really don't know what to do about this. Obviously I want the locket but I think I'd feel guilty about accepting it because I intend to finish things. What do you think I should do?

Well, it would be a bit unfair of you to accept a present as expensive as a gold locket if you're intending to finish with your boyfriend shortly afterwards.

It's a bit awkward, we know, when he's already bought this locket for you, but we still feel it would be wrong to accept it.

We know it's going to be difficult, but we really think you should finish with him before your birthday. He may still want to give you the locket anyway — in which case, if he insists you take it, well, you'll just have to accept as gracefully as possible.

It's a horrible situation, we know, and we hope everything turns out well for you.

DEAR CATHY & CLAIRE — My boyfriend, Scott,is very dependent on me and I feel this is quite a responsibility. You see, he comes from a children's home and he's never known his parents. I don't really know if that has anything to do with it, but he seems to need the security of a steady relationship.

My mum and dad think the world of him and he often stays at our house for the weekend.

Well, I'm beginning to feel this is too much for me. I feel as if I've got a weight round my neck all the time.

I really think I should finish with him but I'm scared to. Can you help?

Well, this is rather a difficult situation but if you really are beginning to feel tied down and unhappy, you *must* do something about it before you get more involved.

Scott is *not* your responsibility, you mustn't feel guilty if you want to finish with him. If you do finish, though, you could always try and stay friendly. This isn't easy, but he'd probably appreciate it if he could still come and visit your home.

Going out with Scott because you feel sorry for him won't do him any good. He's got to learn to stand on his own two feet and, strange as it may sound, your finishing with him might help him do just that.

So try not to worry and do what you think is best — we're sure everything will work out fine.

DEAR CATHY& CLAIRE — I was at a disco last Saturday with my friends and we were all pretty bored. There was this really weedy boy there and one of my friends dared me to ask him to dance.

Well, I did and all my friends started laughing at him and I felt really ashamed that we'd made a fool of this boy. Just before the dance ended, he turned round and said,"That was a really horrible thing to do. I hope you're pleased with yourself." Then he just walked away.

I feel really sorry about it and we all want to apologise to him. It was just a stupid thoughtless action and we feel really bad about it.

Do you think we should approach him at the next disco and apologise?

We're glad you realise this was a really nasty thing to do. This boy was obviously very hurt and he probably lost a lot of confidence through your actions.

We don't think that all of you should approach him if you intend to apologise to him and, since it was you who asked him to dance, and you who accepted the dare, we think it should be you who apologises.

It won't be easy but we think you should do it as soon as possible because the longer you leave it, the harder it will be.

We think you've learned your lesson so we won't lecture about this, but do think twice before you do anything like it again.

Just think to yourself — would you like it?

I DON'T WANT TO END UP LIKE HER!

DEAR CATHY & CLAIRE — I get so depressed when I think about growing up and getting married — the thing all girls are supposed to want.

You see, my nineteen year old sister's married and I really don't fancy her sort of life at all. There's her and Jim and the baby living in one room, they have to share the kitchen and bathroom, and the place is always a mess, with nappies drying everywhere.

I'm sure my sister never cleans up, and when they come round to our house, Jim wolfs his food as if he hasn't had a proper meal in months. My sister used to be so pretty and full of fun, but now she looks a mess all the time and never stops moaning.

Is this what I'm going to be like in four years time?

Why on earth should it be? There's no law that says you must be married by nineteen, and even if you are, you can put off having a family till you've got somewhere decent to live.

There's no reason at all for you to suffer what you consider your sister's awful fate — in fact, simply by observing what's happened to her, you can take steps to see you *don't* go the same way! At present you seem to see marriage as the only thing you can do in the future. Why not think a bit more about getting a good job — travelling around a bit — growing up yourself before you have to help your children grow up? You're in control of your own life, and you can make it as good or as bad as you like.

Meanwhile, don't be too hard on your sister. Getting married doesn't instantly make a perfect cook and housewife out of a lively, pretty girl — that's something she'll need time to learn, and it'll be harder for her with a baby around.

So why not help her out a bit? Go round after school and offer to take the baby out and get her shopping, so she can tidy up the room. Or send *her* out while you do the cleaning up. It'll be a great help to her and it might make you a bit more tolerant of what she's going through . . .

Printed and published by D. C. Thomson & Co., Ltd., 185 Fleet Street, London, EC4A 2HS.

HOW'S YOUR CHRISTMAS SPIRIT?

How's your Christmas spirit? Are you the fairy at the top of the tree who goes out carol singing from July until December, merrily throwing mistletoe and spreading Christmas cheer wherever you go — or are you the one who sits in the corner like a Christmas pudding and trips over the fairy lights? Have a go at our Christmas game and no cheating! It's just like Snakes 'n' Ladders only you climb up the Christmas trees and slide down the yule logs. Merry Christmas!

41 — All the pine needles have fallen off your Christmas tree.

42 — It's Christmas Eve and you still haven't bought any presents.

43 — Santa's got stuck in your chimney.

44

45 — You're the fairy at the top of the Christmas tree. FINISH

40 — You go carol singing and people throw you money to go away.

39 — You remembered to send Great Aunt Flora a card.

38 — You're asked to switch on your town's Christmas lights.

37 — Your snowman is the last to melt.

36

31 — Santa leaves *you* a glass of milk and a jaffa cake.

32 — You give your dad socks — again!

33 — There's a polar bear wearing mittens in your garden.

34 — Your Christmas list is under 3 feet long.

35

30

29 — You remember to sign your cards before you've sealed all the envelopes.

28 — You won't go out sledging with the gang because you don't want to get wet.

27 — The fairy lights blow up.

26

21

22 — You live next door to an abominable snowman.

23

24

25

20 — Cousin Albert catches you under the mistletoe.

19

18 — You thought Yule Log was a famous actor with a bald head.

17 — You go to school in a sleigh.

16 — You find all the pennies in the Christmas pudding.

11 — The bows you tie on your presents look like wet cabbage leaves.

12

13

14 — Mum catches you opening the crackers.

15 — You've burnt the mince pies.

10 — You bought and wrapped all your presents in July.

9 — You're chosen as the fairy in the school play for the third year running.

8 — You throw a snowball at your teacher — and get caught.

7 — Madge is baking a Christmas cake.

6

1 — START

2 — Danny's building an igloo.

3

4 — You put tinsel on the budgie's cage.

5 — You never shake your presents to find out what's inside.

26 December 1981